My Dear Friends,

I received so [...]
after my departu[re ...] [...]me to
thank you all.

I have never [...] [m]oved or humble as
I did when [your] cards started to arrive. I
thought the supporters ~~are~~ I. were close but you
don't realise how close. I have so much to thank
you all for over the last two seasons and
am proud to have been part of The Everton
Revival.

Everton will always ~~have~~ be a special place
for me as it gave me two of the happiest
years of my life. All I basically want to say
is "Thanks for The Memories" you the fans, Howard
Colin, Mick, Terry, Clinks for putting up with and
to the best bunch of lads & I have ever
worked with. God Bless You All And May Your
Amazing Success Continue.

Your Mate Forever,

Aud. G

22nd June 1985.   ASTON VILLA F.C
                    VILLA PARK.
                    B/Ham 6.

Dear Ken, I hate to be to presumptuous but I
wonder if you could do me a small favour. I
received so many cards and letters since I left
that it would be impossible for me to write to
everyone thanking them individually. So I wonder if
you get the space could you print these few
words. I would very much appreciate it,

My Thanks In Anticipation,

BORN
NOT
MANUFACTURED

KEN ROGERS

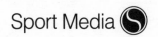

This book is dedicated to:

Evertonians everywhere with whom I am so proud to align. I salute them for their knowledge, pride and passion in a club that has given all of us so much joy. As the famous saying goes: 'Evertonians are born, not manufactured'

Harry Rogers – my father, who gave me my love of all things Everton

© Ken Rogers

First English Edition
Published in Great Britain in 2016.

Published and produced by: Trinity Mirror Sport Media,
PO Box 48, Old Hall Street, Liverpool, L69 3EB.

Managing Director: Steve Hanrahan
Commercial Director: Will Beedles
Executive Editor: Paul Dove
Executive Art Editor: Rick Cooke
Marketing & Communications Manager: Claire Brown
Editing & Production: Roy Gilfoyle
Statistics: Gavin Buckland

ISBN: 9781910335499

Photographic acknowledgements:
Ken Rogers personal collection, Trinity Mirror, PA Photos.

Printed and bound by CPI Group (UK) Ltd, Croydon, CR0 4YY.

Contents

INTRODUCTION

A grand old team to support... and report on

KEN ROGERS was the regular Street Ender from the district of Everton who, from the late 1960s onwards, suddenly found himself inside Goodison Park's corridors of power.

As a young weekly newspaper reporter with access to the Bellefield training ground, he gained a special insight into the world of Harry Catterick. Ken would ultimately become the Liverpool Echo's chief football reporter during Everton FC's most successful era – Howard Kendall's glorious 1980s – and was Echo sports editor from the early Nineties. In 2001 he was named Northern Sports Journalist of the Year.

Ken has written numerous well-received history books about the Blues, not least his official 1992 stadium centenary title '100 years of Goodison Glory' that has been reworked and reprinted several times as the definitive story of the club's famous field of dreams.

In this latest title, he has steered away from the obvious history subject matter to take supporters on a personal, revelatory and sometimes surprising Everton FC journey, with a determination to confirm the long held belief that 'Evertonians are born, not manufactured'.

Ken was closely involved with the Merseyside football scene during six decades, in which time 23 Everton and Liverpool managers sat in the Goodison and Anfield hot seats.

While travelling home and abroad with Everton and Liverpool during this period, it is hardly surprising that Ken collected a wealth of inside stories about some of the most eventful happenings in the modern history of Merseyside football.

While he was Echo sports editor, he launched the official Evertonian magazine in 1994 with the club's full support and would be its executive editor for the best part of 20 years. He also launched the rival and unofficial 'Kop' magazine in 1994. The latter would enjoy a lifespan of two decades before publishing for the last time in July 2015. Meanwhile, the 'Evertonian' magazine has gone from strength to strength under its new 'Everton' banner.

Ken was not only on the original panel that elected the Everton Giants, the club's first Hall of Fame in 2000, he also chaired the panel of former players that would name the official Liverpool FC Hall of Fame in 2006. This indicates the remarkable trust Merseyside's Big Two placed in him.

Down the years Ken secured countless major football exclusives for the Liverpool Echo and the inside story of many of these are featured within the pages of this book.

INTRODUCTION

In 2002, Ken recognised that the world of publishing was changing and that titles like the famous Saturday football editions in their old form were now seriously threatened after serving local football communities for 120-plus years.

He launched a visionary new venture for Trinity Mirror, the Echo's parent company, and became managing director of the successful Sport Media business unit that now has official publishing partnerships with some of the UK's leading football brand names. These include the likes of Chelsea, Arsenal and Tottenham in the capital; Aston Villa and West Bromwich Albion in the Midlands; Manchester United in the North West; Celtic in Scotland, plus – of course – Everton and Liverpool on Merseyside.

Sport Media is now the number one provider of official club publications in the UK.

Ken left Sport Media in late 2014, providing the time to pick up on his previous writing ambitions. Having already published 11 books, he immediately began to write 'Born Not Manufactured' – a pointer to a lifetime covering the ups and downs of the Blues.

This book will give you a fascinating insight into the life and times of one of English football's most famous brand names.

It's a fly-on-the-wall view of all areas of club activity, enabling you to grasp and understand life on the inside, iconic players and legendary managers, owners and high powered executives, indeed everyone who has helped shape the club from the pitch to the corridors of power across nearly half a century.

Written by a declared and proud Evertonian specifically for the army of Blues Noses he firmly associates with, Ken Rogers has always believed Everton are a grand old team to support – and report on!

Ken's other Everton FC books include 'Everton Greats' and 'Everton's Z-Stars'.

He was also one of the driving forces behind Sport Media publications 'If You Know Your History' and 'Dixie Dean Uncut'.

On an Everton district theme, he penned the best-selling 'Lost Tribe of Everton & Scottie Road' social history book and its well-received followed up 'Everton – The People's Memories' which both major on the street clearances that changed the Everton district forever in the 1960s.

It's clear that Ken Rogers' mind never strays far from his boyhood home.

'Oh, we hate Bill Shankly and we hate St John, and most of all we hate Big Ron'

I'M an Everton boy, brought up in Melbourne Street, off Netherfield Road North, in the 1950s. It was a tight-knit community of back-to-back Victorian terraced houses, clinging for dear life to crumbling foundations on some of the steepest streets in the city. These swept down in spectacular fashion from the summit of Everton ridge to the dock gates. We all think our childhood districts are the centre of the universe, but I felt mine was extra special as it was so close to one of the most famous football brands in the world.

As a district, we were clearly split by colour. For clarity it had nothing to do with racism and, surprisingly, little to do with football, even though there were over 100,000 rival Evertonians and Liverpudlians living side by side.

No, the colour split I am referring to in those post-Second World War years was directly linked with the Orange and the Green. Every July 12, Netherfield Road was prime marching territory for 46 Orange Lodge bands that congregated in and around Everton Valley to prepare for their annual outing to Southport.

To reach Liverpool city centre, the Lodges paraded through predominantly Protestant territory in the north end of Everton while also drumming and piping their way through the largest Roman Catholic parish in the United Kingdom at the south end. As a young north ender, albeit one with no Lodge connections, I didn't actually see these marches as some sort of religious statement. Rather, the kids in our street were just excited because the 'bands' were coming – and what a sight it was.

We would stand at the bottom of Melbourne Street and hear the skirl of bagpipes and the heart-pounding sound of a base drum that told us that the show was about to begin.

The crowds would be several deep the entire length of Netherfield Road as we excitedly watched individual band leaders sway from one side to the other in sharp contrast to the disciplined straight lines of their bandsmen. A silver mace would be launched roof high and caught in full marching stride by one of these competitive front men, inspiring a deafening roar from the watching crowd.

All of this might have had religious undertones, but to us kids it was pure theatre, although I'm certain this was not how our young Roman Catholic counterparts saw it.

The only thing that inspired a louder roar than the mace

acrobatics was the sight of King Billy seated on his white horse, ironically a role usually played by a girl dressed in 17th century finery and waving a ceremonial sword high in the air to symbolise the victory of King William III over the Irish Catholics at the Battle of the Boyne in 1690.

Of course, the other major talking point that separated us, not just in inner city Everton but across Merseyside, was football's colour coded rivalry, quite simply Blue v Red.

It goes without saying that I was a Blue Nose, instinctively supporting the team my father and grandfather supported.

In the summer of 1967 I was an excited teenager regularly standing proudly on Goodison Park's Gwladys Street terraces, shoulder to shoulder with my fellow Evertonians as we roared out our favourite song . . .

'Oh we hate Bill Shankly and we hate St John
And most of all we hate Big Ron
And we'll hang the Kopites one by one
On the banks of the royal blue Mersey'

Of course, the hanging reference was a metaphorical statement of fan fervour, a symbol of our blue-blooded family passions. We all had Liverpudlian mates who only became persona non grata on derby days.

I have already alluded to the 'King Billy' who rode a white horse on Netherfield Road to grab the undivided attention of thousands of members of the Orange Lodge.

The football chant, of course, referred to the other 'King Billy' – the little Scot whose passion had stirred a massive

Sixties revival at Liverpool Football Club and a man who was the inspirational leader of the 'enemy' – Bill Shankly.

Little did I realise as 1967 dawned that, within a matter of months, I would find myself out of school and working as a young sports journalist for a local newspaper, the Liverpool Weekly News. By late 1968 I would have a professional requirement to interview the stars of Everton and Liverpool and in March 1969 I would finally come face to face with Shankly who, just a short time before, had been on the receiving end of my vitriolic Gwladys Street chants.

Would we be able to put football before our clear red or blue football loyalties? I would soon find out.

Unhappily, our first meeting was like a Tommy Smith tackle on the genius that was Alex Young. In other words, everything about it was over the top. Shankly, eyes popping out of his head and his voice rising to a shrill scream, would accuse me, or rather my newspaper, of seeking to unsettle the Anfield crowd over a sensational substitution he had made involving Kop idol 'Sir' Roger Hunt.

"Sorry Bill," I said. "I'm only a boy from the streets of Everton, so I'm hardly influential with the Kop."

Shankly was in such a rage that any points I made were totally irrelevant. Indeed, he suggested that any football reporting career I might have been planning at Liverpool Football Club was over before it had even started.

I was tempted to give him a personal chorus of that famous Gwladys Street battle hymn, but as his finger was pointing menacingly in my face, I thought it more sensible that, for now at least, I would keep my powder dry.

My Goodison road to a Shankly bust-up and what happened next

SO what was behind my unexpected confrontation with 'King Billy' of Anfield, a personal 'derby' clash I was clearly not going to win? I need to rewind a few months.

In the winter of 1967, and attending Evered High School in Walton, I took a landmark decision in the middle of my 'A' levels to turn my back on school and accept an unexpected job offer to become an 'Apprentice Journalist' with a company called Swale Press in Widnes.

I loved English at school, had achieved English Language at GCE 'O' level and was in the middle of my 'A' level English Literature and History courses when my mother spotted an advert in the Liverpool Weekly News. This was a small local newspaper, no longer in business, that I regularly purchased because it majored on amateur football. It printed all of the local Saturday and Sunday League results, fixtures and league tables and carried match reports for even the most menial of games.

I had been playing for Clubmoor side St Columba's in the Liverpool Sunday School Union and later for Old Swan and then Mersey Royal in the enormous Liverpool Sunday League which boasted about 12 divisions, featuring some of the most feared amateur sides in the city. These included the big dock teams whose managers included 'legends' like John Slocombe and Harold Hughes, nicknamed 'Big H'.

Playing at Edinburgh Park in Townsend Lane was akin to a local primary school side playing against AC Milan in the imposing San Siro stadium, except that the threats from the line at Townsend Lane were always taken far more seriously than any Italian mafia threat in Milan.

If you were involved at that time, you will know what I mean. I should add, just in case any former players from those old dock teams are still around, that they always had class players as well who would purr through games if you let them, which most sides did. But back to the Weekly News. My mother spotted this advert for a 'Junior Journalist' and urged me to apply. Modestly, I told her that there would be hundreds of applicants, but you never said 'no' to my mother who had this remarkable belief in my ability to achieve anything in life.

"You want to be a star and appear at the London Palladium? No problem, I'll give TV impresario Val Parnell a ring and get you an audition."

"You want to be a real life cowboy and live on the American ranch of your hero Roy Rogers? No problem, he's on at the Empire theatre next week with his golden horse, Trigger. I'll pop into the Adelphi Hotel and have a word."

Mum, like my dad, might have come from an inner city environment, but she set her standards sky high, especially for her only son. So I sent an application to the Weekly News head office in Widnes. The company published newspapers in Widnes, Liverpool and Runcorn.

I was stunned when I got a first interview followed by a call back at which I was offered a job, aged 18, as a junior journalist on a three-year apprenticeship. On the day the confirmation letter arrived, in February 1967, mum smiled knowingly as if it had never been in doubt. Okay, the London Palladium might now be a 'no-no' and Roy had moved on to another cowboy town, but here you go Kenny (I never got my full name 'Kenneth' unless I had stepped out of line). You are now on your way.

With a massive smile on her face, she set out my immediate action plan. "Get into school today and tell them you are quitting your 'A' Levels, leaving on Friday and joining Swale Press."

I must admit, the job sounded a much better bet than school exams, although headmaster Charles Hogg was aghast at my decision and said: "Be it on your own head."

Nothing like a bit of encouragement from the top!

And so a week later I had hung up my school uniform and was sitting in Widnes behind a large Underwood typewriter, waiting for my first exciting assignment. Editor Ray Miller didn't take long to break the silence. "Kenny, get your coat on and get out and about to collect the latest funeral forms and wedding pictures for use in the next edition."

This didn't sound very glamorous and suddenly the London Palladium was looking a much better option. However, the next day I was despatched outside the office where three large tyres had flown off the back of a lorry and demolished the window of the shop next door. Now this was more like it, proper journalism. I wrote up the story, only to be summoned into the office of managing editor Ron Carrington, an inner sanctum rarely seen by staff unless something was wrong.

"A reporter has left in Liverpool," said Mr Carrington, not even looking up from his desk. "You start at our Bold Street office on Monday under your new editor Keith Charlton. Don't be late."

Late? My journey time to and from work had suddenly been cut by two thirds and this was the newspaper I read every week to keep up with the amateur soccer scene.

On my first day I met a brilliant bloke who would become a first class colleague, and a great friend. His name was Alan Parry and the only thing wrong with him was that he was a Liverpool FC fanatic and Kopite who didn't seem to be aware that Everton Football Club even existed.

He had started two football columns in the Weekly News, alternating each week between Bill Shankly's 'Colossus' Ron Yeats and his fellow Scot, striker Ian St John. This didn't seem balanced to me, but then the thought clearly never crossed Alan's mind.

Parry is still a Reds fanatic and doesn't seek to hide it, although these days he delivers the balance I once questioned while operating as a top commentator for Sky TV, having also worked at the highest level for both BBC and ITV as a leading athletics and football commentator which included a spell on Match of the Day.

I had not been at the Bold Street office very long when our openly biased sports editor was offered a new job by the emerging Radio Merseyside that launched in the winter of 1967. Yippee, I was suddenly the new Weekly News sports editor just two days before my 19th birthday.

What a turn-around. At the end of the 1966-67 season I had been on the Gwladys Street terraces. Now, as the 1967-68 season began to unfold, I was suddenly at Liverpool's Melwood training ground or Anfield every Monday, introducing myself as the 'new' Alan Parry to one of Liverpool's greatest ever captains.

Congratulations Mr Yeats, a dyed-in-the-wool Evertonian is now your new ghost writer.

I also had to get my young head around potentially dealing with other LFC heroes and the aforementioned Mr Shankly who had emerged on the Merseyside football scene eight years earlier and was now deemed to be a messiah by those unlucky enough to have been brought up as Reds.

How would this Blue Nose, raised in Everton and fiercely proud of it, strike up any kind of professional rapport with the man I had been professing my 'hatred' for in a famous Goodison battle hymn just a few months earlier? The answer would come very quickly and it's fair to say it didn't go well.

As a Blues fan, I had stood proudly at Goodison on derby days and scanned the Liverpool dug-out. Even I had to accept that Bill Shankly had this remarkable aura, a figure capable of standing on the steps of St George's Hall and silencing a 100,000 crowd just by raising his arms in the air.

Unlike our manager Harry Catterick, the Liverpool boss was the definitive man of the people. "We won this cup for YOU," he would shout, personalising his praise as if he was speaking individually to every single supporter. "I've drummed into our players time and again that they are privileged to play for YOU; if they didn't believe me then, they believe me NOW!"

Shankly's players would nod and the crowd would roar as one, captivated by this inspirational Scot who genuinely put the fans first in every situation.

I wanted Catterick to be like this, but it was chalk and cheese. Harry was a class act, but was much more reserved.

So what would it be like for a young Evertonian journalist such as me to meet Shankly for the first time? Would I immediately declare my Everton allegiance on the basis that honesty is always the best policy?

In March 1969, I would find out.

I had travelled up to Anfield as usual to interview Ron Yeats for his column. The previous Monday, Liverpool had lost 1-0 at home to Leicester City in an FA Cup fifth round replay in front of over 54,000 people.

Shankly's boys had only scored two goals in their previous four games, a disappointing return, but 1966 World Cup hero Roger Hunt had netted both of them, one in a home win over Sheffield Wednesday and the other in an away draw at West Ham.

The manager was clearly unhappy with the general goal drought and in the second half against Leicester he opted to do something about it. He decided to try out Scottish forward Bobby Graham. Hunt was beckoned to come off for the first time in his illustrious Anfield career and he looked at the dug-out in total disbelief.

Now anyone who knows Roger Hunt will understand that he is the complete gentleman, quietly spoken and remarkably modest for such a national hero. Completely out of character, he pulled off his famous red shirt as he passed Shankly, Paisley, Fagan and Moran and threw it on the floor. Anfield was in uproar and it went from bad to worse, Liverpool crashing out of the cup 1-0.

Unlike the Echo at that time, the Weekly News had a state of the art web offset colour press and we also produced our newspapers in a tabloid format like the big national titles. We had just taken on a fairly experienced sub-editor/designer who had previously worked for the Daily Mirror.

He had helped introduce an inside sports pull-out section entitled Sportspot, again ahead of its day, and on page one he decided that we should carry the word BOYCOTT in giant white out of red letters to capture the mood after the sensational Hunt substitution.

The story suggested that Liverpool fans would boycott Anfield for the next home game unless their hero 'Sir Roger' was reinstated into the side. I didn't write the story or the headline and didn't even think twice about it when I set off for Anfield on the Monday to interview Yeats for his column.

We met in the reception and big Ronnie had a wry smile on his face. I looked over his shoulder and saw none other than Bill Shankly marching apace down the corridor from the players' tunnel where he had his small office. My first thought was: "Wow, there's Shankly. I wonder who he is about to meet?"

My second thought was that he was heading directly for me. He grabbed the lapel of my jacket, walked me towards the reception wall and shouted: "Boycott! Liverpool fans boycotting Anfield. You've come here for the last time son. You've reported at this stadium for the very last time." As he wheeled me round he grabbed the heavy metal door with his other hand and manhandled me out into the car park.

It was over in seconds. He stepped back inside and disappeared back down the tunnel.

I didn't have a car at that time and took a 17C bus back into the town centre. I had just turned 20 and it appeared my journalistic career was now over before it had even begun, at least on one side of the park. How would I tell my editor, Keith Charlton?

My head was spinning. Shankly had grabbed the 'Hunt boycott' story by the throat and was now boycotting me.

Who did he think he was? Some kind of untouchable football manager who acted first and asked questions later? I determined that this was exactly how Shankly operated and wondered what it must have been like in the Liverpool dressing room after the Hunt substitution.

Was it all sweetness and light, everyone accepting that the

right decision had been made and that was the end of it? No chance. Shankly had not minced his words with me and he would not have been slow in letting his players know that things had to improve. I recall Phil Thompson telling me about his debut for Liverpool Reserves as a young defender. He was determined to keep things simple and avoid any rash passes that might put him and the side under pressure.

Phil sat down in the dressing room at the end, quite pleased with his 'Steady Eddie' display. He then looked up and saw an angry Joe Fagan, eyes bulging, staring him straight in the face. With every other player listening, Fagan shouted: "Tommo, I know it was your first game son, but can't you play the ball forwards? Use this as an experience and have the confidence to be more positive."

It was a simple statement and the young Kirkby boy realised straight away that 'Steady Eddies' don't influence football matches. Fagan had made his point and Phil never forgot it.

I realised that in the new journalistic world I was in I had to get used to the fact that I would not be immune to criticism or passionate anger, not now, not ever. I had to get over it and deal with it.

We had moved from Bold Street to a new office in the Albany building in Old Hall Street. I sat down at my desk and sent Shankly a letter, typing with two fingers on my old-fashioned typewriter. I said that I understood his anger, but explained that I believed I had earned the respect of big Ronnie Yeats over a number of months.

I suggested that he might have possibly over-reacted

in ending my Anfield reporting career before it had even started.

I didn't add that the previous year I had been one of 40,000 Evertonians singing 'We hate Bill Shankly and we hate St John' at the derby game. Quite sensibly, I thought that might have tipped the balance against me.

I still didn't expect a reply or believe for one minute that I would get one. Two days later the phone rang bright and early in the office and one of the lads said: "It's someone claiming he is Bill Shankly and he wants to talk to you." I thought it was one of my colleagues around the corner messing about and I was fairly sharp in my response.

Then I recognised that familiar Scottish accent: "Son, I got your letter this morning. Come up and have lunch with me today and meet some of the lads. See you at Anfield at 1pm."

The phone went down and I looked at a sea of faces staring in my direction from all corners of the office. "The boycott's off," I said. "That's Shankly's boycott of me, not the Liverpool fans' boycott of Anfield! Bill and I are having lunch later."

There was a big roar and I managed a half-smile. I had now witnessed two contrasting faces of the gritty Scot in a few remarkable days. I realised he was very different from most of the other top bosses, many of whom couldn't care less about football fans and certainly had no time for football reporters, regardless of how young, old, or experienced they might be.

My dream first meeting with Harry Catterick is more like a TV game show!

THIS football journalism business was clearly going to be interesting to say the least. Despite the Bill Shankly experience and the friendliness and support of that giant Anfield character Ron Yeats, my prime aim was now to re-balance the sporting content of the Liverpool Weekly News to feature more big Everton interviews.

Of course, it was reliant on a certain Harry Catterick allowing a 20-year-old rookie reporter near the Bellefield training ground which, at that time, was known, even by the most senior of local reporters, as Colditz after the impregnable Second World War prisoner of war camp.

My plans were clearly going to be easier said than done... but what a challenge!

While I was plotting my new Bellefield agenda, this passionate Evertonian also had to somehow retain the trust of Ronnie Yeats while seeking to understand the little man at the Anfield helm who was viewed by all Liverpudlians as nothing less than a football god.

These two symbolised the very essence of Liverpool FC, the general off the pitch and his commander on it. They clearly belonged to a mutual fan club. I was in Shankly's office one day when the phone rang. He picked up the receiver and said: "Hi big man. Yes big man. No big man. Aye, that will be fine big man. I'll see you later big man." He then put down the phone, looked across at me and said: "That was the big man!"

I would never have guessed. At least I was deemed relevant enough to get into Shankly's inner sanctum. Cracking the code at Harry Catterick's Bellefield training ground was going to be doubly difficult. He didn't even give the big guns from the major nationals the time of day so why would he want to talk to a young reporter from a small weekly paper with a paid-for circulation of just 15,000 copies? The Echo was generating nearer to 200,000 copies a night at that time.

I now set myself the challenge of securing an early interview with 'The Cat'.

As it turned out, Bellefield's 'Colditz' reputation was not a figment of someone's imagination. It would be several months before Catterick opened his door to me, ironically in the week preceding the December 1969 Goodison derby. This was right in the middle of a season that would finish with my team as champions.

My long sought-after interview with the manager at 'Colditz' – or was it the camp commandant – would contribute to my journalistic education, but not in the way I had envisaged.

I actually rang Jean, Harry's Bellefield secretary, twice a week for over six months to ask for an interview, showing all the tenacity of a Canadian 'Mountie' whose famous motto was: 'We get our man.'

I had no trouble getting through to Jean who was always pleasant and professional, but she might as well have recorded her answer on a tape recorder and played it back to me every time I phoned because it was always the same: "I will ask the boss and let you know."

She never did. Summer turned to winter, but it was a good winter. Everton were top of the league going into December 1969, playing some magnificent football with an outstanding goalkeeper, a rock solid defence, a sublime and imaginative midfield and a significant goalscoring threat.

Much was rightly made of the influence of Messrs Ball, Harvey and Kendall in midfield, later to be become known as Everton's very own Holy Trinity. As fans and journalists we possibly over-egged this side of Everton's team game, something that Brian Labone always highlighted in a typically tongue-in-cheek manner. "We were the only club in the history of football to win the league title with three players," Labby would joke. But in the December, everything was still to play for and arch-rivals Liverpool were next up at Goodison in a long-awaited derby clash.

As usual, I rang Jean on the Monday. "Would Harry have

any time to see me this week?" I was waiting for her to switch on her tape recorder when she said: "Just a minute, I will ask."

Maybe I had worn her down. Maybe I had worn him down. Whatever the case, she came straight back on the phone and said: "The boss will see you at noon."

I was stunned, shocked, elated and ready to claim a totally unexpected derby week exclusive for the Liverpool Weekly News. I still didn't have a car and duly took the 75 bus up to West Derby before walking through the Bellefield gates. I headed towards the large complex that contained the dressing rooms at ground level, the players' dining room above, and beyond that Catterick's office. I was quickly ushered inside.

It was unexpectedly small and a room that, in later years, would become extremely familiar to me during daily meetings with managers like Howard Kendall and Colin Harvey. Catterick pointed to a chair opposite his desk and, quite bluntly, said: "What do you want?"

I had written out 20 questions that I believed every Evertonian wanted answers to during this week of weeks.

Surely it was important to prepare for a fast and furious derby match in a different way to a normal league game?

Could he highlight the key elements that had taken the Blues to the top of the table – and could we stay the distance?

How did he compare his management style to that of Bill Shankly?

How proud was he to have inspirational players like Ball,

Kendall and Harvey in his side going into such a big game, players with huge domestic ambitions?

How important were the local lads in the squad, like Brian Labone, Tommy Wright, Colin Harvey, Johnny Morrissey, Joe Royle and Alan Whittle?

Could we go on and win our first league crown since 1963 (the first great team Harry had built)?

Another 14 questions had the potential to tease out at least one great derby angle, but I had kept my most important to the last, a query that would have had a certain Bill Shankly waxing lyrical.

How important are the fans to your title quest? I assume the Goodison roar will be a vital weapon on Saturday?

As a fan, I desperately wanted him to say we were crucial to the cause and that he admired and respected every single one of us.

When my moment came, the Everton manager I had waited six months to meet and who I respected above all of his contemporaries, including Shankly, Revie, Clough and anyone else on the scene at that time, had all the answers.

The only problem was that he wasn't going to share them with me. He answered pretty much every question with a quickfire 'yes', 'no', 'I don't know', or 'kiss my backside'.

I made the last one up, but that's how I felt as my two-minute audience drew to a close.

We stood up, shook hands, and he followed me out of his office onto the short corridor by the kitchen. I was going to head out the way I came in, through the players' lounge with the lads starting to make their way in there after training. Instead, Harry steered me left and pointed me down a steep staircase that led to the emergency side fire exit. In his school master manner, he said: "Go out this way and shut the door behind you."

Within seconds I was out in the fresh air and making my way across the car park towards the Bellefield exit gate. I walked down towards the 75 bus stop to make the return journey into town. On the bus I studied my questions and Harry's answers.

A famous and popular quiz game show entitled 'Take Your Pick' had just finished on TV after a marathon 13 years on the box. Host Michael Miles was renowned for his 'Yes/No' interlude with competitors. He held a gong and asked them questions and they had to avoid saying either 'yes' or 'no'.

"Your name is Arthur?" *It is.*

"You come from Liverpool?" *I certainly do.*

"Are you an Everton or Liverpool fan?" *Everton, of course.*

"They play in blue don't they?" *Yes.*

GONG!

Michael had won again. It had been a tantalising and near impossible TV test for competitors and I had just played my very own version with Harry Catterick.

It was unprofessional, I know, but I decided that this was the way I would play my article for that Thursday's Weekly News sports pages. My intro indicated that I had just taken part in a derby version of Michael Miles' 'Yes/No' game.

I printed my questions in all their fine detail and gave Harry's answers: 'Yes, no, or kiss my backside!'

On the Saturday our title charge took a temporary and very painful knock. Liverpool won 3-0 at Goodison. Like all the fans, I was devastated. But then a young man named Alan Whittle came onto the scene and, despite his inexperience, he started to share the load with the ever-improving Joe Royle as our title charge gathered pace.

We would go on to claim a famous championship triumph and during the run-in would exact satisfying revenge on the old enemy with a 2-0 win at Anfield thanks to the magnificent Royle and an on-fire Whittle.

Catterick clearly had a huge talent and deserved total respect for what he had achieved, my one moment of 'Yes/No' madness apart. Again, it was all part of my journalistic learning curve.

Later in my career I had advanced from Weekly News rookie to experienced Liverpool Echo sports production editor. By now 'The Cat' was reaching the end of his famous and successful career and was embarking on his testimonial season.

He had two contrasting championships under his belt and one FA Cup triumph, but after suffering a heart attack in 1972, caused by the stress of his high profile role, Harry had been moved 'upstairs' as a non-executive director. The logic was that he would be available to offer advice to the man who replaced him, one of his former players Billy Bingham, although the reality was that Harry's influence was now minimal where it was once absolute.

His former secretary Jean, yes the same one I had contacted twice a week for six months, rang me to see if the man she still called 'the boss' could come into our Old Hall Street office and discuss publicity options around his testimonial season.

I smiled, immediately recalling my Bellefield experience all those years before. Clearly, Harry had written down a number of questions for discussion.

"Would I support his testimonial year with regular information in the Echo about events and ticket prices?"

"Could we do a series in the week of his special game highlighting the positives around his career?"

We looked at each other across my desk. I don't know why but a certain Michael Miles leapt into my mind. The words 'yes', 'no' and 'kiss my backside' suddenly flashed through my brain and I could hear a loud GONG ringing in my ears.

There was a moment of silence before I blurted out: "Of course we will, Harry. You have been a magnificent servant for Everton. It will be a pleasure and an honour to support your testimonial every inch of the way."

And I meant it. He really was someone we needed to support, an Everton legend who had earned his place in the Goodison Hall of Fame.

Baby Blue in the arms of the Boys in Blue at my Goodison Park baptism

MY passion for all things Everton FC had been cemented on a sunny Saturday afternoon in May 1950 when my father, Harry Rogers, formally claimed me for the club in his own inimitable way. The venue was Goodison Park's impressive Bullens Road Stand. I was just 18 months old.

The circumstances of my Everton FC 'baptism' and the story of how, as a toddler, I not only became one of the boys in blue, but was actually apprehended by one, will become apparent shortly.

But first, I would like to reflect on the ritual and symbolism of my first ever Everton match, the coincidences it threw up, and the omens it provided, offering a hint as to what might lie in store for me in the years ahead. I'm talking first and foremost as a lifelong Evertonian, but also as a former chief football writer and then sports editor of the Liverpool Echo.

I have no doubt that Dad bedecked me on that May day in 1950 in the colour that would ultimately dominate my life. His treasured blue and white Everton family scarf would have been draped proudly around my neck.

No sponsor names or words were emblazoned on it, of course. It was just an old fashioned knitted version made up of blue and white rectangles that Dad would later swear was held aloft at the 1933 FA Cup final where Dixie went from Goodison god to football immortal.

That day the great man scored a key goal at Wembley in the 3-0 win over Manchester City and, as captain, lifted the famous trophy in front of the Duke of York, who later became King George VI, football royalty putting true blue-blood royalty into the shade. This was the year players wore numbers on their backs for the first time, Everton 1-11 and City 12-22. It was therefore Dixie's first game in the number nine shirt that encapsulates his legend. Incredibly, he would never actually wear the number nine again.

The cup final kit was immediately locked away in a Goodison store room and it would be 1939 before the Football League made the numbering of shirts mandatory, despite the successful Wembley trial six years earlier.

By this time Dixie had played his last game for the Blues, but the ongoing importance to Evertonians of the number nine would forever be linked with his glory days and the legend of 60 league goals in one amazing 1927-28 season, a record that will never be beaten.

The great centre-forward's towering status meant that everyone had to have a 'Dixie' reference point, a story about meeting him, touching him, talking to him.

To truly understand the amazing story of William Ralph Dean is to know what being a true Evertonian is all about.

So my dad's scarf was like a holy relic – and we know that not all holy relics are genuine! To wear it was not just a sign of our family allegiance. It was a symbol of our football roots – and mine were firmly embedded in and around the famous football district of Everton.

I might have only been a toddler in 1950, but I was now about to be 'baptised' in a football sense and claimed for EFC, squaring the circle after my church baptism at nearby St Mary's, Kirkdale.

Sadly, I have to put to bed the myth of Dixie and my dad Harry's 1933 'Wembley' scarf. My father certainly could not have held it high under the old Twin Towers.

He was only nine in 1933 and had been in and out of hospital, initially with a hole in the heart problem, which reminds us of Asa Hartford who was at Goodison between 1979-81. When he was at West Brom a big move to Leeds fell through because of a similar condition. Dad also suffered a debilitating diphtheria episode that was unfortunately par for the course in those pre-Second World War days.

Inner city kids like those in the Rogers clan – Tommy, George, Harry, Albert and youngest brother Ronny – would be top and tail at various times in one attic bed that was held together by an old military belt. The brothers, who lived in Copeland Street, Everton, would be covered on cold winter nights by an Army Great Coat to keep out the biting cold (but not the biting bugs!).

Dad's Wembley scarf story was symbolic of his passion for all things blue and it provided the mystique that ensured I would feel the power of 'Dixie' and the great traditions of Everton FC whenever I wore it in the years that followed, and at my first Goodison game at the end of an uneventful 1949-50 season.

It was Everton's final match and we were entertaining Manchester City, the team we beat in '33. There was huge interest in the occasion for different reasons.

The legendary and veteran Ted Sagar – in his 13th season with the club (not including the war years) – was back in the side that day for the first time in over four months. He was reclaiming his jersey from George Burnett to make his 459th appearance of an eventual 497. What a record!

The Blues had not won any of their previous three games, losing at Derby, drawing against Burnley and losing at Sunderland. Dad was clearly desperate that my fan 'debut' would be a winning one, setting exactly the right tone for the rest of my life.

He had some cause for optimism. A young centre-forward by the name of Harry Catterick had scored in three of the previous four games, taking his league tally for the season to seven in 19 games as he continued to try and establish himself as the next in line of the great number nines.

Of course, anyone trying to fill the boots of pre-war giants like Dean and his magnificent successor Tommy Lawton would be on a hiding to nothing. Neither of us could have imagined that 18 years later I would be playing the Michael Miles 'Yes/No' game with a belligerent Catterick.

My father died in 2014 in his 90th year. He never tired of re-telling the tale of my first game. They say you should never run before you can walk. At 18 months, I was at best toddling, but dad wanted me to hear that Goodison roar.

With 'Dixie's' scarf swamping me, he carried me towards the Bullens Road turnstiles and actually paid for the two of us. The operator accepted the money, even though Dad had carried me over the turnstile. He recalls that a row immediately erupted as the men behind him began to argue with the operator that the mechanism had only turned once and therefore Dad should have only been charged for one.

This rumpus was still going on as my father began to make his way up the steep steps at the back of the Bullens, emerging into the sunshine to a sight that never failed to make the hairs on the back of his neck stand on end.

The Gwladys Street terrace to the right was already in full voice while the Main Stand, rising majestically on the other side of the pitch, resembled a giant Mersey liner.

Its angled upper stand was like the first class deck of a classic Cunard ship with people waving scarves and hankies as if they were about to set sail from the banks of the Mersey.

Down below was the engine room, the all-standing and massive angled area that stretched from the Stanley Park End to Gwladys Street. It swept back under the towering seated section and appeared capable of accommodating, in its own right, half the population of our football-mad city.

In the centre of all of this was the small black tunnel from where the gladiators would soon emerge. The Z-Cars theme and the carefully orchestrated pre-match razzmatazz of records and announcements had still to be invented, but the expectation and the roar was no less deafening.

You will have to accept that I'm making it up from this point. After all, I was only 18 months old. But this was not about visual memories. For my dad, like all Evertonian fathers, it was about my inner consciousness and a tribal bond that would live with me for the rest of my life.

He became engrossed in the game, not least because Catterick would score twice in a memorable 3-1 victory over City, Tommy Eglington getting the other goal.

After Catterick's second hit the back of the net, Dad's rapt attention was finally diverted from the pitch. He thought he heard someone shout: "Does anyone 'own' this toddler?" He looked along the row to his right and a policeman, fittingly one of the boys in blue, was holding me high above his head, pretty much like my dad had done just before kick-off, but this time I was facing the crowd and not the pitch.

"Here," shouted Dad, embarrassed that he had allowed me to crawl free along the row, no doubt in search of Catterick's autograph. "He's mine."

He reclaimed me and replaced 'Dixie's' scarf around my tiny neck with a half smile on his face and with fans all around pointing and laughing.

Dad had done his duty. I was now formally a fully fledged member of the Royal Blue Army and we had won convincingly. He knew this would stand me in good stead for the rest of my 'Everton FC' life – through good times and bad.

Now, like every Blue Nose worth his salt, I would begin to dream about playing for Everton. I would even appear on an 'official Everton pitch' – but it would be for Major Lester Primary School in Stanley Park.

In the years that followed I would actually travel on the official Everton team bus – but as a football journalist in the wonderful Howard Kendall era and not as the Goodison right winger I so desperately wanted to be.

I would forge an interesting relationship with a certain Harry Catterick – but he was now the manager and I was not the baby-faced fan in the stands. Rather, I was an emerging member of the media with whom he conducted a daily love-hate relationship, more hate I should add.

Ironically, I would soon find myself on the receiving end of some of that conflict early on as I've already described, but I still held him in the highest regard.

I would come across the legendary Ted Sagar in my trainee journalist years, but by now he was well past his glory days and running the Blue Anchor Pub in Aintree while I was a young sports reporter eagerly collecting interviews with one Everton legend after another for a 1968 series I had begun to write entitled 'The Mersey Football Hall of Fame' – any excuse to meet my heroes.

Most important of all was the fact that my new role would actually open up the Birkenhead front door of my all-time sporting idol – William Ralph Dean.

Sadly, I have to report that my dad's 'Dixie' scarf was snatched from the window of a railway carriage as I sped towards my first Everton away game at Burnley on September 5, 1964. I had joined the travelling blue army on a steam special to Lancashire where I desperately wanted to see our fairly new striker Fred Pickering, who a week earlier had scored a hat-trick at home to Tottenham.

The team Catterick selected at Burnley was: Andy Rankin, Alex Parker, Sandy Brown, Jimmy Gabriel, Brian Labone, Brian Harris, Alex Scott, Alex Young, Pickering, Roy Vernon and Derek Temple.

I had tied the treasured scarf to the window lock, wanting to show my true colours as we sped past every station along the way. As we slowed down passing through one Lancashire town, a rival fan snatched it from the window and I was devastated.

I had to face Dad when I got home. He just shrugged. "How did we get on?" he said. "What was atmosphere like? How did Pickering play?"

That was my dad. Nothing fazed him – unless it was a policeman shouting: "Does anyone own this toddler?"

Football, or Everton FC in particular, continued to dominate my father's life and got him into further trouble.

It didn't matter that my mother, May, had given him down the banks when he had cheerfully related losing me in the Bullens Road stand during my Goodison baptism.

I should explain that most things went over my dad's head. Mum was always the dominating force in our house which stood on one of those steep streets between Netherfield Road North and St Domingo Road.

Dad had this knack of standing in the face of a withering volley of criticism and letting it go over his head. "Thick as two short planks" was one of my mother's favourites, but my father would rise above it.

I was now eight and had been attending Major Lester School for three years in Everton Valley where I had proved good enough to play, first for the 'B' team and then, when I was 10, for the 'A' team.

We had a decent side. I scored 28 goals from the right wing one season while my attacking partner Raymond Johnston, a blond and pacy boy with great skill and power, bettered that with 32 goals of his own.

Our school was within a short walk of Stanley Park and so, like the original St Domingo pioneers, that was where we played. I remember we were caught up in a fairly tight game against one of the Scottie Road school teams, probably Penrhyn Street, when we got a penalty.

As usual, Dad was an engrossed figure on the touchline. Our school master, Mr Jim Harker, turned to him and said: "Who should take the penalty, Ray or your Kenny?"

Dad desperately wanted me to take it, but his modesty and sense of fair play got the better of him. "Let Jonno take it!" Ray duly obliged as he always did. His shot didn't hit the back of the net because we didn't have any, but it probably made the opposing keeper run 30 yards to recover the ball.

As we carried the posts from the park back to Everton Valley, dad was still debating his decision with Mr Harker as they walked side by side along Walton Lane. Then: "Bloody hell, I've left the baby in the park!"

The baby was my sister June, just a few months old at the time. Mum had insisted that Dad take her to the game in her pram to get her settled. He sprinted back into the park and the green pram was just where he left it. She was fast asleep.

Now losing your toddler son in the Bullens Road Stand is one thing. Leaving your baby daughter in Stanley Park is another. I can predict my mother's response. The only fitting thing I can say is that she would have turned the air blue!

Like most boys, I continued to play street and playground football every day and night between the ages of five and 15. Indeed, I continued to play competitive amateur football until I was 50 when I broke my left ankle with nobody near me on a pot-holed pitch in Manchester, turning out for the Collegiate Old Boys Vets, Brian Labone's famous old school.

I was football crazy throughout my childhood and would now go to Goodison on my own, first in the Boy's Pen, but sometimes finding my way onto the Gwladys Street terraces at three-quarter time. With the gates open to allow many fans to leave the stadium, hundreds of kids like me would be dodging the stewards to get in for our first ever taste of proper terrace life. It was sheer magic.

5

Dreams of being a star number seven and then I meet the real 'Wizard of the Dribble'

I WAS never hard to buy for as a kid. My parents knew that I would always be satisfied with a new plastic ball without an egg in it and I would be out there in the street pretending to be my hero Davy Hickson. At times, because I was a right winger at school, I usually imagined I was one of those well known Goodison number sevens.

One of these was Jimmy Harris who had been a centre-forward until the Cannonball Kid returned to the club in the 1957 close season when Jimmy switched wide right to great effect. I recall he scored a hat-trick in the infamous 10-4 defeat at Spurs in October 1958. There was an American TV programme showing at that time called Highway

43

Patrol starring Broderick Crawford and the call sign for the police cars was '10-4, over and out'. This became a painful rival football chant in the months that followed.

Another more short stay number seven was Mickey Lill until Irish international Billy Bingham claimed the shirt. By the time I was old enough to watch home and away, the skilful Alex 'Chico' Scott was our seven and he increased my boyhood dream of playing on the wing for the Blues.

Every Christmas I would be bought the latest 'Big Book of Football' with colourised images of greats like Tom Finney and the 'Wizard of the Dribble', Stanley Matthews. I once had the honour of sitting next to Sir Stanley at a football dinner. I told him that, Dixie Dean apart, he had few football equals in my book and I reminded him how he had transformed football, not with his famous dribbles, but with his own brand of boot that you could only buy at the Co-op.

My mother worked at the Frost's department store on Walton Road, a busy match day bar these days. Opposite was a large branch of the Co-op and looking in their window one day, I spotted a pair of football boots that resembled nothing I had ever seen before – and I had to have them.

For one thing, they had Stanley Matthews' name down the side and were described as 'exclusive' to the Co-op.

Prior to that point, our boots had been ankle high, made of tough leather and with solid toe caps that were perfect for a certain type of long ball game – known round our way as 'ale-house football'. The soles of these old boots featured nailed-in leather studs which became as sharp as knives as they began to wear down, making them lethal weapons.

Before every new season I would run to the Polish cobblers on Netherfield Road and ask him to hammer in a brand new set for a few coppers. I would also buy a tin of brown, sticky Dubbin that I would rub in to soften the tough leather.

The Matthews boots were cut just above the ankle and were made of a lighter synthetic material. More significantly, they had rubber studs. Ale-house football would become a thing of the past; cloggers would become almost ballet-like (don't you believe it) and the game would be changed forever.

Stanley smiled when I related this story to him. 1950s defenders didn't take prisoners and to a man they had attempted to kick him off the park on a weekly basis throughout his remarkable career, determined to literally 'nail' the genius dancing in front of them. He had become the first European Footballer of the Year, the first Footballer of the Year in England, the oldest player to play for England (at 42), and the first player to be knighted.

I mentioned that my amateur career ended aged 50 playing for Collegiate Old Boys Vets. Matthews was still playing in football's highest echelon at that age. He deserved to be one step ahead in those ground-breaking Co-op boots, and as he signed my menu card. I asked him to personalise it with my mother's Co-op 'divvy' number for good measure!

These early school days were an innocent period. You could have an allegiance with another club while never forgetting your true football love. Major Lester's 'B' team had blue shirts, but the 'A' team played in the colours of Arsenal – or 'the Arsenal' as Dad called them – red shirts with white sleeves, white shorts and red and white hooped socks.

It was no surprise, therefore, that on Christmas Day 1957, my first ever football kit was in the colours of 'the Arsenal'. I was out in our terraced street before 8am, bedecked in Highbury's best and proud to have a new Frido football to hammer against the wall in front of our house. There was actually big time football on Christmas Day, this being the last year that happened.

Later that week, on the way to the local corner shop, I spotted a bubble gum lapel badge in a rain-filled gutter. I picked it up and it featured the face of Manchester United's skipper and Busby Babe Roger Byrne, circled by the words: 'Roger Byrne Fan Club'.

I immediately pinned it to my jumper and would later wear it proudly in school. I was devastated when Byrne was one of those killed in the 1958 Munich Air Disaster. Thirty years later I had the honour of actually interviewing Sir Matt Busby at Old Trafford. By now the former Liverpool captain had stepped down as United's iconic manager, but was on the board and retained an office at the ground.

We sat together and reflected on his own playing days in Liverpool and his respect for both sets of fans on Merseyside. He said he always loved playing at Goodison Park.

I related the Roger Byrne story to him, how I had found that badge in the gutter on my way to school and wore it with such pride. He got quite emotional and even tearful. I asked him to sign a book I had brought with me and he inscribed it simply: 'To Ken, All best wishes, Matt Busby.'

I still have it as the definitive reminder as to how football has changed so dramatically, even in my own lifetime.

Reporting a cup final from the best speck in the house – on the hallowed turf!

I'VE recalled the unexpected outcome of my first meeting with Harry Catterick in his tiny Bellefield office during that glorious 1969-70 championship season, but I need to rewind two years to provide an insight into the challenge I now had as a young journalist, seeking to secure the exclusives I craved to give to the long-ignored Evertonian readers of the small but lively Liverpool Weekly News.

I have mentioned how previous sports editor Alan Parry – a Kopite with a notebook, pen and a passion only for the team that Shankly built – saw our sports pages through red-tinted spectacles. I was determined to bring some royal blue balance to the mix, but it was never going to be easy.

This became patently clear towards the end of April, 1968,

47

less than six months after the Weekly News had given me my dream sports editor's job and what I thought would be my very own 'Access All Areas' pass to the Bellefield training ground with a route to meet all of my personal soccer heroes.

As that '68 season accelerated towards its climax, Johnny Morrissey had scored the lone goal that beat Leeds United in an FA Cup semi-final at Old Trafford, a victory that would take us back to the famous Wembley stadium for the second time in two years.

In 1966, Everton folklore had been written under the Twin Towers when a famous and unexpected double from Mike Trebilcock and a classic strike from Derek Temple earned us a historic 3-2 victory over Sheffield Wednesday.

I had watched much of that game through the window of a television shop in Warrington town centre where, as a schoolboy, I had a Saturday job working for a national chain of tailors in the days when men actually used to get their suits made to measure.

What a day, what a victory and what a sight as my hero Brian Labone hoisted the FA Cup high above his head. Staring at the unfolding action through that shop window, I will also never forget Gordon West's smile lighting up Wembley that day.

Labby was a good mate of my former Evered High School sports master and mentor Ken Webster, both being Collegiate old boys.

On one memorable occasion Brian had accepted an invitation to present the prizes at a school football tournament for which medals were up for grabs for the very first time.

I tried doubly hard to ensure my team came out on top, not because the little trophy on offer had any real merit or value, but because it meant I could step forward and receive it from the Everton giant who was Brian Labone. I still have it over 50 years on, a personal reminder of the Last of the Great Corinthians, as Brian became known.

In the summer of '68 Labby's only thought was to lead Everton to another FA Cup final victory at Wembley, this time against West Bromwich Albion. Forget watching the match while standing outside a town centre TV store, my 1966 experience. I now had a passport to football's most famous press box. At least I thought I did.

I despatched my Liverpool Weekly News application letter off to the Football Association using our smart blue and red Swale Press headed paper and requested a press box ticket for myself plus a pass for our photographer John Callen.

Within a week I had a formal reply, immediately recognising the officially embossed FA envelope. I ripped it open and scanned the words on the page. "We are sorry, but you do not qualify for a place in the Wembley press box. Seats are being restricted to those journalists working for the major evening and national newspapers."

I was devastated, but there was an extra paragraph. It said: "You can have the photographer's pass you have requested and also an accompanying messenger's pass to support your photographer on the day."

I read this twice and then twice again. They appeared to be saying that I wasn't important enough to sit among the high and mighty of my new profession, men like Liverpool Echo sports editor Michael Charters.

However, I could sit behind the goal alongside my Weekly News photographic colleague John Callen and act as a runner between him and the Wembley darkrooms. This was assuming John needed me to do so which I knew he didn't because we were a weekly title with no immediate or overnight urgency.

Wow! I suddenly realised that, by default, I had actually been offered the best seat in the house in the days when the photographers could take vantage points about six feet behind the goal of their choice, almost able to reach out and touch the players on the pitch.

As a kid, Wembley appeared to me to be a football cathedral. Its immaculate green turf was used only for a handful of internationals each year plus the greatest show on earth, the FA Cup final. The pitch, with its perfectly mown tramlines, seemed to have mystical qualities. It was so lush that it had the capacity to drain the legs of even the fittest of players.

Every year we watched with baited breath to see who would be the first star to go down with a devastating and painful bout of cramp in the closing stages of the final. It always happened, often a game changer that had 100,000 fans holding their breath.

As a schoolboy, I had kept one cup final scrapbook after another, pasting in classic match reports.

On the day of the final, I would always sit transfixed in front of our tiny black and white TV in heartland Everton.

Colour sets were still few and far between, and yet I somehow knew just how green that famous pitch was.

Now I would actually be walking on it during cup final day and sitting behind one of the goals. I couldn't care less about the press box. I have a treasured photograph of myself from 1968. I'm walking across this field of dreams minutes before kick-off with someone who would later become a valued colleague, Echo chief photographer, the late Neville Willasey.

I'm heavily laden with John Callen's photographic equipment, carried in a large bag, but my beaming smile stretches the width of the Twin Towers. I would now join the Weekly News photographer in a position right alongside the left hand goalpost of Albion keeper John Osborne.

I desperately wanted to see him beaten by a soaring Joe Royle header; a close range effort from Alan Ball; maybe even a classic long range shot from Colin Harvey or Howard Kendall. Anything in the back of the Albion net would do.

Before the kick-off I asked our photographer for one of the small plastic film containers. Forgetting I was now an official member of Her Majesty's Press, I dug up a little bit of green Wembley turf and forced it into that small container. I wanted a special souvenir for my dad who had given me my passion for all things Everton.

I was recently telling Colin Harvey about this and he smiled knowingly, saying: "Before we moved out to Fazakerley, my family lived in Leta Street just behind Gwladys Street. We shared a house with my mum's sister. Everyone billeted up those days in small two up, two down terraced properties. The great thing was that we could just walk around the corner where my dad would put me in the old Boys' Pen before he went into the Street End.

"Dad was a big Everton fan and always told me about the last day of the season in 1954 when he went to Oldham to see the Blues gain promotion back to the old First Division. Thousands of Evertonians went and because of the traffic, many didn't get there until half-time and had to climb over a wall to get in. Dad was one of them.

"We won 4-0 and he ran on the pitch to celebrate, bringing a piece of the Boundary Park grass back home in an envelope as a memory of a famous day."

Colin's great story didn't make me feel too bad about digging up a piece of the hallowed Wembley turf in 1968. It would be a frustrating cup final for Blues fans.

The match kicked off and we had our chances. I constantly had my heart in my mouth when suddenly an inviting ball fell to Albion centre-forward Jeff Astle at the other end of the pitch, allowing him to strike possibly the greatest shot of his life. It flew past Gordon West.

We continued to attack, but Osborne's goal appeared to have a spell on it. I recall a teasing Jimmy Husband cross just clearing the heads of the in-rushing Everton strikers. It was tantalising.

I was as close as anyone could be to the Albion keeper. Osborne kept turning round every few seconds and nervously asking: "How long to go lads?"

"Loads of time," was my constant reply, but the seconds ticked away and suddenly it was all over. We had lost and the players were devastated. Mass security prevents any incursion onto the Wembley pitch these days, but things were more relaxed in 1968. I suddenly found myself wandering towards the centre circle where Labby and his team-mates were gathered, most of them kneeling down, unable to take in a devastating defeat.

One thing I remember is Harry Catterick, not the greatest of fan motivators and the nemesis of all journalists, asking the lads to put their personal despair behind them to go and salute the Everton faithful. It was hardly a speech, more of an arm pointing in the direction of the blue and white masses, but it struck a chord with me.

I lingered on that lush green turf, probably long enough to go down with my own bout of cramp. My first Wembley sojourn had proved bitterly disappointing for this emerging football journalist who was still thinking and acting like a fan.

In the years ahead, these thoughts would have to be tempered with a more measured approach (up to a point!). Even Alan Parry found that out.

I would never see or meet Albion keeper John Osborne again. I had been tempted to send him the watch I had worn at Wembley that fateful day with the fingers frozen in time before Astle's winner, but I couldn't change football history.

Thankfully, I would return to Wembley many times where I would ultimately see two Everton captains lift the treasured FA Cup.

I put 1968 down as a unique day in my career from which I could learn different lessons.

I might not have made the press box, but at least my dad, the man who inspired my Everton dreams, got his little piece of the turf where Dixie had once played. Sometimes you have to just count your blessings.

23rd January, 1967.

Mr. K. Rogers,
20 Felmersham Avenue,
Norris Green,
Liverpool, 11.

Dear Kenneth,

Following your interview here last week I am prepared to start you as a trainee on six months probation and on the other conditions explained to you. I would like you to start as soon as possible.

I am not sure which office you will be attached to first but, in any event, please report at head office to complete formalities. Let me know by 'phone or by letter the date you can start.

Yours faithfully,

R. Carrington

R. Carrington,
Managing Editor.

P.S.   If your parents have any queries about the position, I should be happy to deal with them.

Appointed by the Weekly News in 1967. The following year I would be reporting on an Everton cup final at Wembley

People's Game, People's Club, and a seismic football revolution

I COUNT myself very lucky to have started reporting on football in the late 1960s . . . the winter of 1967 to be exact. It was still very much the people's game in this era. The £20-a-week maximum wage for footballers had only been abolished six years earlier. Even the game's greatest players were still living on the same planet as the fans.

My journalistic career bridged a series of football revolutions across nearly four decades. Many changes were for the better, like the advent of the new all-seater stadia post-Hillsborough with improved safety and dramatically enhanced facilities as we moved into the Nineties.

However, the great game of the working class suddenly changed beyond all recognition as big business and seismic investment created a massive chasm between the 'haves' and the 'have nots'.

It was still the national game, but not as we once knew it. For instance, football tourism was born with clubs like Manchester United and Liverpool attracting an army of fans from all over the country, indeed the world.

The balancer for a club like Everton FC was that it retained its local heart to subsequently inspire the tag the 'People's Club', but Evertonians are realistic enough to accept that consistent success in Europe breeds a much wider audience – and we were denied the opportunity to achieve that after English clubs were banned from Europe following the Heysel Stadium disaster.

But back in 1969-70, the logic that football would be over-run by commercialism and what Roy Keane ultimately described as the 'prawn sandwich brigade' seemed inconceivable.

The Sixties was an era when a typical goal salute was a player clasping his hands above his head or leaping joyfully with hands in the air. This has been overtaken by the modern preference for a scowl with an arrogant finger up to the lips, a so-called 'celebration' I detest.

We see the totally cynical kissing of the badge, or the finger pointing to the name on the back of a shirt, typifying the 'me-me-me' culture of a new breed of football mercenaries.

This may all seem over the top. There is no doubt that current players are fitter, faster, and more skilful in a sideways, pass-pass-pass kind of way.

But the soul of the game has changed with insanity reigning at times, typified by the sight of a football institution like Glasgow Rangers being relegated into near oblivion and even threatened with closure while still playing in one of football's great cathedrals, all down to living beyond their means.

As 1968 unfolded and I got into my journalistic stride, the rewards players received were still fairly modest. This meant they remained grounded and could relate much more closely to the fans paying their wages. It also meant that life was much simpler and easier for the media as they went about the daily task of seeking exclusive interviews and news stories for readers.

Gordon West was the first Everton star I interviewed. It was a joy and an honour to discuss football with one of Goodison's greatest characters. Of course, I also had to go to Anfield and I will use one of those sorties to explain just how dramatically football has changed.

In 1970, as England's preparations for the Mexico World Cup reached a climax, I decided to seek a chat with Liverpool winger Peter Thompson, a mazy dribbler who thrilled Liverpudlians with his skill on the left flank. The players trained at Melwood in those days, before taking a coach back to Anfield where they had lunch or received treatment for any knocks.

Still without a car, I waited in the Main Stand car park as the likes of the emerging Ray Clemence, Ian Callaghan and Emlyn Hughes appeared and set off for home. The last one out was Peter.

All the England players had been given a special edition

white Ford Cortina called a 'Mexico' so I knew Peter was still there. He finally emerged into a totally deserted car park where I was encamped with my notebook right next to his car.

I asked if he would mind doing a short interview for the Weekly News and when he said he had to go for his pre-World Cup injections, I thought this was polite code for "Thanks, but no thanks." Peter then said: "But if you wait here, I'll come back in 15 minutes."

I nodded and he jumped into his speedy new motor and disappeared through what became the Shankly Gates. I was like Billy No-Mates and didn't expect to see Peter again until after the World Cup.

I kept looking at my watch and it got to 14 minutes. Suddenly this white Cortina Mexico swept back in through the gates and a smiling Peter pulled up. "Jump in," he said. "Now how can I help you?"

These days, the superstars of the Premier League don't need to cross the road to talk to anyone except their agents. At times, many players show what can only be described as contempt for supporters, highlighted perfectly by those high tech earphones many wear, locking them inside their own closeted world as they transfer from team bus to players' entrance.

Many players genuinely do great work behind the scenes for the various club community initiatives, but you can't compare the way it was with the way it is. Perhaps we shouldn't try, except that the football revolution has been seismic to say the least.

No car between us, so an Everton star agrees to an interview on a 75 bus!

IN the Sixties and into the Seventies, Bill Shankly insisted that his Melwood training ground should be accessible every day to the public, and therefore the media, although I have already highlighted that Harry Catterick did not necessarily concur with this open door policy.

Modern training grounds have more security than the famous MI5 spy headquarters on the banks of the Thames, but back in 1968 even Everton's Bellefield complex was not a complete no-go area. As a young reporter, I was allowed through the gates into the car park, but no further.

As explained, the routine was that you would wait for the players to finish training and then approach them for a chat as they walked towards their cars. Even the superstars of the day would not think twice about inviting you to sit inside a gleaming E-Type Jaguar to conduct these interviews and I was quickly into this routine.

Over a period of months – and with the support of Everton's magnificent captain Brian Labone – I built up an impressive portfolio of exclusives with the likes of Alan Ball, Howard Kendall, Colin Harvey, Joe Royle and the rest as Everton once again began to develop under Catterick's astute leadership as a team more than capable of reclaiming the league championship.

Having won it in 1963, the Blues had finished third, fourth, eleventh, sixth and fifth before finally looking genuine contenders again in 1968-69 when they finished a credible third. It was clear this was a side with genuine star quality. Catterick's strongest team that season was: Gordon West, Tommy Wright, Sandy Brown, Howard Kendall, Brian Labone, Colin Harvey, Jimmy Husband, Alan Ball, Joe Royle, John Hurst and Johnny Morrissey.

Along the way, one or two others had their moments and one of these was a young Welsh Under-23 international by the name of Gerry Humphreys. In mid-September 1968 the Blues entertained Sheffield Wednesday at Goodison and I was in the press box to witness an outstanding 3-0 victory.

The rout started with a remarkable strike from Humphreys who was making just his third appearance on the left wing with Morrissey injured. The young Welshman picked up the ball just inside the Wednesday half and began to make ground towards to Gwladys Street End. He suddenly let fly with a left-foot shot that flew into the roof of the net.

The crowd roared its delight and I made an instant note that I would try to interview Gerry at Bellefield the following week for the Liverpool Weekly News. On the Tuesday, I waited in the car park and when he emerged from the dressing room complex, I approached and asked if he could give me a few minutes.

I explained I didn't have a car and asked if we could sit in his car for the interview. He said he would do the interview, but explained that he too didn't have a car. We looked at each other and I was suddenly thinking on my feet.

Could we go down to the small cafe on Eaton Road opposite Alder Hey Hospital where many of the Everton and Liverpool players went for lunch? I had been there a couple of times to ghost-write Ron Yeats' Weekly News column. It was a mile and a half to walk, but Gerry agreed and we set off on this unexpected expedition.

When we reached the main road, I suggested it might be better if we waited for a 75 bus. Again, Everton's Saturday goal hero agreed and we stood there chatting about his debut and his wonder goal. Almost immediately, the bus arrived and I generously offered to pay the fares. Well, it was only right and proper!

We jumped off outside Alder Hey and were soon inside the cafe, completing the interview over a coffee.

That day always comes to my mind when I think about today's super-rich players with their mega salaries and high-powered cars. It's not unusual for Ferraris and the like to jostle for position inside modern training complexes. I recall a Daily Mail news story in March 2016 with the headline:

"Is this why fans can't relate to today's mega rich stars?" It accompanied a picture of Samir Nasri, leaning nonchalantly with his foot against the wall of an old terraced property in Wilson Street close to Manchester City's training ground. He was tapping away on his mobile phone without a care in the world as three policemen inspected the registration papers for his new car – a £330,000 Lamborghini Aventador Pirelli – which was later impounded.

The owner of the house, John Miller, summed up the disconnection between most fans and players when he said: "They just fly past behind their darkened panes." His neighbour Pauline James declared: "The street has become a rat run for these City players in their multi-million pound cars."

Nasri could have bought four houses in Wilson Street for the price of his high powered super car. When I read that story, I smiled and remembered that day in 1968 when an Everton player who had scored one of the goals of the season joined me on a 75 bus to conduct an interview.

Can you imagine any current star walking a mile and a half through the streets to a public cafe for a press interview, or agreeing to jump on an old double decker for the privilege of a chat with a young reporter? Answers on a postcard, please!

Soccer slave,
World Cup giant,
Blues hero
– and undertaker!

ONE of the most down-to-earth and remarkable characters I ever met in the world of football was Ray Wilson, or Ramon Wilson to give him his Sunday name.

He was possibly the only Everton star to totally refuse all of my polite requests for a Bellefield interview in season 1967-68, but I fully understood his reticence to speak during a campaign in which he was dogged by an injury that would soon hasten his departure from the club.

Ray had been one of my favourite players and had earned the right to be in any British Football Hall of Fame as one of only 11 individuals to have played in and won a World Cup final with England.

He struggled to get 100 per cent fit after picking up a

problem in the final game of the 1967-68 campaign, just three days after he had appeared in his second FA Cup final for the Blues.

Unable to shrug the injury off, he was replaced in the first-team by the play-anywhere Sandy Brown and our 1966 Jules Rimet hero would play in only five more games that season before leaving on a free transfer to Oldham Athletic.

It would be over 20 years before I eventually got the interview that had evaded me. It came after I was asked by publishers Breedon to produce a book entitled 'Everton Greats' – naming the 10 best Everton players I had ever seen, a massive challenge, but one I accepted with relish. It meant I could get back on the Ray Wilson trail.

The joy of finally meeting him that day in 1989 and discussing his eventful career took on a whole new meaning in April 2016 when it was reported that our World Cup hero was suffering from advanced dementia and sadly could no longer remember his glory days for club and country.

It's remarkable to reflect that Ray was approaching his 30th birthday when Harry Catterick chose to sign him for Everton in the summer of '64.

But despite his age Wilson wasn't just any defender. He was a man whose international pedigree was amazing, considering he had given his best years to Huddersfield Town, mostly in the old second division.

One of Ray's biggest achievements was therefore to destroy the popular misconception that you have no chance of progressing on an international stage unless you are sitting pretty with one of the game's aristocrats. Wilson secured an astonishing 30 England caps while he was still operating in this country's second tier and would add another 33 to his collection after he joined Everton.

Catterick's instincts that Ray still had much to offer would be mirrored years later by Howard Kendall's astute move for veteran Manchester City full-back Paul Power who helped the Blues claim the 1987 league title. Clearly, Howard had learned well from the old master.

Ray would not only win the World Cup as an Everton player in 1966, but could also reflect on a famous FA Cup triumph that year.

Of course, Wilson's eventful career was long behind him in 1989 when I travelled across to the small West York-shire village of Slaithwaite where he lived to secure that long overdue interview. He had a reputation for being a bit dour and had long put the glamour of football behind him, taking the highly unusual decision to become an undertaker, running the family business.

I wanted to know why he had stayed outside of football's top flight for so long with Huddersfield Town before finally joining a giant like Everton. He immediately refuted any logic that it might have been linked with a lack of ambition.

He said: "When you signed for a club in those days, it was for life, unless it suited your employers to sell you. There was absolutely nothing you could do about it. They had you over a barrel and we were soccer slaves. The only reason Huddersfield finally let me go to Everton was because I was almost 30 and they decided it was time to cash in. It was the best favour they ever did me."

In my mind, Ray had no reason whatsoever to be grateful to his former employers and at Goodison Park he quickly grasped the difference in class. He told me: "It was only when I had been at Everton for two or three weeks that I began to understand what I had been missing for the previous 12 years. I'd won 30 international caps, but only played in six top-flight games. My only regret in life is that my career wasn't the other way round, playing for Everton from the word go."

We began to reflect on how the boy from the pit village of Shirebrook climbed the ladder to become a national hero and World Cup winner, an achievement he is very proud of. He said: "Many people think Alan Ball was an Everton player during the World Cup, but I was the only one."

Terry Darracott once gave me a player's insight into Wilson. He said: "He was a brilliant footballer and a true gentleman. I'll never forget being drafted in to replace him for a game in the season when he was out with a knee injury. He was a great influence and an outstanding full-back whose cultured left foot would stick out a mile in any situation. He could also be very strong if the game turned that way, but he was renowned for his class and could knock as sweet a pass as you would wish to see from a defender."

Class is the first word that comes to mind when talking about Ray Wilson. The second word is modesty. I remember him telling me: "As a young player, I was actually offered a trial by Everton, but chose to go to Huddersfield in case I finished up with nothing. I was never ambitious in trying to plan my life. I've just gone up different roads. If you're relaxed, it often works out better. I never wanted to be a millionaire. Dreams must be attainable."

This immediately conjures up the third phrase to describe Ray: totally grounded. He played in an age when young players, far from being pampered as they are now, had an intensive workload that had nothing to do with football, but everything to do with building character.

He told me: "We were called soccer apprentices, but that probably contravened the Trades Descriptions Act. We would sweep the terraces, wash the kit, clean the boots – and then they would give us a ball!

"It was really tough to break through with 40 to 50 players on the ground staff. They had to take three or four team photographs to get everyone in."

Ray is in a very select group, having played for Bill Shankly at Huddersfield and Harry Catterick at Everton. Johnny Morrissey also played for both legendary Merseyside bosses. He described Shankly as inspirational and Catterick as tough. "Harry ran the club with an iron fist," said Ray. "He was never afraid to take on players with a big reputation. He used to weigh us every week and we had to clock in every morning. If you were late or overweight you were immediately fined."

Yet Wilson revelled in every minute of his Everton career and it was his view on the supporters that filled me with particular pride. He said: "The fans had a very special feel for the club. It wasn't a case of four big games a season like I had been used to at Huddersfield. There was a new challenge every week. Every day was a pleasure."

In 2002, Ray chose to sell his treasured World Cup medal for £80,750. It would be re-sold a second time by Sotheby's for £136,000 in November, 2014. The purchaser was well known memorabilia collector Nigel Ray.

It's sad that Wilson chose to part with this solid gold treasure which was inscribed 'FIFA World Championship Winners, Jules Rimet Cup' – the ultimate reminder of the part he played in the greatest day in English football history.

But he is not the first legend and he won't be the last to take such a decision, coming from that era when rewards were nothing like they are today. The reality is that you can't live on your memories, something that really hit home in April, 2016, when Ray's wife Pat revealed that his dementia had become advanced, her treasured husband having lived with the condition for 12 years. Ray now spends much of his time sitting at the kitchen table drawing images that she dutifully puts up on the wall. On one of them, he had penned the words: "I am a happy man."

She said: "I love his art work, but they are weird. They are all pen drawings and most of them are happy. The eyes on the figures he draws are bright and they're normally smiling, although some of them do look like aliens!"

Ray may no longer be able to personally recall the immense part he played in Everton and England football history, but the fans who were lucky enough to see him play will continue to carry those wonderful memories on his behalf.

And despite the club securing two league championships and two FA Cups since he left, I would still include Ray Wilson in my Everton greats top 10. He was world class.

I find Dixie, the legend of 60 goals, working in a tiny hut in a city centre garage

WILLIAM Ralph 'Dixie' Dean will forever be the greatest Everton player of all time. That's a bold statement when you try and take in the status and history of our club, but I have still to meet a single Evertonian who would dispute it.

In the previous chapter about Ray Wilson, I reflected that he was included in a book I was asked to write about Everton greats.

I was told I could name just 10 with the proviso that I had seen them in action. After much deliberation, I opted for: Dave Hickson, Brian Labone, Alex Young, Colin Harvey, Ray Wilson, Alan Ball, Howard Kendall, Bob Latchford, Andy Gray and Neville Southall.

It's enough to say that every Evertonian, depending on his or her age in 1989, would have produced a different list. I would have liked to have included Joe Royle in my personal 10, a local boy who enjoyed a great playing career, but I opted to seek decade balance.

I envied those senior fans lucky enough to have watched the Blues in the 1920s and 1930s and witnessed history in the making at Goodison Park, the first School of Soccer Science era.

Their star selection would have always had one name in large capital letters at the very top . . . DIXIE.

His 60 league goals in 1927-28 were secured against centre-halves and defenders who were allowed to tackle waist-high and crush opponents with lethal shoulder charges without ever being booked or sent off. Dean's haul will forever stand as an unbeatable top-flight scoring record.

This alone confirms him as the 'Prince of Birkenhead's North End, and the King of St Domingo Road' to quote from Gerry's Murphy's emotive song: 'The Ballad of Dixie Dean'.

He was and remains the brightest star in Everton's royal blue heaven. Obviously, I never saw him play, but I have already described the talismanic power of my father's so-called 'Dixie' scarf and how people like Dad desperately wanted to have a link, no matter how tenuous, with this football immortal.

Dean was the definitive king of the air and while there was clearly much more to his game than this, his heading power was the stuff of legend. My father and grandfather would both suggest that he could head the ball from his own half deep into the opposing penalty area and out-jump or out-jostle any defender in the world in his personal domain – the penalty box.

I was ready to believe anything about Dixie Dean. In late 1968, I got the chance to ask the man himself. I had started my new 'Mersey Hall of Fame' series in the Liverpool Weekly News and set myself the challenge of interviewing as many former local football heroes who were still alive at that time as possible.

On the Everton front I was able to sit with the likes of Tommy Lawton, Warney Cresswell, Ted Sagar, Jimmy O'Neill, Gordon Watson, Joe Mercer, Jackie Grant, Eddie Wainwright, Tommy Clinton, Cyril Lello – and the amazing Dave Hickson.

Of course, my number one interview target was William Ralph Dean. The Weekly News office was in Bold Street. I heard that Dixie, now the legend of 60 years as well as 60 goals, had been given a job by Everton chairman John Moores, working in a large Littlewoods garage behind Renshaw Street. It was effectively a cavernous shed, inside which was a small hut where Dixie whiled away his days.

The garage was just two minutes from our office and I was soon over there on a daily basis. Dixie humoured me, relating the great stories of his playing era which he must have told a thousand times. I just sat their mesmerised, taking notes and making sure he knew that he was my dad's number one hero. I even apologised for losing our treasured 'Dixie' scarf en route to Burnley circa 1964.

Dean might have been the greatest, lauded by everyone he met, but he was the definitive man of the people and an unshakeable Evertonian. He had lived for a spell in a club house in the shadow of the ground when his local pub was the Winslow, opposite Goodison's main entrance.

He would drink in there and on match days would walk the 50 yards to the main entrance, exchanging jokes, stories and gossip along the way with the fans. He didn't know what the word pomposity meant.

The only time I ever saw him on a football pitch was at South Liverpool's old ground, Holly Park, where he once kicked off a charity match in the 1960s, but even I couldn't claim this as a tick on my all-time Everton greats list.

However, I count myself as one of the luckiest people in the world to have had the opportunity to get to know Dixie, albeit sitting with him in a cocky-watchman's hut, as we used to call them, in a colourless and cavernous city centre garage, although 'cocky' he most certainly was not.

I felt it would have been more fitting for John Moores to have simply given him a weekly retainer based on everything he had achieved for the club. The reality is that Dean still wanted to work as a matter of pride.

That work ethic and the importance of it swamped his eventual Goodison successor Tommy Lawton. After Tommy's playing days were over in Nottingham, he also secured a job, but lost it, leading to a period of genuine financial instability. He was too embarrassed to tell his wife and at one point was setting out for 'work' in the morning and coming home at night while keeping his little secret.

This was ultimately solved when the local newspaper, the Nottingham Evening Post, offered him a paid-for football column. I would see this instantly recognisable figure at Everton away games at both Notts County and Forest and would make a beeline for him. Like Dixie, he loved to recall his Goodison days. Some people argued that he might have even been a better all-round player than Dean.

I put this to Tommy and he said: "No-one was better than Dixie. He was, and always will be, the greatest centre-forward of all time and he made me feel so at home when I first arrived at Everton in 1937. I was effectively bought to replace Bill Dean as his magnificent career began to wind down, but he was at Lime Street to meet me on the day I arrived and was the one who immediately began to show me the ropes."

Everton arranged a testimonial match for Tommy Lawton in 1972, a gesture he never forgot. Dean would also enjoy a famous testimonial night and would regularly attend football functions all over Merseyside until he died in 1980 – ironically at his beloved Goodison Park.

On May 8, 1971, Merseyside's historic Football Echo had launched a much-anticipated series of interviews with Dixie Dean that would run for an astonishing four-and-a-half months. The great centre-forward had spent several weeks sitting with the Echo's sports editor of the day, Michael Charters, who typed 30,000 words on an old fashioned typewriter in which he inserted a piece of carbon paper to ensure he had a copy before it was sent, first to the sub-editing team and then to the printers.

The Echo's library staff, the holders of the company's rich archive of pictures and cuttings, asked Charters if they could have his original manuscript which they duly filed away along with the series press cuttings.

Thirty four years later responsibility for the Echo archive fell to me as part of my wider remit with parent company Trinity Mirror, running the company's Sport Media publishing unit.

I found myself researching one day in a fairly dismal and dusty library storage room in the basement of our Old Hall Street building.

I pulled open a drawer in a large metal cabinet and couldn't believe what I found. Neatly filed away was a brown envelope marked: 'Dixie Dean Football Echo series, 1971.' To have a complete set of cuttings from that series was fantastic enough, but it was the accompanying and completely unedited manuscript, originally typed by Charters, that was football gold.

Sub-editors inevitably have to cut back stories and features to make them fit into an allocated space. I suddenly had the complete uncut version in my hands on 450 neatly-typed pages. I also found Michael's accompanying rough notes. He had clearly taped Dixie and then transcribed his words over a period of weeks.

We immediately decided to turn this football treasure into a book: 'The Lost Interview – Dixie Dean Uncut.' It revealed the Goodison legend's innermost thoughts and some truly remarkable anecdotes. Many years earlier, while writing my 1992 official centenary book '100 Years Of Goodison

Glory', I set myself the challenge of finding out once and for all just how good Dixie actually was. Was it a case of the legend almost going before the facts?

I reviewed all the Everton match reports from the famous 1927-28 season of 60 league goals, home and away, analysing his performance level in as much detail as I possibly could. Did he start quickly? Did he drift out of games and then score with one moment of magic? Was he an ever-present threat to opponents? Was he just a natural king of the air or did he have other attributes? Was he stronger on one side or the other or could he strike the ball naturally with both feet?

I wanted to be as scientific as I could be based on contemporary reports and comments. I wasn't disappointed. Indeed, Dean appeared to have it all at his peak. He wasn't just a goal taker, but someone who could set up attacks on both flanks with deft flicks of that famous head.

He was mobile and had a great football engine. He was also powerful, refusing to be intimidated or bullied by big centre-backs who, in those days, each had a 'licence to kill'. Dixie took a lot of stick, but he handed it back in good measure and the fans loved him for it.

He scored goals with both feet and his name would pop up in every phase of every game. He was a true giant, but with a modesty that made him the definitive working class hero.

We often see photographs of him later in his career when he was carrying a bit of weight and beginning to look his age, bearing in mind training and diet then was not the scientific subject it is today.

But look at the young Dean in his pomp and you will see the perfect football specimen, ideally balanced to destroy the game's greatest defences. His eyes reveal his pride in all things Everton. At the end of my research I knew that he truly was and is the greatest of them all.

My favourite four Dean stories from that epic Football Echo series are captured in the chapter that follows. If you ever doubted he was a complete one-off, read on.

A ticket stub from the famous 1933 FA Cup final where Dixie Dean scored one of Everton's goals and (below) a treasured autograph from the great man

My favourite stories that confirm Dixie was truly an Everton immortal

THE EXTRAORDINARY NIGHT-TIME TREATMENT REGIME THAT KEPT THE 60-GOAL DREAM ALIVE:

In 1927 Middlesbrough's George Camsell scored 59 goals to set a new Football League scoring record, but this was achieved in the old second division.

The following season, Dixie Dean was on course to set a new mark, this time in the much tougher surroundings of the top flight. It wasn't going to be easy. With two games left, Dixie still needed to score seven goals.

He made an incredible start, grabbing four in a midweek game at Burnley during the final week of the season. The achievement was all the more remarkable because he was being marked that night by big England centre-half Jack Hill. The elation of the Everton staff was immediately tempered when Dean pulled a thigh muscle in the second half.

The great man recalled: "Our trainer, old Harry Cooke, was shaking when he found out about it. He was really worried that I would not be able to play in the final game at home to Arsenal on the Saturday.

"He wanted to put hot plasters on my leg to get the muscle right. These needed to be left on pretty hot for up to 12 hours, but Harry wasn't content with that.

"He wanted to change them every two hours so that the heat of the plasters would really work. I went to bed, but he sat in a chair in my bedroom and woke me up every two hours so that he could put a fresh plaster on. He did this for three nights on the run – on the Wednesday, Thursday and Friday before the Arsenal game.

"He put hot towels on as well and without him I would not have played that day and would have missed out on the record. Every morning I would run Harry home to his house in Wallasey before we returned to Goodison for more treatment. I don't know how he stuck it for three nights with so little sleep."

I've got this image of old Harry in Dixie's Birkenhead bedroom, asking Mrs Dean to move over in the middle of the night while he changed a hot poultice on the great man's leg! It was dedication beyond the bounds of duty – and it worked.

On the Saturday and with three goals needed for the

record, Dean inspired one of Goodison's biggest ever roars when he won and then scored a penalty. Just before half-time he rifled a second into the corner of the net.

The crowd were on pins as Arsenal tightened things up. The game went into the final eight minutes with Cooke increasingly concerned about Dixie's thigh muscle. The Blues secured a corner on the left.

Alex Troup sent over a typically precise kick and Dean leapt to bullet a trademark header into the back of the net. Fans invaded the pitch and he recalled: "I got more whiskers on my face from the Scotland Road lads than Soft Joe."

The record of records was in the bag and he left the pitch shortly before the end to a standing ovation. He didn't actually receive anything from the club to mark the 60 goals, but the supporters club gave him a big wooden shield on which smaller shields recorded each of his 60 goals as well as displaying his remarkable medal collection.

THE NIGHT DIXIE SILENCED HAMPDEN PARK, ONLY TO BE CRITICISED BY A BLAZER-WEARING FA OFFICIAL:

In 1927, Dean was selected to play for England against Scotland at the mighty Hampden Park. He recalls the occasion as one of the greatest days of his life because he scored twice to silence the Scots and inspire a 2-1 victory.

His first goal was a 30-yard drive with his right foot into the bottom corner of the Scottish net. He said: "You could suddenly hear a pin drop at Hampden."

A few minutes later he repeated the exercise, this time with his left foot into the other corner. After the game, the elated England team were all smiles in the dressing room when members of the FA committee, all amateurs, came in.

One of them stepped in front of Dixie and said: "Well, I don't know Dean that you had such a great game, but you got two goals."

It's enough to say that the official was lucky not to be immediately shoulder charged into the deep bath at Hampden. Players only got caps in those days for playing against Scotland, Wales or Ireland.

During the following mid-season, Dixie grabbed a hat-trick in a 9-1 win over Belgium, another treble in a 5-2 victory over Luxembourg, and two in a 6-0 win against France.

He was on £8 a week at Everton, but the England fee during the summer was just £6 per match. The night before this successful summer series, another FA official had the audacity to stand in front of the England players to ask a shock question: "Do you all want your £6 fee per match, or would you prefer the medal for representing your country?"

All the lads looked at each other. "I'll have the medal," said Dean, proud to be an Englishman and play for his country. He treasured it all his life.

DIXIE'S MIND GAMES AS THE BLUES PREPARED FOR THEIR 1933 FA CUP FINAL AGAINST CITY:

In 1933, Dean led the Blues to a famous FA Cup final victory against Manchester City, having won the championship the previous year. The FA had a strict pre-match Wembley ritual and a commissionaire came to the dressing room door and said: "Get ready to come out. The Manchester City players are already in the tunnel."

Dixie turned to his team-mates and said: "It's alright. Don't worry. We'll catch them up later. Shut the door."

The players began to suggest they should hurry up, but the captain looked across at old defender Warney Cresswell who was sitting in the corner as calm as ever, smoking his pipe. Dean recalled: "To keep him company I lit a cigarette and said to the lads 'There's plenty of time, let them wait.'

"When I eventually got out there alongside City captain Sam Cowan he was holding a football in his hands and he was shaking. I knew it was going to be our day – and it was."

GERMAN CAPTAIN FINDS OUT THAT NO-ONE MESSES WITH EVERTON:

Dixie recalled an Everton pre-season tour in Dresden before the war. The Blues had taken a supply of size five footballs with them and the Germans agreed to use them.

Dean recalls: "When I went to toss up with the captain, he was carrying a size four ball that he wanted to use. It was just a kid's size and we were not going to have that. I said to him 'This is the ball we are going to use' and put the size five down on the centre spot.

"He kicked it away and put his smaller ball down so I kicked that away. The referee was trying to stop all this when I said to the captain: 'All right, give me your ball.'

"He did with a half smile on his face. I carried it over to the touchline, followed by the Dresden skipper and the referee. When I got to the line, I kicked the size four right over the stand and out of the ground.

"I turned to the referee and said: 'Right, now we'll play with this one – the size 5.' We did and we won. No-one messed around with Everton."

LABBY'S PROUD DEAN EPITAPH:

When I was considering someone to write a foreword for the 'Dixie Dean Uncut' book, there was only one man I could genuinely turn to, that other remarkable Evertonian, Brian Labone. He told me: "I was privileged to know Dixie Dean, or Bill as he preferred to be called. For all he achieved, he remained a down-to-earth fellow and a hell of a character.

"When Dixie was to have his leg amputated in 1976, I went to visit him at Birkenhead General Hospital with his great friend and former Everton team-mate Gordon Watson. The staff told us that Bill had needed a major blood-transfusion and we needed to tread softly.

"We tiptoed into his room, expecting to see him in a poor state and wired up to various tubes.

"Bill was sitting up watching the racing on a portable television with a bottle of beer by the side of his bed. He looked over at Gordon and myself and said: 'That flaming Lester Piggott has just let me down again.'"

Brian added: "I was with Dixie on his final day on this Earth, fittingly at Goodison Park on March 1, 1980, and I was so proud to be a pallbearer at his funeral along with Gordon West, Bob Latchford and Mike Lyons. As I sat there with my memories, I thought: 'What a man.'"

Legend Bally demanded 'nothing but the best'

DIXIE Dean, the irrepressible giant of the Twenties and Thirties, was undoubtedly the all-time king of Goodison Park, but that didn't stop a popular chant ringing around our famous stadium in the late Sixties: 'He's the greatest of them all, little curly Alan Ball'.

The club's newly-arrived 1966 World Cup winner was sensational in the Everton side that claimed championship glory in 1969-70.

Ball was high up my list of target interviews as that famous season unfolded and I waited patiently in the Bellefield car park one Tuesday lunchtime to see if the pocket dynamo Harry Catterick had captured from Blackpool in August 1966 would agree to speak to me.

He was just 23 and one of football's hottest properties with that World Cup success already under his belt. I was just 20 and still a comparatively unknown entity, working for a tiny weekly newspaper compared to the big evenings and nationals of the day.

In some ways, I was also still a fan at heart and a little bit starry-eyed, something that would be hammered out of me in the years to come.

Alan came out of the Bellefield complex, no doubt wanting to go straight home. I approached and asked if he could give me 10 minutes. He pointed to his smart light blue E-Type Jaguar and I gratefully climbed into the passenger seat.

I can still remember the first question I fired at him: "Alan, you've achieved so much in the game for such a young player. What are your aims and ambitions with Everton FC?"

He glanced across at me and didn't have to think twice about his answer. "I've won absolutely nothing in the game," he said, completely ignoring the glory of Wembley '66. "That is why I have signed for this club. I believe we can go on to achieve great things with this side. I'm proud to be here and playing for these fans."

As an Evertonian, that was exactly what I wanted to hear. I knew instantly that we had a real winner on our hands and he would live by his word. The Blues would finish that season in the championship driving seat and Ball would confirm his place as one of the greatest and most inspirational players we have ever had.

Everton's midfield engine room, ultimately dubbed the 'Holy Trinity' of Ball, Harvey and Kendall, were in a class of their own throughout that title-winning campaign, but this was a side with a perfect balance in every area.

After the World Cup, top clubs all over the country had wanted to sign Alan Ball, including Liverpool's Bill Shankly. But the one who made the first play was Leeds United's Don Revie. Indeed, Revie had tried to sign Alan when he was at Blackpool and was clearly not a manager who worried too much about underhand tactics.

In his 1978 book 'It's all about a Ball', Alan provided a fascinating and yet disturbing insight into the way Revie operated, although I'm sure the Leeds boss wasn't the only manager at that time prepared to bend the rules. Alan revealed: "I received this call from a stranger who asked if I was interested in speaking to Revie. I knew of him by reputation for, although Leeds were not then the power they would become in the next 10 years, it was already obvious to most of us in the game that things were starting to buzz at Elland Road.

"I then received a call from the manager himself and he said that with me, Billy Bremner and Johnny Giles in the Leeds team, it would be unbeatable. He then demonstrated his ruthless streak when he said: 'Make yourself a real rebel at Blackpool and they will want to sell you.'"

Ball pointed out that the longer he refused to sign a new contract, the more money it would cost him, £100 a week to be exact. Revie told him not to worry and that Leeds would cover it.

The end product was illicit meetings on the moors on the other side of Manchester at which Revie would hand over an envelope containing £100 a time. There were at least three such meetings.

Clearly, the Leeds boss didn't care that he was breaking football's biggest rule about tapping up players still under contract at other clubs.

The ultimate irony was that the Leeds board refused to pay Blackpool more than £100,000 and the astute Harry Catterick immediately topped that by 10 grand to get his man, a club record fee. Revie could do nothing about the illegal cash he had handed over on the moors. In many ways, it was football justice.

Alan admitted he was wrong to do what he did, but it confirmed in his mind that football at the highest level was a cut-throat business. The only thing that mattered to Evertonians was that he was now in a blue shirt.

One of my favourite Alan Ball stories illustrates the influence his father Alan Senior had on his life. Alan had married his girlfriend Lesley Newton in May, 1967, just after his 22nd birthday.

Alan Snr remained a dominant figure in his life and he warned his son that if he ever showed any sign of breaking the rigid code of conduct he had set, on and off the field, he would be in serious trouble.

Alan was going through an unusual bad patch with Everton and arrived home late with Lesley after a Saturday night out in town. He was staggered to find his father waiting for him. Son greeted father in the usual warm way, but all he got was a belt that nearly put him on the floor. Ball Snr said: "Don't give me all that 'good to see you' stuff. Look at the bloody time. It's 2.30 in the morning and here's you, playing like a mug, but still going out and enjoying yourself.

"I saw you laughing and joking like a couple of kids. You're living in bloody fairyland, son. You know what you've become, don't you? A bloody prima donna!"

Young Alan had not even been aware his dad was at the match that day. Ball Snr was manager of Preston at the time, but had forsaken his own team to watch his son.

Alan recalled: "He had taught me all my life to fight for my football future, and he was now teaching me that I still had to fight if I wanted to remain at the top."

The story had a remarkable conclusion. The following home match at Goodison Park, Alan chased and fought for every ball. That night, when he got home with Lesley, his father was waiting again and advanced towards his son.

Alan Jnr was expecting another right hander and instinctively ducked, but instead his father put his arms around him and said: "You were still rubbish out there today, but at least you were fighting again. Keep that up and in three weeks you will be playing as well as ever."

Sometimes managers are the inspiration behind players, but here was a father doling out tough love and Bally would soon be back to his brilliant best.

I left Alan after the interview he gave me in the Bellefield car park, supremely confident that a momentous season lay ahead for the Blues – and it did. The Blues went top with eight games to go with an Alan Whittle strike at Spurs.

The young Whittle would also score in the next five games, but Joe Royle was still a giant influence on the side, completing an ever-present championship season with 23 league goals.

Gordon West was also an ever-present, as was John Hurst and Tommy Wright. My own hero Brian Labone frustratingly missed the run-in with an injury that enabled Ball to take over as acting captain. He never stepped back from speaking his mind in the dressing room, which didn't always go down well, but no-one doubted his single-minded determination, drilled into him as a young boy by his father.

And anyone who scores twice on his debut against Liverpool and was only on the losing side in four of 13 derby games would always have the heart and minds of the fans. Incredibly, Everton's title-winning side would begin to break up after two years and Alan was sensationally sold to Arsenal midway through his sixth Everton campaign.

Catterick doubled the money he had paid for him, but Evertonians felt they had lost an inspiration and a leader. Ball would later have two spells with Southampton. Ironically, his very last top flight game was in October 1982 . . . against Everton! Almost fittingly Alan missed a penalty that day against the Blues.

Alan would later tell me: "The thing you ultimately miss most about football is not being able to play. The things I missed most about Everton and Merseyside was the people. Evertonians are probably the only supporters who got to me. I played for a great club in Arsenal and a smashing outfit in Southampton as well as playing for Blackpool as a boy, but only one crowd made my head turn and my hair stand on end and that was the one at Everton.

"I instantly felt their respect and passion, but that's probably because of more great advice from my dad. He told me that there was never any point in walking in anywhere like a sheep. You walk in like a lion and if you aren't good enough, then possibly you come out like a sheep."

Ball was certainly not a shrinking violet, cutting a distinctive figure with his white boots and red hair.

Alan Ball had an outstanding playing career, but could never match it as a manager. That didn't mean he ever lost any of his drive and passion. In writing my 'Goodison Greats' book, I travelled down to the less than glamorous surroundings of Exeter City where he was boss between 1991 and 1994.

I arrived early after a marathon drive and sat in the small stand while Alan finished off a training session. He was coaching the Exeter forwards and drilling them in a series of dead ball situations. These were players who were not fit to lace his boots, but his enthusiasm and passion had clearly never waned one jot.

Later, as Echo sports editor, I invited him to be our main speaker at the annual Merseyside Sports Personality of the Year event in the year Liverpool's Michael Owen claimed the trophy. Michael was sitting at a table immediately in front of the stage.

With the crowd totally silent, Alan spoke directly to the young striker, not just paying tribute to his goals and the great year he had enjoyed, but telling him that you never stop learning if you want to become a truly great football player.

It was like a father talking to his son. I'm sure Alan's words mirrored the high standards set by his own dad. Michael just sat there, totally mesmerised like the rest of us.

Ball was a realist, a driven figure who set himself and everyone around him incredibly high standards. Towards the end of his top flight career at Southampton, the engine that had once purred was finally beginning to splutter. I actually found myself tearful as I read Lawrie McMenemy's superb autobiography "A Lifetime's Obsession" in which he recalls sitting in his manager's office at the old Dell and hearing a knock on the door. Lawrie called out, but there was no reply so he went to see if anyone was there.

The corridor was empty and silent, but when he looked down he saw a pair of white boots in his doorway. It didn't need a big speech. A legend had signalled in his own inimitable way that he knew it was time to move on.

Alan died in shocking circumstances in his Hampshire garden on April 25, 2007, having a heart attack as he tried to deal with a fire.

His family had lost a man who was totally devoted to them.

Football had lost one of its greatest. Evertonians had lost one of their very own.

Cannonball Kid has me for dinner in a charity game and I'm so proud

MY first Everton hero was the irrepressible Dave Hickson. When the Cannonball Kid went to war on a football field, opposing defenders donned their tin hats and prepared for a mighty battle. Author Dr Percy Young wrote: "Hickson was not built for finesse, nor did he particularly try to cultivate it. He had fire in his nostrils."

It's not often that you are lucky enough to get close to someone you idolised as a boy. I not only managed to forge a great friendship with Dave during my three decades on the Echo sports desk, but also had the honour of playing with him and against him in his twilight football years.

When you review Dave's former clubs and his 400-plus league games and 182 goals between 1951 and 1963, you see names like Everton (two spells), Aston Villa, Huddersfield Town, Liverpool, Cambridge City, Bury and Tranmere Rovers.

In his records you will definitely not see any reference to his final club, the Over The Hill Mob.

Yet in many respects his many games for the charity side, run by dedicated Evertonian Ivor Scholes, rate as the most remarkable in his eventful career, if only because they sum up his all-consuming passion for football.

It didn't matter whether the venue had soaring stands and terraces like Goodison or Anfield, or was a muddy park pitch with a tin shed for a changing room. It didn't matter whether he was an ambitious 15-year-old at Ellesmere Port, a superstar at Everton, or a 60-year-old leading lads who, in the main, were not fit to lace his boots in the Over The Hill Mob. I should add quickly that I don't includes OTHM team-mates like Everton's Ronny Goodlass and George Telfer among the latter. The only thing that mattered for Dave Hickson was that he was playing the game that he loved.

And yet the young Hickson couldn't get a game in that disastrous 1950-51 season when Everton suffered relegation for only the second time in their history. However, he was making a big impression in the reserves and scored five against the Sheffield Wednesday second string. This encouraged the club to give him his big break early in the 1951-52 season when he replaced Harry Catterick at centre-forward.

Everton failed to bounce back into the top flight at the first time of asking, but in 1952-53 a remarkable FA Cup run saw the Blues reach the semi-finals. Along the way they met one of the big form teams of the top flight, Manchester United, and this Goodison clash remains one of the finest cup ties ever seen on our famous ground with Hickson at the heart of it.

Jack Rowley had given United the lead after 27 minutes before Tommy Eglington equalised. But just before the interval disaster struck when Hickson was led off with a badly cut eyebrow and it looked as if he would be unable to do much in the second half. There were no substitutes in those days.

Blood was streaming down Dave's face, but he was still diving in where it hurts and heading the heavy case ball. The Echo columnist covering the game said: "Never in my life have I seen a player perform with such guts as Davie showed. Twice the referee suggested he should go off. Davie waved him aside and his bravery paid off after 63 minutes."

Eglington squared a pass to the number nine who had two United defenders on him. He beat one, side-stepped the other and rattled a shot into the back of the net to give Everton the lead. The atmosphere was electric. Dave was playing with five stitches in an eye wound, but he still met a curling cross and bulleted a header against the United post. His eye split open again and there was blood everywhere.

The victory took Everton into the quarter-finals where they beat Aston Villa with another Hickson cracker and on the final whistle hundreds of fans chaired him from the field.

The Blues failed to take the final step to Wembley, but their classic semi-final against Bolton would be described by all Evertonians as one of our greatest cup ties of all time. Bolton's defenders were renowned as the roughest and toughest in the top flight. When Hickson clashed with Bill Hartle after just 15 minutes, the Everton star was clearly concussed and had to leave the field. Before he came back 15 minutes later, Wanderers were 3-0 up thanks to the famous Nat Lofthouse who quickly added a fourth.

When Tommy Clinton missed a Blues penalty right on the break, the Evertonians in the crowd were losing hope.

The second half was a total transformation. A double from John Willie Parker and a third goal from Peter Farrell had Bolton clinging on desperately to their 4-3 lead. The Blues never quite made it, but think on this. Bolton's subsequent final clash with Blackpool is still talked about as one of the most iconic Wembley occasions of all time. The Seasiders won thanks to a Stan Mortensen hat-trick, inspired by the legend that was Stanley Matthews. It is still called the 'Matthews Final' but it could easily have been the 'Hickson Final' if lady luck had been a little kinder in the semi-final.

However, Dave's only focus was now on helping to inspire promotion for the Blues and he helped the club achieve that aim at the third time of asking in the 1953-54 season.

Evertonians were shocked when Dave left for Aston Villa for £20,000 in September, 1955. He then joined Huddersfield Town, managed by the emerging Bill Shankly. His battling qualities were constantly on the lips of every Blues fan and it was no surprise when Everton brought him home again in July, 1957. He had been away for just 18 months and the club made £13,000 profit on his departure and return – a significant sum in those days.

When Everton signed Alan Shackleton from Leeds, the Goodison board were talking behind closed doors about cashing in once more on a player they believed was now expendable. One man who had no doubts about his continuing ability was Shankly who now made an audacious £11,000 bid to sign him again, this time for Liverpool.

Controversy raged across the Liverpool Echo letters pages, an accompanying comment declaring: "Never in the history of football in this city has there been such a rumpus about a player from one club joining neighbours and rivals."

Some Liverpudlians were declaring that if Dave Hickson signed for them, they would boycott Anfield.

As it turned out, Dave did cross the park but only because he suddenly felt unwanted by the Everton board of the day. And just to prove that fans can be among the most fickle people in the world, Hickson scored twice on his Liverpool debut and suddenly he wasn't such an anti-hero after all. On the same day Everton lost 8-2 at Newcastle!

All I can say is that while Dave Hickson might have carried his boots across the park to Anfield, his heart always remained at Goodison Park.

His glory days had long passed, but it was still an honour to be able to play with and against a man I had idolised.

First came an occasion when I found myself marking him towards the end of the Seventies. The Liverpool Echo football team played a friendly at Metal Box in Speke against a team of former Everton and Liverpool players. Derek Temple, who I had also admired and respected from the Goodison terraces, was in the Mersey All-Star XI that day.

They won a corner on the right and Derek, Everton's glorious 1966 FA Cup final match-winner, curled a ball high into the box with pace and accuracy. As the Echo's centre-half, I found myself marking my idol 'Dirty Dave.' I was about 30 while Dave was approaching 50.

I got as tight as I could and prepared to jump to try and head clear when a hand suddenly grabbed my shirt, held me down and used me as a lever to rise and send a bullet header into the back of the Echo net.

My moment of potential glory against a legend had suddenly gone so horribly wrong, but I was proud rather than deflated. I just smiled, shook his hand and said: "Superb Dave." It was an honour to have been 'done' by my idol.

Later, I played up front alongside him for the 'Over The Hill Mob' charity team. Dave was now approaching 60 and I was 40. He was a constant source of encouragement and inspiration.

Off the pitch he was the opposite of the fiery Cannonball Kid, quiet and unassuming. Everyone who met him would comment about how approachable he was. When I broke my ankle playing in a Vets Cup game, my father Harry – one of his number one fans – mentioned the injury to Dave and he was quick to contact and encourage me in Birkenhead's Arrowe Park Hospital.

Bill Kenwright summed up a player who was also his hero perfectly when he declared: "The Dave Hicksons of this world helped you to dream and believe that you could achieve the impossible."

14

Brian Clough warns me: 'Don't try and put words in my mouth, son'

AS the 1970s dawned, I was now becoming more confident as a young sports journalist, even though I was still working for the diminutive Liverpool Weekly News. I continued to write a weekly column for Ron Yeats while interviewing all and sundry at Everton's Bellefield training ground.

However, in seeking to find a different way of previewing the big weekend games on Merseyside, I tried my hand at ringing the managers of opposing clubs to see if they might give me an insight into their plans.

The first boss I phoned was the vastly experienced Ted Bates of Southampton. He had played for the Saints between 1937 and 1953, a war-disrupted career that still delivered over 200 appearances. He would then manage the club for an astonishing 18 years between 1955 and 1973.

Having seen it all and done it all, I didn't think for one minute that Bates would take my call one Tuesday morning in late 1970. Incredibly, I was put straight through and he was soon discussing his side, players who were injured, in-form stars, and how much he always looked forward to his Goodison Park visits. We seemed to be chatting about football for ages and I thought: "What a great bloke. I've got more than enough for a fantastic preview."

I always compared moments like this to my experience with our very own Harry Catterick. Remember the demoralising 'Yes/No' interlude?

I was just about to draw my chat with Mr Bates to a satisfactory conclusion, when he started to interview me. How are Everton playing at the moment? Is anyone injured? Have they been showing any particular weaknesses?

It was dawning on me that I was suddenly being utilised as Southampton's Merseyside-based chief scout. Bates questioned me for so long that I started to do a Catterick and become almost bland in my answers, terrified that I would reveal something that might cost us the match.

We actually beat them 4-1 that weekend with a Joe Royle double, plus strikes from Johnny Morrissey and Alan Whittle.

Later, Southampton would erect a statue outside their stadium to mark the remarkable career of Ted Bates. He thoroughly deserved it, not least for being arguably the most approachable manager in football.

Around this time, a young boss was emerging whose face would soon dominate the headlines on a daily basis. His name was Brian Clough. After a couple of years learning the ropes at Hartlepool United (Hartlepools United as they were then known) he was now making a big name for himself at Derby County, securing them promotion from the old second division and ultimately winning the league championship. I rang the Baseball Ground and, once again, was stunned to be put straight through to the manager. He must have thought the Liverpool Weekly News was Merseyside's premier paper. I had prepared loads of questions that might secure me a decent headline for that Thursday's paper.

However, my first mistake was to make a statement rather than ask one of those questions. I said: "Everton are a great side, having won the championship last season. You must be looking forward to the challenge at Goodison on Saturday."

He immediately clicked into the brash Brian Clough mode that would soon become par for the course when clashing with journalists all over the country. "Listen, son," he said. "Don't try and put words in my mouth. Now ask me a proper question and I'll give you a proper answer."

Clearly, this was going to be a different challenge to speaking to Ted Bates. I also assumed he did not want to use me as Derby County's Merseyside chief scout. I should add that his answers were first class and full of the vision and confidence that would win him numerous honours.

Here was a very unusual character who knew what he wanted out of the game and was determined to get it. He brought his Derby side to Goodison on the Saturday and grabbed a 1-1 draw, highlighting their improvement while we edged into a disappointing campaign that would see

Everton, as reigning champions, finish just 14th.

At a sportsman's dinner, I once sat next to one of Clough's most talented players, his captain John McGovern. It was fascinating listening to him talking about the irrepressible Clough. He told me that after one midweek defeat, when Forest lost because a free-kick went straight through the defensive wall, Clough said absolutely nothing in the dressing room after the match.

At the next session, the players were on the training ground as usual, waiting for the manager's analysis of the previous game. Clough marched towards them and demanded they set up the same defensive wall formation that had conceded that crucial goal the previous day. He then instructed John O'Hare, the Forest player with the hardest shot, to place the ball 10 yards from the wall and blast it at them.

McGovern recalled that the wall blocked the shot, but moved slightly. "Do it again," Clough told O'Hare, moving the ball two yards closer. This time the wall held firm, but someone blinked. "Do it again," instructed Clough, again moving the ball even closer.

"Let them have it," he told O'Hare. The Scot obliged and this time the wall, knowing what was coming next, stood tall as a unit and the shot rebounded well clear.

"Training over," shouted Clough as he marched back to the dressing room. They all stood there, looking at the other trainers to see what they should do next. Lesson learned.

I always thought about that phone conversation I had with Clough. I had learned a short, sharp lesson. Don't make statements, ask questions. Enough said.

15

Colin Harvey – hailed in a Goodison Park banner as the 'White Pele'

I WELL recall the day when a banner was hoisted high on the Goodison Park terraces declaring: 'Colin Harvey – the White Pele.' To any outsider, the sentiment might have been deemed over the top. To Evertonians, it was simply a reflection of our admiration for someone who would serve our club magnificently as a player, coach and manager.

The fact that I named my own son Colin highlights how much I personally rated and respected a key member of Everton's Holy Trinity – our unmatchable midfield of Ball, Harvey and Kendall that encapsulated skill, mobility, drive and inspiration in that magical period at the end of the Sixties when the Blues were simply irrepressible.

It was always doubly difficult for a local lad to make the grade, but Harvey was a special talent, highlighted when Harry Catterick showed total trust to give him a sensational debut in the intimidating surroundings of the San Siro stadium in 1963.

That Colin came through with flying colours against the mighty Inter Milan was a clear signal that we had a very special young talent on our hands. We didn't know then that he would also become an inspirational coach and leader in the magnificent 1980s, working alongside Howard Kendall during the most successful period in EFC's history. Ultimately, Colin would take on the almost impossible job of managing the Blues following Howard's shock departure to Athletic Bilbao.

He can look back on what he achieved at Goodison with nothing less than total pride. As a young fan, I remember the playing qualities that made Colin Harvey so special.

He was a marathon man who loved the discipline of training and who worked hard on his conditioning throughout his football career. Terry Darracott summed this up when he told me: "Colin was a self-made player. He was dedicated, hard-working and always determined to do that little bit extra. I would see him putting in an extra half hour at the end of training, no matter what he had done in the morning.

"He always had time for the younger players in the squad and I admired him for that. It costs nothing to go over to a kid and say: 'Hey, I noticed you doing something this morning. It wasn't quite right.' Or, if a lad had impressed, say: 'Well done, I thought that was smashing.'

"If one of the senior pros ever spoke to me, I would float all the way home. Colin was that type and it went towards making him a great footballer and an outstanding coach."

Harvey was brought up in Fazakerley, an Evertonian from the word go like his father and grandfather. He was a real talent at school, and Liverpool soon spotted his potential. He attended a trial at Melwood where he played alongside a man who would later make over 800 appearances for the Reds – Ian Callaghan.

Colin recalls: "Ian was head and shoulders above the rest and I thought to myself 'That's the standard I must attain'.

"They called me back the following week, but I was then invited for a trial at Goodison. This used to take place at the Stanley Park end where the car park is now. After that, there was no way I was going back to Liverpool."

He has vivid memories of his first appearance in a blue shirt. It was mid-October, 1958. Colin said: "I'd played in the morning for my school team Cardinal Allen, and then had to make my way to Bellefield where Everton's Les Shannon had told me I had to report for a match with the 'C' team. I grabbed all my stuff and set off for West Derby.

"I had been told the club's training ground was in Sand-field Road, but didn't actually know where Bellefield was. Fans are aware that the small entrance was fairly well hidden between some semi-detached houses. I walked right past and carried on, almost as far as Queens Drive. I saw a lad carry-ing a pair of boots and asked if he was going to Bellefield.

"Luckily he was, and I turned round and walked back down the road with him. I played in the game but hurt my knee. Tommy Fairfoul was running the 'C' team and he instructed me to go for treatment with trainer Harry Cooke Snr at Goodison the next day.

"This was 24 hours after the first-team had lost a famous game 10-4 at Spurs where one player who had done himself justice was Jimmy Harris. He finished on the losing side despite scoring a hat-trick. I was surprised when I found myself sitting alongside him at Goodison where he was also getting treatment."

Ironically, Colin's first full-time job was not training and working at Bellefield as an apprentice, but as an NHS clerk in Upper Parliament Street. It was 1961 and he was just 16. Coach Shannon was horrified when he found out and on the following Monday, Everton's chief scout, Harry Cooke Jnr – grandson of Cooke Snr – turned up at Colin's home.

Harvey was offered professional terms and so ended the shortest career ever in the NHS. Over the next two years he began to make outstanding progress and was impressing in the reserves.

Colin recalls: "We had played at Sheffield and stopped in Manchester on the return journey for something to eat. I knew the first-team squad was travelling to Italy on the Monday for the European Cup clash against Inter. Gordon Watson phoned to say three or four of us were on the trip."

Colin was convinced they were all called up to carry the skips and stood back accordingly when Harry Catterick read out the team on the day of the game: West, Parker, Harris, Stevens, Labone, Kay, Scott, HARVEY, Young, Vernon and Temple.

The news caused a sensation and Liverpool Echo correspondent Michael Charters was quickly filing the story back to the city. Colin said: "I was well aware that Inter had world-class stars like Suarez and Jair. I knew all of their names, being an avid reader of World Soccer magazine. I was suddenly in the centre of this incredible experience and when I stepped out onto the San Siro pitch, the atmosphere was incredible.

"It did me no harm and I didn't feel overawed. I was nervous, but that suited me. If I ever felt calm before a game I was worried."

The first leg at Goodison had been goalless. In the end, the return was settled by a strike from Jair, one of the fastest wingers in the world.

It's interesting to reflect on the Echo match report the following night: "The gamble of playing Harvey was an enormous one, but it nearly paid off. This young Liverpool boy will look back on his first senior game with some pride since he fought hard, played at times with a veteran coolness and could have been a scorer with either of two overhead flips when standing with his back to goal."

Many years later, I would ask Harry Catterick about his decision to play Colin that night. He said: "Colin was always going to be a great competitor. He was a quiet lad, introvert as a player, but with superb skills. He was very quick and had a lot of mobility, the ideal professional. He was the kind of lad who could exercise his skills both defensively and deep in opposing territory."

Catterick's expert assessment could not have been bettered.

Colin would play only two more games that season, but he was very much on his way. He established himself in the first-team and in 1966 played a key role as the Blues claimed the FA Cup at the expense of Sheffield Wednesday.

I particularly loved Colin's comment about the importance to Evertonians of seeing that famous trophy back in the Goodison trophy cabinet. He said: "My granddad had told me all about his hero Dixie Dean and the way he had carried the cup through the streets of Liverpool on the back of a horse-drawn carriage. The fact that my granddad was up in the Wembley stands in 1966 with about 50 relatives and friends made the day extra special for me."

Now Colin would repeat Dixie's journey from city centre to Goodison. I love one of his favourite moments from the final. As Everton held on to their slender lead, the battling Jimmy Gabriel took the ball right up against the corner flag. He was surrounded by three or four hacking and increasingly desperate Wednesday players, but with skill and strength he finally won a throw-in, thrusting his arms into the air like a champion boxer who had just knocked out an opponent.

The Everton roar from the Wembley terraces summed up how everyone felt about the performance and the achievement of this Everton side of which Colin was now a key member.

Of course, 1966 would see Harry Catterick building for the future with great signings and belief in the club's emerging talent. Perhaps the two most significant acquisitions, certainly as far as Colin was concerned, were the purchases of Alan Ball and Howard Kendall.

It's worth reflecting what Colin told me in my 1989 'Everton Greats' book about his partnership with Ball and Kendall. He said: "I used to love playing with Bally because he could do some brilliant things. He was my favourite player of that era. I would have happily paid to watch him every week, so to have played alongside him was an honour.

"Howard was a magnificent first-time passer of the ball. He could play it short or long and was one of the best tacklers I have ever seen."

I was lucky enough to be a young journalist in the Goodison press box on April 1, 1970, when that great Everton team won Catterick his second league title and it was doubly fitting that the opposition was West Bromwich Albion, a club that had dealt me one of my bitterest blows in football two years earlier in the FA Cup final at Wembley.

From an earlier chapter, you will recall that I watched that game lying behind the goal of a certain John Osborne, the Albion keeper, who kept turning round and asking me how long there was to go.

This time, Osborne had no time to do anything except keep his total focus on a game that Everton dominated in front of an ecstatic 58,000 crowd. Colin Harvey and Alan Whittle scored the key goals, but it was Colin's second-half strike that will forever stand out in my memory.

He collected the ball deep in Everton territory, advanced down the left and turned back in his tracks to lose two defenders. He then carried the ball into a more central position before rifling a 25-yard shot with his right foot to leave Osborne helpless. This was the goal that clinched the title.

The boy of 16 who had made such an impression all those years earlier in Italy had now become the complete midfielder. I'm elated when players can relate things to their own supporter days. Colin said: "As a youngster, I had stood in the old Boys' Pen at Goodison and cheered on the Blues. As a young professional in 1963, I had raced back to Goodison from an 'A' team game to see the championship being won against Fulham.

"I thought then what a magnificent moment it must be for a footballer to win the title and be able to parade the trophy in front of his own fans. Suddenly I was one of 11 men accepting the plaudits of the crowd. It was one of the highlights of my playing career."

In researching my 'Everton Greats' book, I came across an Echo cutting from December 9, 1972, that sums up Colin Harvey perfectly. It said: "Although slightly built, he could win the ball in tackles with the power and timing of his challenge. He could use it with immense skill and precision. He could dribble, beat men, shoot, score goals and his work-rate was phenomenal, while his sharpness off the ball was remarkable. To this abundance of football talent he added enthusiasm, a competitive spirit and a whole-hearted dedication which forced him, in every match and training session, to give everything."

Perhaps that Goodison Park banner declaring Colin Harvey as 'The White Pele' was not as over the top as it might have seemed.

Latch got £192 and a £5,000 tax bill from his £10,000 goal jackpot!

IN many respects, it's fitting that I encompass the unfulfilled and fairly desolate 1970s in one single chapter.

It's also fitting that I dedicate this section to a striker who scored 138 goals in 286 appearances for the Blues between 1974 and 1981. If I had to express just one disappointment about Billy Bingham capturing Latch from Birmingham for a club record £350,000, it would be the fact that we had to release our skipper Howard Kendall as part of a deal that also took young defender Archie Styles to St Andrews.

In a perfect world we would have retained Kendall and given ourselves a much better chance of building on that famous 1970 championship success. Of course, many fans would also point to the loss of Alan Ball to Arsenal.

As it was, Everton's dreams would wither and die on the 70s vine although the quality of football played at times and the reality that the Blues were not a million miles away from fulfilling their potential should not be completely dismissed.

It's worth assessing our top flight finishing positions in the 10 seasons following the 1970 championship triumph: 14, 15, 17, 7, 4, 11, 9, 3, 4, and 19.

Clearly, the opportunity to drive on as title holders evaporated in those three bitterly disappointing seasons immediately after we stormed to the title, but three top four positions beyond that up to 1979-80 suggests it wasn't a total disaster. We also reached three FA Cup semi-finals in the period, as well as the League Cup final.

Okay, that's putting a gloss on it. Evertonians tend to block the Seventies out of their minds, but in the early part of the decade we still had much of the talent that had taken us to the top. And we could cheer outstanding newcomers like classy midfielder Martin Dobson, the effervescent Andy King, the showman who was Duncan McKenzie, rock-solid players like Bruce Rioch, Mike Pejic and Mark Higgins, and flying winger Dave Thomas.

And let me make a case for the local boy who would run through a brick wall for Everton, Mike Lyons. I don't care who you are, you don't pull on our famous blue shirt across 12 seasons without having character, ability and true grit. He also scored 59 goals for good measure, captained the side and dedicated the best years of his football life to the club he loved. I won't hear a word said against any local lad with his record. What would I have given to have worn that blue shirt just once, let alone 473 times? There are dreamers and there are those who fulfil the dream.

Clearly, the Seventies were frustrating for all Blues fans. No-one remembers the runners-up or the nearly teams, be it in a championship race or any cup final. But it can suggest you were on the brink of something big.

We finished third in 1977-78 and while Kingy and McKenzie shared 17 goals between them, it was really all about one man, Everton's King of the Seventies . . . Bob Latchford.

This was the season when his impressive goal haul reached its zenith on a late April day in '78 when he stood on the brink of claiming his 30th league goal of an outstanding campaign with a £10,000 jackpot within his grasp. The Daily Express, aware that no striker had achieved that total in the previous five years, had put up the prize.

The incomparable Dean might have secured his glorious 60 in 1928, but in this era any player reaching half that number could reflect on a truly outstanding season.

Latchford needed two goals that day against Chelsea and 40,000 Evertonians turned up, desperate for him to do it.

Incredibly, the Blues swept into a 3-0 lead without a single strike from the big centre-forward. It looked like it might be one of those days, but he suddenly delivered one of the two goals required with a second-half header.

Everton scored a fifth, but it was greeted not so much with a roar as a sharp intake of breath from the supporters. Mike Lyons told me: "I scored the fifth, tucking the ball into the bottom corner. I turned away to celebrate, but because I had not knocked the ball back to Latch, who was in a great position, everybody just stood and looked at me. It's the only time I've scored at Goodison and felt sick about it."

However, Latchford would not be denied. His memorable 30th league goal of the season came from the penalty spot and the stadium erupted.

When I spoke to Bob about his £10,000, he revealed that it proved a curse rather than a bonus. It certainly did not boost his bank balance. He explained that part of the deal was that £5,000 would go to the Football League and Professional Footballers Association Benevolent Fund.

Bob decided to share the rest with his squad mates who had supported his goal haul that season. Everybody received the princely sum of £192, but Bob was later stung with a £5,000 tax bill which it took him three to four years to resolve. He said: "If I'd have known I would have told them to keep the damn money."

The final irony of Bob's jackpot day was that it coincided with a print strike at the Liverpool Echo. We therefore never recorded his fantastic achievement in the paper the following Monday and no photographs appeared to record that glorious day. How ironic is that.

Latchford played for the thoughtful taskmaster who was Billy Bingham and then the football-mad bundle of energy that was Gordon Lee. At the end of 1976, Bingham had given the side what appeared to be a massive boost when he added to the squad the contrasting figures of Bruce Rioch of Derby County and Duncan McKenzie of Anderlecht. I recall going to the Prince of Wales Hotel in Southport to see Bingham unveil his new stars. Remarkably, the two newcomers would only play in five games for their new boss before he was sacked on January 10, 1977.

It would be Lee who would ultimately lead the players out at Wembley against Aston Villa after the Blues reached that season's League Cup final. This game gave me the chance to take my dad, Harry, to his first Wembley final. We were offered a lift in a friend's car, only to be told very late on that only one seat was available. I told Dad to go in the car to smooth his Wembley experience and managed to claim a place on one of the fans' coaches that eventually got caught up in a terrible traffic jam a few miles from the stadium.

We were clearly going to miss the kick-off and I jumped off about a mile and a half away and started to run. By the time I reached Wembley Way it was totally deserted. I could hear the roar of the crowd inside and started to sprint, eventually getting to my seat 10 minutes into the first half, more exhausted than anyone out on the pitch.

I needn't have rushed. It was a fairly disappointing game that finished goalless. The irony of the replay, at Hillsborough, was that both goals in the 1-1 draw were scored by Everton players! Roger Kenyon gave Villa the lead with an own goal, Latch taking things to a second replay with an equaliser in the final minute of normal time that led to a deadlocked extra-time period.

This meant a second replay, this time at Old Trafford and when the prolific Latchford gave us the lead I was convinced it was finally going to be our day.

Then, with just nine minutes to go, Villa's Chris Nicholl

scored an absolute thunderbolt from close on 40 yards to level things.

Just a minute later Brian Little gave Villa the lead and it looked all over until the never-say-die Mike Lyons snatched a sensational equaliser. In extra time it looked like the game would go to penalties until Little grabbed his second and Villa's third with just seconds to go to take the trophy to the Midlands.

The Everton players were shattered and as I stood among the devastated Evertonians who had given such incredible support I convinced myself that nothing else that season could possibly be more demoralising.

How wrong I was. Just 10 days later, on the other side of Manchester at Maine Road, controversy and absolute frustration lay ahead of us in the semi-final of the FA Cup against arch-rivals Liverpool.

The Blues looked to be on course for a second Wembley experience, only for referee Clive Thomas – a man who often liked to steal the headlines from the players – to rule out what we all know to be a perfectly good goal for an alleged offside against Bryan Hamilton. The tie finished 2-2 and the frustrations of April proved just too much for the Blues in the replay that Liverpool won comfortably 3-0.

Trying to be positive, Lee's men had proved themselves capable of beating anyone on their day and that memorable 30-goal season was now about to unfold for Latch.

Once the frustrating 1970s were over, it was time to look forward to the greatest era in our club's history, the remarkable 1980s.

My city centre 'Over the Top' fight night with the Anfield Iron

YOU will have gathered from the opening chapters of this book that I was born to be a Blue Nose, supremely proud to have been brought up in the district that gave our club its famous name and lucky that my whole working life was steeped in all things Everton FC.

As a boy, standing first in the Boys' Pen, then the Bullens Road Paddock and finally on the famous Street End, I could not have dreamt that I would step up from my inner city environment to ultimately spend my whole life writing about players and legends I could previously only idolise from afar.

I have already alluded to the fact that when I was appointed sports editor of the former Liverpool Weekly News at the age of 19 following the departure to Radio Merseyside of declared Kopite and Liverpool fanatic Alan Parry, I decided that it would be my immediate challenge to transform our Liverpool FC-biased pages into something Evertonians could finally relate to and want to read.

Over three years I feel I achieved that as I began to learn my new profession and develop as a writer and journalist with big ambitions in the thrilling world of publishing that I had now committed my life to.

I would ultimately become chief football correspondent of the Liverpool Echo and then sports editor and during this period I ensured every day that Everton FC would get the balanced and considered coverage it deserved. I also ensured that, at every given opportunity, the Evertonians themselves would be saluted and highlighted for being among the most passionate, knowledgeable and inspirational supporters in the entire country.

Yes, I had to seek journalistic balance in our football-crazy city because one half of my role was catering for the red side of Merseyside, but I never tried to hide my Everton passion, not to Bill Shankly, Bob Paisley, Joe Fagan, Ronnie Moran, Kenny Dalglish, Graeme Souness, Roy Evans, Gerard Houllier – or any of the leading LFC figures of the day.

At one stage I found myself ghost writing the Echo columns of a certain Tommy Smith and I informed him on day one that a true blue was now going to be interpreting his views in the foreseeable years ahead. I had this idea for a new inter-active Echo fans platform for the Anfield Iron that I fittingly decided to call: 'Tommy Smith – Over the Top'.

It was a simple concept. Fans would send in their local

football views and Smithy would offer his own acerbic thoughts. If he agreed with their viewpoint he would respond with a 'Fair Tackle' answer. If he was in the middle on a subject, highly unlikely I should add, he would give a 'Bounce Ball'. But if he fiercely disagreed, he would go 'Over the Top' in his reply.

This Echo section transformed the number of letters we received from a handful, usually written by the same few people, into an absolute avalanche of views. Rightly or wrongly, I initially determined that Tommy would also answer the Everton letters as well. He was a regular in the Goodison press box, watching as many Everton matches as Liverpool games. It was clear that most readers actually wanted him to respond with an 'Over the Top' reply which instantly became a badge of honour.

I liked Smithy. He was a local boy who loved the city he was brought up in. He didn't suffer fools gladly. I always felt that if he liked you, he would be your friend for life and do anything for you. If he disliked you, he would hate you forever. There was no middle ground with Tommy.

I sat next to him at Goodison every home game and it was 90 minutes of kicking and elbowing each other which went to a completely different level on derby day when money was on the table as a matter of colour-coded pride.

I feel proud that the 'Over the Top' letters platform was actually the forerunner of the now familiar radio phone-ins. Indeed, Radio Merseyside rang me one day to ask permission to transfer the format into a popular post-match slot every week with Smithy responding to callers in the way he did in his hugely successful Echo column. I was happy to agree, providing they gave our pages a regular plug. Soon all the local and national radio stations were broadcasting interactive fan platforms.

Ultimately I chose to bring in Howard Kendall to answer the Everton letters to provide the balance some Evertonians were asking for, but it was Tommy's reputation for speaking his mind in every situation that had been the spark for this very successful exercise.

At one point in the Nineties, Tommy Smith was named as one of 100 Football League Legends and I joined him at the accompanying dinner. He had enjoyed his evening and at the end of it we were having the usual Everton and Liverpool banter. I asked him to sign my place setting. We'd both had a few drinks.

"What do you want me to write?" asked Smithy. I replied: "Come On You Blues – Tommy Smith" which he did without even thinking. I still have it and always threatened to publish a photo of it in the Echo – usually while we were jousting on those battling press box derby days.

I also never stopped reminding Tommy that, like me, he was brought up as a youngster in one of those steep Everton streets between Netherfield Road and Great Homer Street, in his case above a coal yard. This made him an Everton boy which he always railed against, once again leading to another good natured pushing and shoving episode.

However, it got much more serious than that when I joined him at the Liner Hotel alongside Lime Street Station for a charity dinner that was tagged: 'A Tribute Evening to

Tommy Smith'. It went really well with Tommy the main speaker. Everyone appeared to have had a fantastic time and when it was all over we went to sit in one of the adjacent lounges.

Out of the blue, literally, a bloke stepped in front of Smithy and started hurling abuse at him, clearly not prepared to take part in the 'tribute' night spirit. Tommy had a mate known as 'Big Mike' who went round with him because people confronting Tommy was not an unusual event.

Mike stepped between Tommy and this guy who continued to rant at the Anfield Iron. It was getting a bit out of hand, and someone held Big Mike's hands by his side in case he suddenly let fly at the individual causing all the trouble. Within a second this bloke had lashed out at Mike and from that small beginning the so-called 'Tommy Smith Tribute Night' developed into what can only be described as a saloon brawl that went out into the street.

I'm always the calm peacemaker, trust me, but I found myself in the middle of this. It was over as quickly as it started. We went back up into the lounge and I said to Smithy: "If anyone reports this back to the Echo tomorrow, I'm getting the sack, either that or a few people will be waiting for me outside the building!"

Tommy just smiled; it was just another day at the office for him. As it happened, the uproar didn't make the front page and I forgot about this moment of madness. A few years later I was organising the annual 'Merseyside Sports Personality of the Year' awards – the Echo's prestigious annual event held at a city centre hotel.

I popped to the gents during the evening and found myself standing next to a guy dressed like me in a smart black evening suit and bow tie. We exchanged pleasantries, as you do, and agreed it was shaping up to be a great evening. He then asked me if I remembered a certain 'Tommy Smith Tribute Night.'

Apparently, he had been with those individuals who started the uproar that evening. I assume they were not Liverpudlians. We just looked at each other and burst out laughing because it had been a bizarre experience. You have to cross the blue and red divide at times. Unlike in other cities like Glasgow, Liverpool families can have split loyalties.

I would write Tommy Smith's autobiography 'My Anfield Secrets' and Phil Thompson's autobiography 'Stand Up Pinocchio.' I would also pen Kenny Dalglish's 'My Life' book. They all knew my strong Everton FC roots, but gave me their absolute trust in big personal projects which I interpreted as recognising my professionalism as a journalist.

But it wasn't always a case of joining hands across the park. I revealed in an earlier chapter how Bill Shankly had ejected me from Anfield and then admirably demonstrated his other side. Inevitably, I had many rows with football figures down the years because football is a passionate business, but this was par for the course and you had to be prepared to stand up for yourself.

I recall another Echo Sports Personality dinner when Liverpool FC's very own sergeant major Ronnie Moran joined me as one of my guests. Halfway through a very pleasant evening he suddenly decided to ask an interesting question across the dinner table which was clearly heard by all of my guests.

In simple terms, he asked: "What the f*** do you know about football? You've never played the game. What right have you got to be critical of us in the Echo?" The conversation around the table immediately stopped.

Tongue-in-cheek, I was going to explain that I had actually played 100 games for St Columba's in the Sunday School Union; 120 games for Old Swan and then 98 games for Mersey Royal in the tough Liverpool Sunday League; 180 games for the Daily Post & Echo in the Liverpool Business Houses Midweek League and another 250 in the Business Houses Sunday League; 30 games alongside Dave Hickson and Ronny Goodlass playing for Ivor Scholes' charity side the Over The Hill Mob; and a further 80 games for Collegiate Old Boys before breaking my ankle aged 50 playing in a Vets Cup game in Manchester. This meant that in terms of playing the game, I had actually beaten Ian Callaghan's remarkable LFC appearance record of 857 by one!

Of course, I understood Ronnie's drift and acknowledged his tactical superiority, but I clearly didn't agree with his fundamental logic. He was suggesting that if you had not played professional football, how could you have any clue about what was happening out there on the pitch at Anfield and Goodison every weekend?

I decided to respond in a different way. "Are you suggesting," I asked "that every fan in this room knows 'f*** all' (to use his words) about football because if that's what you are inferring then I'm happy to step up onto the stage and give you the microphone so that you can express that opinion to a wider audience."

Ronnie looked at me and I could see what he was thinking. "Clever arse Evertonian!"

I didn't take offence. I'm sure he didn't either. I knew that his confrontational approach to me was no different whatsoever to the way he spoke to his own players in Anfield's inner sanctum first-team dressing room on match days. He famously once threw a bag of championship winning medals into the middle of the dressing room at Melwood and said to the players: "Take one if you think you deserve it!"

His role in that backroom team was being bad cop to Joe Fagan's good cop, or should that be bad kop, good kop.

Once you got your head round the fact that you were being treated no differently to anyone else, you could deal with it. You had to. There is no room for sulkers or shrinking violets in football.

But to say that football fans can't have an opinion about the professional game they support with their turnstile cash is disrespectful and wrong. Football is nothing more than a game of opinions – and that's what makes it so special.

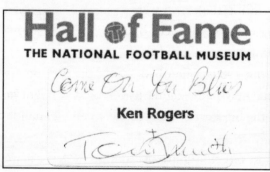

Tommy Smith's tongue in cheek message of support for Everton that I cajoled out of him!

18

'Andy Gray is in a Goodison Road newsagent! Are we signing him?'

DURING transfer windows, football journalists all over the country live every day on a knife edge, fearing they might miss out on the kind of major exclusive that can drive newspaper sales through the roof.

The reality is that these days, with the big clubs totally focused on ensuring their own websites and TV channels get everything first, the chances of any local or national newspaper getting a significant 'scoop' are minimal.

But back in the 1980s, when I was covering Everton and Liverpool, your newspaper didn't just hope you might get most or all of the big stories. They expected and demanded it.

When you lost out to a journalist on a rival title, it was

as if you had stabbed your own organisation in the back. There was never any point trying to explain to an exasperated editor how it might have happened.

It was as if you had let everyone down, like scoring an own goal in a derby match or a World Cup final.

You could argue as much as you liked that it was circumstantial and a matter of timing, perhaps due to a surprise announcement by the other club involved, be it an in or out transfer.

But that simply didn't wash. In my case at the Liverpool Echo, I was expected to have an infallible network of contacts with other evening newspaper journalists across the UK and there could be no excuses if I missed out, at least none that an office-based editor who didn't have to work the training grounds or the corridors of power could understand or wanted to understand.

It didn't matter that, in my case, I was one evening newspaper journalist against five vastly experienced national reporters. These guys knew what they were doing and operated as a cartel to ensure they had the best possible chance of cornering the market. They even called themselves 'The Mafia'!

I didn't believe that I would end up with a horse's head in my bed if I crossed them, but they were all hugely experienced individuals at that time like John Keith (Daily Express), Chris James (Daily Mirror), Mike Ellis (The Sun), Colin Wood (Daily Mail) and Matt D'Arcy (The Daily Star).

It meant that I had to develop and maintain first class relationships with Merseyside's top local football managers as well as a personal understanding with other people on the inside, not least influential chief executives like Jim Greenwood at Goodison Park and Peter Robinson at Anfield.

Now I'd like to say that every big story I secured was based on my ability as a leading regional journalist and a contacts book that was second to none, backed up by personal relationships with all the people who mattered.

The reality is that it often never works out like that. Let me give you an example of a Howard Kendall signing that helped transform the Blues in the Eighties. I was sitting at my desk one November day in 1983. Nothing much was happening and I warned the sports editor not to expect anything too exciting for the back page.

Suddenly the phone rang and a Scouse voice at the other end of the line asked: "Are we signing Andy Gray?"

I knew Andy was an outstanding centre-forward on his day and that he had suffered a number of injury problems, but his name had never come up, even in one of those speculative Sunday newspaper transfer columns that linked clubs with all and sundry on the basis that one day they might strike it lucky.

Even though I had regular daily contact with Howard Kendall, he had not mentioned it.

I asked the caller why he was posing the question and he said: "Because I've just seen him in a newsagent's opposite Goodison Park!"

I couldn't get the phone down quickly enough. The 11am first edition deadline was looming and I needed to get back to Howard again, even though it sounded highly unlikely that Gray would be a priority target. Maybe it was just a hoax call?

I immediately rang Bellefield, only to be told: "Sorry, the boss isn't here." This in itself set the alarm bells ringing because Howard was always available, being the most user-friendly manager in the top flight.

My second call was to chief executive Jim Greenwood. I asked: "Do you know where Howard is?"

Jim was vastly experienced and blocked my question with one of his own: "Why do you want to know?"

I replied: "I know this sounds ridiculous, but I've just been told that Andy Gray was seen half an hour ago buying a newspaper opposite Goodison."

The phone went silent for a few seconds. I instinctively knew that Jim had Howard in his office, ready to sign the transfer document. Jim was the master of telling me something without actually saying it.

"Give me 10 minutes," he said, "and do not write anything until Howard rings you back."

I knew it was on, but didn't have time to kick my heels with the deadline looming. I immediately sent a request to our newspaper library for the press cuttings on Gray, plus his photo bags. I also alerted the sports desk and put in a back-up call to my opposite number at the Birmingham Post & Mail.

By the time Howard rang me back to confirm the deal was about to be done, I had a full story written, plus a backgrounder on Andy who had made a big name for himself, first in Scotland with Dundee United and then with

Aston Villa and Wolverhampton Wanderers, who had just accepted Howard's £250,000 offer.

Andy's 138 goals in 308 games was impressive enough, but it was his uniqueness as an old fashioned centre-forward, his remarkable heading ability and his character as an individual who could inspire players around him that encouraged Howard to overlook his injury problems.

I don't know if Andy came through his medical with flying colours, but I can envisage Howard looking at 'The Doc' and saying: "Can he reach down and pull his boots on? Just do it!"

As it turned out, the acquisition of the infectious Gray was one of the key elements in Everton's mid-Eighties transformation. He would play just 68 games for the Blues and score 22 goals, but the stats defy the impact he made on the club and the fans.

He was always a great player to interview, full of opinions and unexpected thoughts and I knew that one day he could develop a new career for himself in the media in exactly the same way that Gary Lineker was always head and shoulders above most of his peers in dealing with the press.

When Gray left Everton, I travelled down to a sports centre in Birmingham and asked Andy if he would write a regular weekly column for the Echo. He agreed and this was one of many key steps towards the Scot becoming one of the game's most influential media personalities.

A national newspaper recognised his potential and he eventually had to contact me to say that he would have to give up his Echo column. I was just happy that we had benefited from his input for so long, and wished him well. He would never look back.

Andy lost a little bit of face with Evertonians when he turned down the opportunity to become the manager at Goodison in 1997 after Joe Royle's departure. Clearly Sky TV paid well and it was less frenetic and risky than taking on one of the hottest managerial seats in the country.

However, Evertonians will always admire and respect Andy Gray for what he did as a player and he demonstrated his class when he wrote to me in those disappointing days immediately after Howard transferred him back to one of his former clubs, Aston Villa, in the wake of the Lineker signing.

Andy asked me to pass on his thanks to the Evertonians he was leaving behind. His words are both moving and modest for a man who had been so influential in a comparatively short space of time. His full letter is printed elsewhere in this book.

Quizmaster Howard's seaside surprise: 'Go on, name today's team!'

MANY managers often struggle to build any kind of meaningful relationship with the media, but Howard Kendall was a master when it came to dealing with the press, particularly in the Eighties when he had to survive turbulent times before going on to reign over four trophy-packed years between 1984 and 1987.

I was fortunate enough to report on most of the landmark games throughout his first spell in the hot seat and built up an understanding with him that was based, first on trust, hopefully respect, and later a genuine friendship that I will always treasure.

The kind of relationship we had was summed up for me during an away trip to Brighton in 1983 as he continued to experiment to find his best team. I had breakfast with Howard and he said: "Fancy a walk?" As we strolled away from the team hotel he surprised me when, with a twinkle in his eye, he said: "Go on then, name today's team!"

Of course, he wasn't actually taking leave of his senses and handing over selection responsibilities for a key game to a local journalist. The reality was that he knew all about my strong Everton leanings and he was clearly interested in what the fans were thinking in this early period of major squad evolution.

As it happened, Howard always loved a quiz. He even invented his own quiz game at one stage and revelled in being the quiz master, coming up with a formula that he believed was good enough for TV consideration. He made contact with key parties, but nothing ever came of it.

And so he had posed me a team question to which only he knew the answer and it was as if a big clock was ticking over my head. I named the keeper and the back four. "Correct," said Howard. "Carry on, give me the two wide men next."

I named my wide midfielders. "Correct," confirmed the quizmaster, who added: "Leave the middle two for now and name the strikers."

I came up with my front two, and he smiled again. "Correct! Now finally the centre midfield partners for today."

The quizmaster waited patiently as I gave the final question some real thought. If this had been 'Who wants to be a millionaire?' with a seven-figure prize up for grabs, I must admit that I was suddenly feeling in jackpot mood.

I had two chances and played my best bet first. "Steve

McMahon," I said, pretty confident that I was within touching distance of the million.

I looked at Howard, expecting him to say: "And is that your final answer?"

Instead, he simply replied: "No, Kevin Richardson for McMahon."

Clearly, it was not a decision he had taken lightly. This was an area of the team where competition was mounting for places and here was an early signal that at this point he saw something he really liked in the versatile young Geordie. Howard also rated the emerging young McMahon and wanted to keep him, but on days like this the player himself would clearly begin to have doubts and soon moved to Aston Villa before enjoying a magnificent career with Liverpool.

Ironically, Richardson would eventually find himself in and out of the Everton team as Steven, Reid, Bracewell and Sheedy became the established midfield tour de force. But Richo remained a massively important option for Howard before joining Watford shortly after the start of the 1986-87 season, a club he had clearly impressed in the 1984 FA Cup final.

Kevin soon impressed Arsenal, succeeded fans' favourite Graham Rix on the left wing, and then operated on the right as the Gunners reached the League Cup final in 1988, and then won the championship in 1988-89. He was in the Arsenal side that secured the title that season with a famous last-minute victory over Liverpool at Anfield and actually had a key role to play as he went down with cramp, meaning there was extra time added on at the end of the game. Ironically his former Everton team-mate McMahon famously held up one finger to signal that there was one minute of added time left when, due to Richardson's injury, there was a little bit more, which allowed Michael Thomas to score.

After a spell in Spain, Richardson became Aston Villa captain and inspired them to victory over Manchester United in the 1994 League Cup final.

Clearly, Howard's early belief in him was justified. As I reflected on the outstanding careers of both McMahon and Richardson, I remember reminding Howard about that little chat we had and the call he made that day in 1983. He said: "Every successful team has to have its stars, but it also has to have its special professionals. Kevin was one of those and Alan Harper was another. They were vital players."

Managers certainly have to make tough decisions on emerging talents and while his Richardson call probably cost him Stevie Mac, Howard had no regrets about the midfield personnel that drove his team to glory between 1984 and 1987.

When the remarkable Mr Kendall ultimately retired from the game in 1999, having spent the final 12 months of his 20 eventful managerial years in the sunny, but less than prestigious surroundings of Greek outfit Ethnikos Piraeus, it didn't sit well with him at first.

I asked him to write a column for the Echo because his respected views deserved a continuing public platform. He was still giving considerable thought and focus to that column until the very end in 2015, always speaking sound sense with a knowledge and passion that never left him.

Howard didn't need a second thought in 2003 when I suggested we work together on a book that would pick out the Eighties games that made history, not just great victories, but testing moments that could have changed the course of this eventful era.

Because he respected them so much, Howard was also keen to give his opinion on every player who contributed to that epic four-year spell.

We met at an Italian restaurant near his home in Formby and this would become our social and working base over several weeks as we jointly pulled together ideas for the book, starting with its title.

I asked Howard what single thing made him think about Everton FC and he immediately mentioned the Z-Cars theme, our traditional call to arms before every game. I said: "How about tweaking the book title to 'Everton's Z-Stars'?" and Howard loved it, immediately throwing in other ideas, including the opportunity to give his 'inside the dressing room analysis' on key matches.

Selecting the games that would feature among Howard's favourites was a challenge in its own right and this took up our first few sessions together.

We came up with 19 contrasting matches: seven from 1983-84; six from 1984-85, which naturally included a couple of absolute classics; just two from the 'oh so close' Gary Lineker campaign of 1985-86; and four from what would be his farewell 1986-87 year before his Bilbao adventure.

I've selected here three of the games chosen by Howard

that will help us to understand some of his innermost thoughts in his first spell as manager . . .

1983-84:
INCHY'S JOY
Everton 1 Southampton 0 (FA Cup semi-final, Highbury, April 14, 1984).
Goal: Heath (117).
Howard's dressing room analysis: "This semi gave me one of those almost impossible selection decisions. I took Graeme Sharp for a walk on the morning of the game and explained I was pairing Andy and Inchy up front. Graeme wasn't happy, obviously with one eye on the final (in which he ultimately played and scored).

"Colin Harvey and I had done a little bit of homework and knew Southampton were vulnerable at set-pieces. Frank Worthington was a skilful forward, but not the most disciplined. He always went back for set-pieces and we felt that if Derek Mountfield jogged alongside him, forcing him to mark our big defender, then it might pay off. Derek got a touch on the cross that Inchy buried at the far post. There is a famous picture of us leaping off the bench, screaming in delight. Now you know why."

BAILS . . . WHERE DID YOU GET THAT HAT?
Everton 2 Watford 0 (FA Cup final, May 19, 1984)
Goals: Sharp (38), Gray (51).
Howard's dressing room analysis: "We had played Watford at Vicarage Road in the February and it finished 4-4, so we

knew we could score against them and that if we could get the ball down and play at Wembley we would win the cup.

"I retained Andy Gray and Adrian Heath in the side, but included Graeme Sharp who came back all fired up to score a fantastic opener. Then Andy climbed all over Steve Sherwood for a crucial second. John Bailey put the top hat on it. He was a remarkable character and produced this giant hat. Don't ask me where he got those Elton John glasses.

"Bails could always lift the dressing room. In a derby game, as the lads lined up to go into the tunnel, he shouted: 'I've seen those Red Noses out there and I can't believe how nervous they are.' He then turned round to face the lads and had his shirt on back to front! It was a typical Bails stunt to raise a laugh and boost team morale."

1984-85:
PICK THAT ONE OUT BRUCIE!
Liverpool 0 Everton 1 (League, October 20, 1984)
Goal: Sharp (46).
Howard's dressing room analysis: "What a difference a year can make in football. In November 1983 we had been struggling for a way forward. Now we had the FA Cup in our trophy room and knew that but for a controversial Wembley refereeing decision when Portsmouth's Alan Robinson allowed Alan Hansen to get away with a blatant handball in the box, we might have had the Milk Cup as well.

"This was our first chance to put that right and travelled to Anfield with our league results on the up. Graeme Sharp's spectacular winning volley is now part of derby folklore.

"Sharpy must have been a nightmare to play against. He was strong and had this knack of jumping early to frustrate defenders. He was an excellent target man and while he could have possibly scored more tap-ins, I'm not complaining. He played his part for us and his final goal tally was impressive with some classic strikes, like that volley that gave us our first victory at Anfield in 14 years."

Sitting with Howard to write the 'Z-Stars' book was a joy, but then he was simply different class.

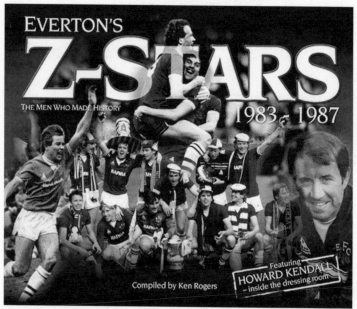

The Z-Stars book that enabled me to sit with Howard and revel in the glory of the 1980s – an era none of us will ever forget

My nightmare match finale as the great Catterick dies at Goodison

THERE are football matches that are fairly straightforward for a reporter – and there are those that suddenly take on a whole new meaning.

On March 9, 1985, with Everton leading the way in the top flight en route to a historic championship triumph, the Blues entertained Ipswich Town at Goodison Park in the sixth round of the FA Cup.

I settled down in the press box and prepared to file my report for that evening's Football Echo. The players had progressed all the way to Wembley the previous year and had picked up their first silverware of the Eighties with a solid FA Cup win over Watford.

It was now time to build on that and while the championship remained the priority with 15 games to go, the fans had tasted the magic of an FA Cup triumph and clearly wanted more.

My phone rang on the front row of the press box at 2.50pm at which point I dictated the team Kendall had selected: Neville Southall, Gary Stevens, Pat Van Den Hauwe, Kevin Ratcliffe, Derek Mountfield, Peter Reid, Trevor Steven, Terry Curran, Andy Gray, Paul Bracewell, and Kevin Sheedy.

Graeme Sharp was injured. I suppose the surprise selection was mercurial winger Terry Curran. He had initially been signed on loan in late 1982 during Howard's second season in charge as the manager tried to inject something a little bit different into a side that was still finding its way at that point.

By this stage Curran had already played for eight clubs in less than 10 years. Everton was the ninth and he would play for another eight after that, a total of 17 in all which made him one of the most travelled players ever in the Football League.

The fact that he would ultimately call his autobiography 'Regrets Of A Football Maverick' perhaps best sums up his character as a player, but he had skill – no doubt about that. Kendall famously signed him in unusual circumstances, which was par for the course with Terry.

In his excellent book 'Only The Best Is Good Enough' Howard recalls: "We were trapped in a downwards spiral and I just felt we needed someone with enough self-confidence to take games by the scruff of the neck and breathe fresh enthusiasm into the Goodison public. I had players in my team who were hiding during matches.

"The man I chose for this difficult task was Terry Curran. He had tremendous talent, but more importantly he was a genuine personality with a reputation for entertaining the crowd. I took him on a month's loan at first from Sheffield United and his impact was such that I attempted to make it permanent."

What should have been a simple transfer exercise for Howard then became something of a saga. It would be the start of the following season before he could confirm the winger as a fully fledged Everton player. Having put a £150,000 valuation on him, Sheffield United suddenly increased their asking price. It ran on towards the March transfer deadline and despite a meeting with player and agent it fell through again.

Howard was bitterly disappointed with Curran's attitude, but then it wouldn't be the first or the last time the player proved controversial.

It would be September 1983 before things were rekindled and settled, the only bonus being that by now the price had dropped to £90,000.

When he was fit, Curran clearly had the ability to lift the crowd, but he was dogged by injuries and his senior chances were limited.

His FA Cup appearance against Ipswich was a rare opportunity for him to show his skill after just a handful of games during that 1984-85 campaign.

Having dictated the teams to the office, I reported the inclusion of Curran and kept the phone line open for the full 90 minutes which was the usual procedure.

The Football Echo report was effectively like a live commentary involving 32 first half paragraphs and 28 in the second half, plus a four-paragraph summary at three-quarter time and a definitive introduction. This would often have to be altered if the score changed in the closing moments.

As it turned out, Ipswich put up a real fight in a 2-2 draw. Kevin Sheedy would score our first goal with a famously twice-taken free-kick, Derek Mountfield grabbing the second with a typical opportunist effort. With a few minutes to go, I noticed some unusual activity on the front row of the directors box straight ahead of me.

Clearly, someone was being lifted onto the roof of the executive boxes immediately below, enabling the individual to stretch out flat with the St John's Ambulance Brigade quickly on the scene. I also recognised the official Everton FC doctor and realised that someone had possibly had a heart attack.

I assumed it was one of the fans. Suddenly a message was passed back that it was Harry Catterick, the man who had been playing centre-forward for Everton and scored two goals on the day when my dad took me, as a toddler, to Goodison Park for the first time in May 1950. Of course, he had later become one of the most successful Blues managers of all time and I had worked with him as a young reporter, a sometimes challenging experience as explained in an earlier chapter.

Clearly, it was important that I reported what was happening for the readers of the Football Echo as that Ipswich cup tie reached its conclusion. The first thing I did was warn the copytaker back at the office not to put the phone down on the final whistle which was standard practice. When this happened it was impossible to get back through. I asked them to inform the sports desk that Harry Catterick had taken ill and that because of his stature it was crucial to delay publication, even for a few minutes, to capture the latest update. I knew this would not go down well with the production team, regardless of the importance of potential breaking news. Deadlines were crucial when it came to the Pink because many fans, having watched the match, went straight to their local newsagents on the way home to buy a copy and relive that afternoon's action. Fans who dallied at the ground would actually find the Pink sellers waiting outside to greet them as they left.

I made eye contact with one of the St John's Ambulance crew standing on the front row of the directors' box, looking down on Harry. I didn't know it then, but the club doc was pumping Catterick's chest to try and revive him.

The manager who, in the Sixties, had restored pride to our club with two league championships and an FA Cup triumph had actually suffered a warning attack in January 1972 while driving home from Sheffield. He still had four years of a ten-year contract still to run at that time. The end game was that Harry was moved sideways into a senior executive role with his former right winger Billy Bingham handed the hot seat.

Now he was clearly having a much more serious problem almost 12 years later, one that I knew could be life threatening. I stood up in the press box and put my arms out wide to ask the St John's man how serious it was. He suddenly put his thumbs up. The doc had revived Harry.

I immediately began to dictate my final paragraphs of the day for the Football Echo:

"Harry Catterick, the legendary Everton manager, collapsed in dramatic circumstances at Goodison Park today after having a heart attack. He was lifted from the directors' box onto the roof of the executive boxes below where he received treatment from the club doctor.

"I am able to report that Mr Catterick responded to this medical intervention, news that will be a relief to his family and all of those fans who were inspired by his outstanding championship-winning teams."

The copytaker was clearly agitated, getting ear-ache from the production team at the office. I was just about to say "you can put the phone down now and run with this" when my St John's Ambulance man suddenly gave me the thumbs down.

"Wait," I shouted down the phone. "I have to go again." I dictated two new paragraphs, using "died in dramatic circumstances" instead of "collapsed in dramatic circumstances."

Then the thumbs went up again. I was now in a state of absolute panic, fearful that I was going to report Harry's death, only for him to be fine, or vice versa. I was imagining Harry having to mirror the legendary words of novelist Mark Twain after incorrect stories of his death appeared in American newspapers. Twain later declared: "Rumours about my death have been greatly exaggerated!"

"Don't put the phone down under any circumstances," I repeated to the copytaker. I heard a groan at the other end of the line!

I glanced down one last time towards the St John's Ambulance man. The thumbs went down again and this time I saw them lifting Harry up on a stretcher to remove him from the roof of the executive box. "Go with the dead version," I shouted, still not believing I had said it. I heard the phone go down. There was no turning back.

I looked up to the blue heavens. Harry had never been the easiest individual to deal with. He had kept that up right to the bitter end.

I raced out of the press box and took the stairs two at a time down to the directors' landing. Harry was being carried towards me. A sheepskin coat now covered his upper body and head.

I then asked the most ridiculous question. "Is he dead?" I didn't need a formal answer, of course, but in the circumstances I just had to ask.

The St John's Ambulance man looked at me. I just shrugged, took a deep breath and blew out my cheeks! I think even the straight-laced Harry would have fully understood where I was coming from.

My sheer relief at not making a catastrophic reporting

error now swamped me. I made my way down to the players' tunnel. One or two of the lads who had not played were first out of the dressing room. "Do you know Harry Catterick has died?" I asked, expecting them to say: "WHAT? HARRY CATTERICK!"

It was a more muted response as they made their way through to the players' lounge, but why should it have been any different? Harry was of a different era, but he had been an absolute Everton giant for fans who had witnessed his glory years.

Those who knew him personally were obviously stunned, not least Colin Harvey who said: "I was devastated. I had a lot of time for Harry. He mentored me as a kid and then right through as a senior player, handing me my debut in the San Siro stadium in Milan. He had been a great manager and Everton servant."

Colin's assessment was perfect. In the following week's Echo, I would proudly write up the 'Harry Catterick Story' and what a series it was.

Introvert he might have been, but the teams he built oozed class and fulfilled all the criteria needed to live up to the club's proud 'School of Soccer Science' tag. What better legacy could any Everton manager wish for?

Debut boy Snods ends up naked in Bordeaux... I end up creosoted!

ON February 4, 1987, I found myself covering a fascinating friendly match as French giants Bordeaux prepared to celebrate the 50th anniversary of their first professional game.

Everton were deemed to be the perfect prestige opponents, particularly as the Merseyside Blues were on course to claim their second championship in this glittering period.

As the Echo's chief football writer, I was allowed to travel to Bordeaux with the official party and turned up at Belle-field to join the team bus on its short journey to Liverpool Airport. I boarded with Neville Southall and we both kept our bags with us rather than putting them into the hold where kit man Jimmy Martin was busy loading the skips.

When we got off at Speke, big Nev left his bag where it was

on the seat, so I left mine, assuming that other people were doing the same and that there would be a final trawl of the coach before everything went through the official channels.

We boarded the plane, had a pleasant flight and then headed to the baggage reclaim at Bordeaux airport.

Player after player grabbed his bag from the carousel and headed towards the team coach to take us to our hotel. Suddenly there were two people left . . . Neville and myself. We looked at each other as the empty carousel went round and round. He was fuming in typical Nev fashion. At least Neville had kit in Jimmy's skips. I had the clothes I was standing up in.

I went to watch a light training session in the afternoon and at some stage, I leaned back on the brown rail around the pitch to make some notes. As I tried to move away, it felt as if my suit jacket was glued to the rail.

Clearly, the French groundsman had been slopping creosote onto the wood to spruce things up before Everton's arrival and I suddenly looked as if a motorbike had driven over my back. We would soon be whisked off to a prestige event involving local city officials at an exquisite venue.

I spent the whole time edging my way around this chandeliered room with my back to the wall. I was being introduced to special guests, but walked sideways like a crab to retain my tactical position and hide my jacket disaster.

Of course, Bordeaux is famous for its wine and the hosts were keen to invite us to one of the premier vineyards in the region. I remember that our small party included Howard Kendall, Jim Greenwood, and popular Everton director

Jack Search. Mr Search was a down-to-earth and upbeat character and we were soon sipping some of Bordeaux's very best in magnificent surroundings.

Feeling that our party had to take a real interest in this session rather than simply having a great time, Mr Search put a fairly long-winded question to the vineyard owner. He asked: "Based on the amount of sunshine you get per year, and the type of soil you have, and the annual amount of rain, does this provide exactly the right nutrients and conditions for growing grapes here in Bordeaux?"

The vineyard owner went silent for a moment, smiled and replied: "Mr Search. Just drink it and enjoy!"

Back at Liverpool Airport, Nev and I eventually got on the team coach to return to Bellefield. There were our bags, on the seats where we had left them.

The important thing was the game, which Everton won 2-1. The French club had given everyone on the trip a special bottle of Bordeaux wine in an inscribed wooden box which I've still got unopened somewhere in my loft.

A couple of years ago I found myself in the grand entrance hall of the Adelphi Hotel in Liverpool where I was meeting Ian Snodin. I wanted him to work with my Trinity Mirror Sport Media publishing unit on a book about his career highlights, well aware that he was a character and a half.

I had previously sat with him at an after dinner event at Goodison Park. We were both on the top table and over the meal he had started to discuss some of the hilarious moments he had experienced throughout his career.

We were both laughing so loud that everyone was starting

to look up to see what was going on. The tears were rolling down my face and I knew at that moment that Snods had a hit book in him, hence our follow-up at the Adelphi.

One story, in particular, struck a very personal chord. He started to talk about Bordeaux and his pride in suddenly being an Everton player. He was so proud, in fact, that he went "out on the lash" after the victory, to use his own words.

Snods later told the ghost writer that we used for the book, Alan Jewell, how he was soon 'plastered' and told his room-mate Alan Harper that he needed to go to bed.

I quote directly from Ian's tremendous book 'Snod this for a Laugh': "I scored in the Bordeaux game and celebrated as if it was the winning goal in the European Cup final. Later, after a real good drinking session, I remember Alan and Kevin Ratcliffe putting me to bed. I woke up in the night absolutely freezing. I leaned over to pull the quilt over my body and grasped thin air. I thought, 'Where is it?' As I did so I heard a bell ring. I opened my eyes and an old couple emerged from the hotel lift in front of me.

"Alan and Kevin had carried me out of my room completely naked and laid me on a settee right outside the lift. I put my hand over my manhood, spluttered an apology and ran back down the corridor to my room completely starkers.

"It was a case of, Welcome to Everton."

If I'd have known at the time, Snods could have had my creosoted suit jacket as a pillow.

And I bet his special bottle of Bordeaux wine is not sitting unopened in its presentation box up in the loft like mine!

Surely UEFA's post-Heysel ban on innocent parties had to be illegal

AS we jetted home from that Bordeaux friendly in February, 1987, life couldn't have been much better for Evertonians, but there was one dark cloud in the sky.

The Blues had claimed the FA Cup in 1984, followed by a league title triumph in 1985 with the prestigious European Cup Winners Cup also in the trophy room. Everton had then come as close as they had ever come to securing a historic league and FA Cup double in 1986 and, as we headed back from that 1987 prestige showpiece in Bordeaux, a second league title triumph in three years was now confidently in the club's sights.

But behind all of this positivity, there was a massive negative, the inability of England's top clubs to prove themselves against Europe's elite because of the ongoing ban that followed the 1985 Heysel Disaster. This not only frustrated every Evertonian, but would ultimately be one of the reasons why we lost the most successful manager we have ever had.

Significantly, Everton would be denied the opportunity to build on those Eighties glory years, prevented from capitalising on their unprecedented domestic success and therefore unable to reap the rewards that can go hand in hand with progress in the major European competitions. This, in turn, hampered the possibility of attracting the kind of business investment needed to catapult the club into the 1990s and the golden era of the new Premier League.

All of this is not to underplay the Heysel Disaster where 39 people died – mostly Italians – prior to their European Cup final clash with Liverpool.

Crowd trouble and the collapse of a wall in a totally inadequate stadium led to what was described at the time as the "darkest hour in the history of UEFA competitions."

Liverpool fans had travelled worldwide from the Sixties without any real issues and our city's fans, in general, had built a wonderful reputation – cemented so graphically the year before Heysel when rival Merseyside supporters travelled together to Wembley for the 1984 Milk Cup final.

It would therefore be wrong to heap the ills of the soccer world at the door of Liverpool FC for Heysel, while accepting that it was a dreadful event that had a tsunami effect on others. We had the upsetting sight in 1985 of a distraught Joe Fagan, one of the most down-to-earth and honest managers in football, reduced to tears and effectively a broken man as

Liverpool FC returned home from Belgium. I don't think he ever recovered from what happened that night.

In the end, Everton and the other leading English clubs paid a shared price.

On reflection, I believe that what UEFA did in ordering a blanket ban on all English teams was not only grossly unfair, but actually against all the civil laws of Europe, let alone the rule book of any governing football body.

Of course, Liverpool FC had to take its punishment – and the club acted with dignity and contrition after the disaster. But is there any court in the world where innocent third parties might be punished for an incident that:

1. They were not even involved in and, indeed, took place in another country.

2. They had no influence over.

3. Might seriously affect their ability to move forward as a business.

The answer, of course, is a resounding no.

UEFA felt empowered and justified in imposing the blanket English ban following a statement on May 31, 1985, by British Prime Minister Margaret Thatcher who asked the FA to withdraw English clubs from European competition before they were banned. Within days of her statement, the ban was imposed for 'an indeterminate period of time'.

The four affected clubs and the PFA fought hard to get the ban overturned, but on July 29, 1985, High Court Judge, Mr Justice Vinelott, threw out an appeal, claiming it was "in the interests of the game and its future."

What an absolute travesty it was for those innocent parties.

The ruling not only ended Everton's immediate European competition dreams, but also those of Manchester United, Tottenham, Southampton and Norwich.

As the years unfolded, 11 other clubs would also suffer: Southampton, West Ham, Sheffield Wednesday, Oxford, Coventry, Arsenal, Wimbledon, Nottingham Forest, Luton, Derby and, of course, Liverpool.

Everton had qualified for the European Cup for the first time in 15 years in 1985. All the affected clubs claimed the bans were "an unlawful restraint of trade, a breach of natural justice, and against European Community Law," as well as being "an interference in contractual obligations."

Incredibly, the appeal judge ruled that the civil courts had no power over UEFA or FIFA. It is little wonder that in the decades that followed, high ranking officials within FIFA would ultimately believe they were above the law.

Back in December, 1985, they threw a few scraps towards the innocent English third parties. It was decided that English clubs were also free to play friendly matches in Europe, but not in Belgium, hence Everton's ability to accept prestige friendly fixtures against clubs like Bordeaux.

After a five-year exile for the English, UEFA finally lifted the ban in 1990-91 on all but Liverpool who served an extra year. But Everton's opportunity to build on their sensational Eighties success story had been seriously compromised, and it all began to unravel on what I expected to be a fairly uneventful day in June 1987.

One paragraph in a Barcelona paper hands me 'Howard Quits' exclusive

I WILL never forget June 19, 1987. It was just another day at the office – at least it should have been.

Instead the morning exploded into a hive of feverish activity as I began to put together the biggest Everton football exclusive I had ever secured up to that point. My daily input usually appeared on the back page. This one would completely dominate the front page and many news pages, stunning Evertonians all over the city.

In a nutshell, the Blues were about to lose Howard Kendall, their newly crowned Manager of the Year, just a matter of weeks after players, officials and fans alike had celebrated Everton's second league championship success in three seasons. During this historic period – the most successful in the club's history – the Blues had also claimed the European Cup Winners Cup and the FA Cup.

It seemed inconceivable that Howard would choose to go at this time, but that morning I had confirmed that it was about to happen. I'd love to say it was a masterstroke of journalism but while these exclusives often come out of a great contacts book, the truth is that the source is sometimes at a much more basic level.

In an earlier chapter I explained how I secured the news that the Blues were about to sign Andy Gray, courtesy of a fan who had just spotted him in a Goodison Road newsagent. This time, the source was genuinely more continental, but was equally rooted in fan passion.

For some time I had been exchanging Everton FC views with a lad called Peter Cail who knew Colin Harvey and who had previously lived close to my former home in Crosby. Peter had moved his family to Spain where he was now running a very successful bar in Barcelona.

Of course, he was always desperate to get the latest news from Goodison and we would chat on the phone in an informal way. I was therefore not surprised when my phone rang on that June morning, although I did immediately recognise that Peter was not his usual chirpy self.

"I've just been down to my local Barcelona newsagent," he said, "and in one of the local papers I've spotted something you might be interested in."

Before I could say anything, Peter blurted out: "There is just one paragraph, but it is suggesting that Howard Kendall is leaving Everton and moving to Athletic Bilbao."

If the call had been about Howard accepting a glamorous new role with Real Madrid, or Barcelona, who he had already been linked with, I would have given Peter's call more credence, but Athletic Bilbao up in the north?

I told Peter, a massive Blues fan, that I would check and promised to get back to him before he had a heart attack. I immediately tried to get Howard. He was not available, which was highly unusual for him.

As usual my next call was to Everton's chief executive Jim Greenwood. The conversation was short and sweet. In actual fact there was no conversation, which was a good thing from my point of view. It went something like this: "Good morning Jim. I know this sounds ridiculous, but I have just had a call from Barcelona saying that the local paper is carrying a one-paragraph story claiming that Howard is going to Bilbao. This is surely not correct, is it?"

I had a fantastic relationship with Jim, someone Howard called "a great tourist" because he always joined in whenever we were away, not least on pre-season tours. Jim had always been prepared to guide me on stories, even if he could not formally confirm or deny anything.

I've explained that Jim's way of giving me the nod was actually to say nothing at all and so when there was a tantalising few moments of silence on the phone, I knew that Peter's one-paragraph filler was absolutely correct. I also knew that Jim would now check out how much I could use and get back to me. Whatever happened, I was now going to stun Merseyside – indeed the world of football – with the breaking news that Howard Kendall was off to sunny Spain.

I breezed into the Echo's morning conference in the editor's office. "Anything happening?" was the simple question. I said: "In terms of an exclusive story that will sell thousands of extra papers tonight, we've got a really big one. But if you are an Evertonian, it will be a bitter pill to swallow. Howard Kendall is leaving to join Athletic Bilbao."

There was a stunned silence and then the whole team leapt into action. I would send for Howard's pictures and cuttings from the Echo library. The planners were deciding how many extra pages to devote on the news and feature pages, let alone the sports pages. A reporter was despatched into the streets to get reaction from the fans.

I just had to calm myself and start to write stories for the front and back pages, as well as a personal backgrounder on the life and times of Howard Kendall.

Why would he want to go? He had an outstanding relationship with chairman Sir Philip Carter and the board. He had a magnificent backroom staff which included his right hand man and assistant Colin Harvey. I was already thinking about what we might report the following day and immediately decided that we would be backing Colin to the hilt to replace his former playing partner and great friend.

I knew that Howard was bitterly disappointed that his English title winners would once again be denied the opportunity to play in Europe after winning the championship because of the ongoing ban caused by the Heysel Disaster.

The Blues didn't just lose the greatest manager in the game at that time. Howard's departure inevitably sparked a period of change and challenge. Significantly, Everton also lost the ability to secure key sponsorship deals and further potential investment in the club.

In his autobiography 'Nil Satis Nisi Optimum' Howard explained the reasons behind his departure. He revealed: "I missed those nights of European glory very much indeed."

He also highlighted the fact that Barcelona's interest, while it had come and gone, had very much whetted his appetite to leave England and try his luck abroad. Bilbao had also done a magnificent selling job on their club, thanks to a man called Fernando Ochoa, who had been despatched to Liverpool in April 1987 at a moment when the Blues were on the brink of claiming another title.

Howard had been impressed, even if Fernando had reasserted the fact that Bilbao would continue with a policy of only signing Basque players.

The biggest enticement for Howard was that he could become a coach once again, getting out on the pitch with the players and leaving the general manager style responsibilities to other people. It excited him and he agreed to fly out to Spain after Everton's end of season tour to Australia, New Zealand and Hawaii. I should add that, like Jim, Howard was also a 'great tourist'.

Travelling via Madrid to Bilbao was what Howard described as a pantomime. He was using a false name, Mr Robinson, to avoid any undue focus. Of course, this caused problems securing his tickets at the airport with a passport stating Kendall. It was the same at the hotel in Bilbao.

Howard has always been keen to emphasise that he never left Everton for "Spanish gold." In simple terms he believed it was the right thing to do at that moment in time – as a person and a football manager.

It would be a journey that would last two and a half years and end in frustration, but I am not surprised that Howard built up a special relationship with his players and fans, although his normally superb relationship with the media had been stretched to the limit by the tough Spanish press.

He recalls a New Year's Day when hundreds of Bilbao supporters turned up to watch training. Impressed by this, Howard told the players that they should stand in a line in front of the fans and shout in unison: "Happy New Year."

The players initially refused until Howard offered them a light-hearted alternative – a five-mile hill run. Soon the players were singing to his tune and the fans roared their approval. This was Howard down to a tee.

This exclusive made it onto the front as well as the back page of the Echo. Howard never liked this headline because of the cash inference, adamant that European competition was the big draw

True blue Colin Harvey – totally dedicated to Everton in every way

BACK at home, Colin Harvey was now beginning his own managerial career at the age of 42 with a 1987 Charity Shield victory at Wembley over surprise FA Cup winners Coventry City. This was followed by an opening day league win against Norwich City.

There's nothing like a winning start, but Colin would soon discover the frustrations of life in the hot seat.

Even though the league programme was reduced to 40 matches that season, Everton played in eight different competitions, including the Charity Shield, while coping with a series of injuries to key players. The fact that the Blues played in 21 cup games indicates that they were still battling and winning matches in the FA Cup, Littlewoods Cup, and

Simod Cup. They beat old European Cup Winners Cup rivals Bayern Munich 3-1 at Goodison in the league's special Mercantile Credit Centenary Challenge; led 2-0 and then lost 8-7 on penalties after a 2-2 draw with Glasgow Rangers in the Dubai Super Cup; and took the familiar road to Wembley in the Football League Centenary Festival where they beat Wolves, but lost to Manchester United.

Everton went on an unbeaten league run that left them third going into the final game of the campaign at home to Arsenal. Despite leading, the Blues would allow the Gunners to recover and claim victory and this pushed Colin's men down to fourth place. But it had been a solid season as he steadied the ship following Howard's unexpected exit.

Colin was anything but satisfied and in his 'Everton Secrets' book he revealed that he had repeatedly told the players, often in some quite heated team meetings, that if they had reproduced their home form in key away games, anything might have been possible for the defending champions.

Clearly, Everton had been lacking a cutting edge. At the same time, change was inevitable. Two goalkeepers went, Bobby Mimms and Alex Chamberlain. Derek Mountfield joined Aston Villa because of Dave Watson's superb consistency and Colin's confidence in Pat Van Den Hauwe who could comfortably fill in at centre-back when needed.

I recently discussed the aptly nicknamed 'Psycho Pat' with Colin while initially seeking an opinion on Ray Wilson, a 1966 World Cup winner with England and former class act with Everton during Colin's playing days. The resulting comments were intriguing.

Colin said: "Ray could be a bit dour in the dressing room, but not in an aggressive way. He'd been forced to do National Service with the Army and subsequently had 'Egypt, Never Again' tattooed across a dagger on his arm. Ray was a good lad, but not like his England team-mate Alan Ball who would light up a room. Ray had a quiet aura about him, but on the pitch was tremendously quick with a great left peg."

Colin then paid a tribute to Van Den Hauwe. He said: "I actually believe Pat was a better all-round player who could switch comfortably between his full-back role and centre-half."

Another departure in Colin's first managerial season included the versatile Alan Harper to Sheffield Wednesday, while veteran Paul Power – a supreme professional who made a solid contribution to the 1987 title triumph – retired to join the coaching staff. The manager tried and failed to bring in the outstanding talent from Barcelona that was Mark Hughes and it would be a further 12 years before he arrived at Goodison. At the same time, Peter Reid's decision to stay halted a potential exchange deal with Newcastle for the talent that was Paul Gascoigne, another who would ultimately find his way to Goodison.

Gary Stevens was increasingly unhappy, not helped by personal problems, and he soon joined Glasgow Rangers.

This was never going to be an easy transition into management for Harvey, not least because of the standards he had helped to set. However, he brought in some quality individuals in Stuart McCall, Tony Cottee and Pat Nevin. Neil

McDonald was another decent addition, but the side had a worrying slump and just one win in eight league games in Colin's second season left the side in 15th place, their lowest position for over four years.

Colin then had to step away from his management duties following a much-needed hip operation and it didn't help when he returned to the hot seat too soon. Adrian Heath departed to Espanyol and all of this highlighted the inevitable changes that were unfolding.

At the turn of the year in that 1988-89 season, the Blues were fourth after 18 games. A run in the Littlewoods Cup ended in surprise fashion at second division Bradford, but Colin guided the team back to Wembley in the Simod Cup final where they led twice before Nottingham Forest recovered to take the game into extra time in which they ultimately snatched a late winner.

Everton also returned to Wembley in the FA Cup at the end of that eventful season and I reported on the semifinal at Villa Park where the Blues played Norwich City. I contacted the office shortly before the game and, as usual, would keep the line open for 90 minutes to enable my Football Echo report to unfold.

The match had only just started when the copytaker indicated that there was a problem in the Liverpool v Nottingham Forest semi-final at Hillsborough. Moments later I was told that reports were emerging of deaths following a crushing at the Leppings Lane end. First it was one, then several, then dozens. Of course, the final toll would be 96.

Trying to concentrate on a football report was virtually

impossible while grasping the tragic events that were unfolding in Sheffield. Pat Nevin scored what proved to be the semi-final winner for Everton after 26 minutes, but suddenly football seemed irrelevant and I really felt for Colin Harvey. He had achieved what should have been one of the greatest moments of his remarkable football career, but stepped quietly into a totally silent Villa Park press room after the game to express his deep felt concern about what had happened at Hillsborough.

In my subsequent match report, I wrote: 'Everton had just achieved a feat that, in normal circumstances, would have turned the M6 into a sea of blue and white. But on the journey home there was no chanting or singing, no banter between supporters who had just seen Everton secure their fourth FA Cup final appearance in six years with a glorious win over Norwich City. There was only a feeling of helplessness and uncertainty. All we could do was tune into our car radios and wince as the death toll rose with every mile we covered between Birmingham and Liverpool.'

I added: 'Merseyside fans have always been able to stand shoulder to shoulder. In that way we are unique. Evertonians recognised that it could have been them at Hillsborough. The recipe for disaster would have been just the same. It was Colin Harvey's greatest day as a manager, but he used his press conference to send a message of sympathy to the families of those who had lost their lives. Suddenly victory had a hollow ring about it. A giant cloud hung over Villa Park and, try as it might, the sunshine just couldn't break through.'

I had secured two tickets for a colleague and so I knew her

son was in the Leppings Lane end. I went straight from Villa Park to her house in Crosby, fearing the worst, but it turned out he was okay. At that stage no-one could be certain that Liverpool's semi-final would be replayed, let alone the FA Cup final confirmed, but I sensed that whatever happened, no-one could truly win.

In the end, the Merseyside giants stepped out under the Twin Towers in a somewhat unreal situation and Ian Rush would have the final say, scoring the extra-time winner.

Reflecting on his second season at the helm, Colin said: "I was proud of my players, but was still striving to find that team chemistry that would bring us another major trophy."

It wasn't to be. In his first three seasons as manager, Colin steered the Blues to fourth, eighth and sixth in the old first division, won a Charity Shield, and secured Wembley appearances in both the FA and Simod Cups. He had not expected to be thrust into the managerial spotlight in 1987. Whoever came in at that time was on a hiding to nothing.

In that third season in charge, Colin tried and failed to bring Gary Lineker back from Barcelona. Colin spoke to talented Norwich midfielder Mike Phelan who, at the last minute, opted to join Alex Ferguson at Manchester United. The Everton boss now made an audacious bid to persuade Ferguson to part with the class midfield act that was Bryan Robson, but received a firm 'no'.

Colin completed one outstanding piece of business when he beat Ferguson to secure centre-back Martin Keown from Aston Villa. Echo back page headlines would soon demand an England call-up for Martin. Mike Newell arrived from

Leicester to boost Colin's striking options. He also captured young Swedish midfielder Stefan Rehn as well as gambling on the fitness of United's Norman Whiteside, who had struggled with a knee problem, but who was still only 24. Colin's final signing that third summer was Dutchman Ray Atteveld who could play in midfield or at full-back.

Peter Beagrie would also arrive that season, a fast and skilful winger from Stoke. Signings invoke departures and all Evertonians were sorry to see Trevor Steven refuse to sign a new contract and follow Gary Stevens to Rangers.

It's pure conjecture how Everton might have fared in that 1989-90 campaign if Colin had signed a Lineker or a Robson, hugely influential as players in different ways. As it was, sixth place was secured.

It will be left to the history books to debate whether Colin deserved to depart in his fourth season on October 31, 1990, with Everton standing 18th of the 20 clubs in the top flight. His Everton managerial record had been vastly superior to many other top flight managers of the day who retained their jobs, but Colin accepted it with the professionalism that had been the hallmark of his career.

One thing happened as it all imploded in October 1990 that summed up for me just how much Everton and everything around it meant to Colin Harvey.

After a Rumbelows Cup defeat at Sheffield United where Dave Watson was sent off, Colin sensed he was out and these words, revealed in the 'Everton Secrets' book he penned with my national newspaper colleague John Keith, summed up his feelings.

He said: "Being a lifelong Evertonian as well as manager made the pain worse. The buck stopped with me. I was the man in charge – and that was it. I felt so bad I didn't go home that night after we returned to Bellefield. I rang my wife to say I was spending the night at the training ground.

"I just sat there and thought about the season we'd had. It was my fourth and while we came close twice, we had not won anything. At Bellefield, our coach Jimmy Gabriel kept me company for a while, but when he went home I just stayed there all night, sleeping only fitfully. Next morning when the staff came in, I got a phone call asking me to go to a meeting. A chill ran down my spine, not because I knew I was losing my job, but because I felt I'd let down the club and myself."

Just the very thought of Colin, alone all night in that large Bellefield training complex, fretting about his beloved Everton and thinking about the fans, says everything about an individual who had actually given us so much. He is up there with the greatest in terms of his contribution to everything we achieved between his sensational 1963 debut as an 18-year-old against Inter Milan in the San Siro to that watershed moment in October, 1990.

Remarkably, on November 6, he would return to Bellefield within seven days, announced as assistant manager on Howard Kendall's shock return.

25

Howard renews his Everton wedding vows, but testing days loom ahead

HOWARD Kendall had spent a year at Manchester City following his return from Spain and would now utter his famous quote: "If City was a love affair, Everton is a marriage."

I was in the room for that November, 1990, press conference and will never forget it. When Bill Kenwright walked in with chief executive Jim Greenwood, followed by Howard AND Colin, the whole place erupted. The media can be cynical at times, hard to impress and difficult to please, but there was effectively a standing ovation, a lot of back slapping, and a feeling of sheer delight that the men who had brought Evertonians so much pride were suddenly and unexpectedly back in harness. Would this revived partnership be the stuff that football dreams are made of?

Bill Kenwright declared it "The Second Coming," adding: "If I put it in a movie, no-one would believe it."

For now, at least, fans and media were prepared to accept that anything was possible as the Blues edged up the table in season 1990-91 to finish ninth. My experience down the years tells me that you will never have a great side without a great manager.

I felt privileged to have been privy to Harry Catterick's tough mindset and controlled regime, reporting on his illustrious 1969-70 championship-winning side.

From the heart of the Echo sports desk I had seen the likes of Billy Bingham and Gordon Lee try and fail to repeat Catterick's glory days. They came close at times, but in the final reckoning each would be forced to take that fabled managerial taxi ride without managing to bring further silverware to Goodison.

I had found myself reporting on the Blues again at the start of Howard Kendall's glorious 1980s era, a 3-1 home win over Birmingham City at Goodison in late August, 1981. In the second match, at Leeds, I gained an early understanding of the new manager's media management style. I was in the press room at Elland Road after a 1-1 draw. The press conference was over, but Howard made a point of searching me out and asking if there was anything else I might need for the following day's paper. This was highly unusual for a manager and I immediately knew Howard was different.

It was the start of a relationship that would stand the test of time and we would finish up as great friends, but football is about the good, the bad and the ugly and if you are doing your job correctly as a reporter it is impossible to work with top football managers without falling out big style at times.

I was there the night the notorious 'Kendall and Carter Out' leaflets were distributed at Goodison Park before a League Cup tie with Chesterfield in 1983. These were severely testing days.

Whenever I walked away from a match after games that had left the fans totally frustrated, they would inevitably stop me in the street and all say the same thing: "Tell the truth in the Echo tomorrow!"

Supporters don't want flannel and you can't pull the wool over the eyes of Scousers. They simply won't have it. Before the 1990s, fans were the acknowledged lifeblood of the game. Sadly, their needs often come second best to a colossal TV agenda these days, but don't get me started on that one.

So when Howard returned for his second spell at the helm in November, 1990, now wedded again to his beloved Blues, I took key members of my Echo sports team to meet his backroom staff for what proved to be a marathon and highly enjoyable 'welcome back' session at a well known restaurant in Liverpool's Chinatown.

Everyone desperately wanted him to be successful again and I said he could rely on our support, while accepting that there might be moments, hopefully few and far between, when we might have to be constructively critical. Howard jumped on the comment straight away so I immediately put it another way. "If you shake a champagne bottle for too long without releasing some of the pressure, the bottle will explode."

Howard smiled and nodded. He knew the score, having always been a master throughout his career when it came to dealing with the press, through good times and bad. Having worked in Spain, he was now also well aware that while the English media could be uncompromising at times, their Spanish counterparts were on a whole different level; lethal, manipulating and always seeming to have the ear of influential club presidents.

As our Chinese lunch unfolded, we were soon revelling in memories of his first successful spell at the Goodison helm. He had lost none of his sharpness and certainly none of his sense of humour.

Here was a manager full of confidence, with a genuine belief that what he had achieved once, he could achieve again. We all desperately wanted to see the Blues drive forward again with Howard and Colin back in the old routine.

I spoke to Colin recently about what it was like to have been the manager with total control, only to suddenly find himself working again as Howard's assistant. Speaking with hindsight, he now believes it was a mistake because, as he put it, there were too many ghosts.

Colin explained: "There was never a problem with our relationship. It was brilliant, particularly before Howard went to Bilbao. We were on the same wavelength and always knew what each other was thinking.

"As manager, he always had the final say, but if I really felt

170

something needed saying, I would say it. He either took it on board or he didn't.

"We had gone our separate ways in management and had both changed a bit, but he called me after I got the sack and asked me to go to dinner. He quickly said that there was an offer on the table for him to come back – and asked if I would be interested in becoming his assistant again. It only took a couple of seconds to say yes, but I made this decision without fully thinking about all the consequences. In retrospect, I should not have accepted the new job offer.

"What about my relationship with the players after being manager? Equally, what about the changes that inevitably happened around my coaching staff? I never thought it through. It became a bit more difficult and a bit stilted in certain ways, having been manager for three years."

For his part, Howard had taken Manchester City from difficult territory onto much more solid ground in his short spell at Maine Road, and he had clearly enjoyed the experience. Everton were at the wrong end of the table when he returned in November, 1990, and the priority was clearly to move towards safety, determined to avoid ending the season in a relegation dogfight.

He always said that top clubs like Everton would be more vulnerable in relegation scraps than teams who had regularly experienced such tensions and who were subsequently more battle hardened.

Howard therefore wanted to secure safety as quickly as possible and by mid-January, 1991, the Blues had edged up to a more respectable mid-table position while securing a

February clash against Liverpool in the fifth round of the FA Cup.

The tie was at Anfield where the talking point at the end of a combative goalless draw was a moment of real controversy when Reds defender Gary Ablett, later to play for the Blues, pole-axed Pat Nevin in the box. I recall that referee Neil Midgley not only waved aside Everton's appeals, but indicated that Nevin had 'dived' and would be sent off if he did it again.

If a player swore at Midgley, he was as likely to get a mouthful back. The experienced Bolton official, unlike many of his peers, had a sense of humour and, in the main, players respected him for it.

He would need to prove he could take a joke when he emerged from the Goodison Park tunnel to take charge of the replay on February 20, 1991. A fan ran forward and symbolically draped a red scarf around the referee's neck to the delight of every Evertonian.

Midgley, a well known and talented individual on the after dinner circuit, who sadly died in 2001, didn't make a fuss, but I'm sure the incident now became part of his act at future speaking engagements where he could lay claim to officiating at what became known as the FA Cup clash of the century.

The replay was an eventful affair in which eight goals were shared in a passionately-fought 4-4 draw. Putting the action on the pitch to one side, if that is possible, this clash proved without a shadow of a doubt that football managers carry an immense and often devastating weight of responsibility at the highest level, not least in a soccer hotbed like Merseyside.

Two days later, on the Friday morning, I attended the 8.30am daily planning conference in the office of Echo editor John Griffith. All the heads of department were there and while sport was normally the last thing to be discussed on the news list, all the talk was still about the drama at Goodison, not least because Griffith, like me, was a big Evertonian. As we moved on to the priorities for that day's paper, there was a knock on the door and Ric George, one of our leading football reporters, popped his head round the corner and asked if he could speak to me.

I stepped outside and he explained that he had made his usual calls to Liverpool FC and that chief executive Peter Robinson had warned him that the Echo should not miss an unexpected 11am press conference at Anfield. Peter refused to expand any further.

I returned briefly to the editor's conference, advising that something big might be breaking, and said that I would get back to Peter Robinson to see if I could elicit what was happening. I had a good and trusting relationship with him, likewise with Everton's Jim Greenwood.

I phoned Robinson and after some gentle persuasion he revealed the reason for all the secrecy. Kenny Dalglish was about to quit!

In telling me this, Peter swore me to absolute secrecy, at least until the start of the Anfield press conference that was timed for 11am. I gave him my word that, apart from speaking to the Echo's hierarchy so that we could prepare ourselves for one of the biggest LFC stories since Shankly quit in 1974, no-one else in the office would be informed.

Having made this promise, I was worried because these things can inadvertently slip out from a whole variety of channels, including club employees, other players, and close family and friends. I told Echo editor Griffith that I had some bombshell news that would wipe anything and every-thing else off the front page that day.

We needed to agree that we would not break the embargo in any way, shape or form. Robinson didn't want the world's media, who were converging on Anfield, to hear the news from any source other than Kenny himself. The club certainly didn't want any misinterpretation of his reasons, be it in an early edition of the Echo, and certainly not on local radio.

John Griffith and I agreed that the Echo's first edition would be set up on the press with no mention whatsoever of the Dalglish information, but that several pages would be prepared by a tightly controlled team, ready to be changed as soon as the 11am witching hour passed. Only a few people in the press hall would be informed about our secret plan.

I penned the page one lead and set off for Anfield where the Main Stand trophy room was packed with journalists and TV cameras. These were the days before mobile phones and the internet. I knew that there was just one public payphone at Anfield, on the first floor landing close to where the shock news was being broken. I stood close to the trophy room door and as soon as Dalglish publicly revealed his resigna-tion, with everyone else still hanging on his every word, I literally ran to that payphone, called the office, inserted a pound coin and confirmed that it was green for go.

And so, within seconds of one of football's biggest exclusives in years breaking, our presses were rolling to inform Merseysiders of this totally unexpected news.

Dalglish had seemed an immovable object. As a Liverpool player he had won five league championships, four League Cups, four FA Charity Shields, three European Cups and one UEFA Super Cup. As a player-manager and manager he had won a further three top-flight titles, two FA Cups and four FA Charity Shields, which included an historic league and FA Cup double.

But he had still been feeling the perpetual strain of trying to keep his side at the top. He had also been badly affected, first by the impact of the Heysel Disaster as a player, but then all-consumed by what happened at Hillsborough.

The tension around the Goodison FA Cup replay was just the straw that broke the camel's back, but Dalglish already knew deep down that his mind and body was telling him that he desperately needed a break from football.

As fans, we demand everything from those leading the clubs we support. I knew Howard Kendall would not be immune from carrying the football burden of his 1980s successes. He dealt with pressure in a different way, but it would still mount as he battled to repeat former glories.

Everton would win the second FA Cup replay against Liverpool courtesy of a Dave Watson goal with Dalglish now gone and Ronnie Moran in temporary charge before the appointment of Graeme Souness. But the Blues would not fulfil Howard's dream of reaching Wembley, crashing out in the sixth round at West Ham. Howard did inspire a Wembley return in the somewhat controversial Zenith Data Systems Cup, but suffered an extra time defeat against what was a decent Crystal Palace side at that time.

Ninth place would be secured in the league, but ultimately it would not be the "Second Coming" Bill Kenwright had so romantically hoped for. There's a school of thought in football that once you've had success, you should never go back.

The trouble is, when you love a club, your heart can often rule your head.

26

I shun the press box for an emotional last stand at the Street End

THAT first season with Howard and Colin back in harness proved eventful in more ways than one.

On May 4, 1991, I put away my pen and notebook and shunned my seat in Goodison Park's main stand press box to join the faithful on the Gwladys Street terraces. It was an emotional odyssey that revived memories of my early days as a proud Evertonian.

This was the occasion supporters stood as one for the very last time in that hallowed area prior to seats being installed in time for the 1991-92 season.

As a young fan, I had been a fully paid-up member of the Street End. I reflected earlier how I had revelled in the atmosphere, the chanting, the camaraderie and the opportunity to salute heroes like Dave Hickson, Bobby Collins, Roy Vernon, Alex Young and the rest.

My journalistic responsibilities, first with the Liverpool Weekly News and then the Liverpool Echo, had kept me off the Gwladys Street terraces for 23 years, but nothing was going to stop me standing there just one last time.

I arrived very early for the game against Luton Town. It was a shame the opposition wasn't more glamorous, but the symbolism was the most important thing. My two young boys, Colin and Peter, were with me. I wanted them to be there so that they could remember being a part of Everton FC history.

We climbed into a central position on that slightly elevated shelf to get the best view, but the game itself was disappointing and the raucous and passionate support that went hand in hand with standing on the Gwladys Street was a little bit muted early on.

After the 35th minute the fans took things into their own hands and a tuneful ditty spewed forth, the lyrics suggesting that the seats planned for this section should be stuck up a certain part of the anatomy.

It was time to get behind the lads and skilful Polish star Robert Warzycha and striker Tony Cottee stepped things up a gear. Possibly inspired by speculation that the Blues were interested in Derby's Dean Saunders, Cottee opened the scoring and it proved to be the only goal of the game, his 22nd of the season.

In the end, victory was almost irrelevant because Goodison would never quite be the same again and while safety and progress meant we had to move forward, somehow we had lost something special.

The one thing I do remember is what happened at the end of the game. In my mind, I had expected the players to have a complete awareness of the historical importance of the day, not just to those on the Gwladys Street, but to all supporters.

There were no special announcements and no special salutes to the Street End before the kick-off or on the final whistle. I assumed the players would make a real effort at the end of the game. I don't know whether they just felt flat because of the nature of a disappointing match or whether the importance of the moment went right over their heads.

The team trudged off, one or two glancing towards the partisan hordes at the Street End and clapping, but the vast majority simply headed for the dressing room. Sometimes players have no sense of theatre or tradition.

Cottee was the only one who broke ranks, jumping onto that hallowed terrace and throwing his shin pads into the crowd. Many wondered if it was a signal that he was on his way.

Tony was Man of the Match on this special afternoon, but any champagne on offer should have been sprayed towards the Gwladys Street faithful.

I remember searching in the Echo's extensive archive and discovering the first ever image of our famous terrace. It was a pen drawing used in the Football Echo when the brand new Goodison Park was opened in 1892. At that time the Gwladys Street end was nothing more than a steep cinder bank without a roof. However, loyal fans that had previously stood at the Kop end of Everton's then Anfield clearly knew that their new venue was in a class of its own and this must have made them very proud.

I have always said that if I could make one football time machine journey it would be to stand on the Gwladys Street terrace, Goodison Park, May 5, 1928, just to hear the roar when Dixie got his hat-trick in the 3-3 draw against Arsenal that made him the legend of 60 goals.

From my own perspective, I remember great days when the noise from this terrace made the hairs on the back of my neck stand on end.

These included that glorious occasion in 1963 when we beat Fulham 4-1 to give Harry Catterick his first league title with a hat-trick from Roy Vernon.

I was covering the legendary Bayern Munich victory in 1985 from the press box, but remember standing up at the end and marvelling, not just at the response of the Gwladys Street faithful, but the whole stadium. That night, for me, was the noisiest, most passionate occasion I have personally witnessed at Goodison. I do remember looking down on those Gwladys Street hordes and wishing I was in there with them.

At least I made it for their last stand, an experience I would not have missed for the world.

Kendall's champagne sundaes and I'm talking like one of the Flowerpot Men

EVERYONE was now wondering how Howard's first full season back at the helm would shape up. I got an early insight after journeying with the team for their 1991-92 pre-season tour to France and then Switzerland. As the Liverpool Echo's chief football reporter, it was usual to travel as a member of the official touring party which gave me exclusive access behind the scenes.

However, this brought its own pressures because if you missed anything, like a major pre-season signing or departure, there would be hell to pay back at the office.

The games themselves were always fairly straightforward. Fans want victories in every game, but most understand that the priority in friendlies is to ease players towards full fitness.

You would very rarely find a top club preparing for the 'Big Kick-Off' against a Barcelona, AC Milan or Juventus. More likely, we would find ourselves in tiny stadiums that even the most knowledgeable supporters had never heard of.

Of course, this never stopped a tight-knit band of dedicated Evertonians from turning up for every single pre-season tour game I ever covered, regardless of the fixtures, where they were played or who the opposition might be.

I got to know many of these fans personally and I was always interested in what they had to say. These were the days before clubs were forced to travel halfway around the planet to appease major sponsors on the basis that he who pays the piper calls the tune.

The first tour game in the summer of 1991 was in north eastern France against Racing Club Strasbourg in a city that is the cosmopolitan home to the European Parliament. It is actually hard to discern whether Strasbourg is French or German, standing right on the border between the two countries while also being close enough to drive across a third border into Switzerland.

The latter was Everton's plan to extend this summer tour and I travelled with the team to report for the Echo alongside then Liverpool Daily Post reporter Philip McNulty, now chief football correspondent for BBC Sport Online.

We jetted out to Strasbourg and soon arrived in an excellent city centre hotel that had a large outdoor swimming pool. Colin Harvey travelled out late, but Howard and chief executive Jim Greenwood, one of football's most respected chief executives, wasted little time in settling in.

Phil and I, having identified our shared room, soon joined them in the sunshine down at the pool. I had phoned the office to catch up on news at home and was shocked to hear that the Echo was running a story revealing that Derby County striker Dean Saunders was signing for Liverpool.

I knew Howard had been tracking the Welsh international for some time and was convinced the deal was all but done. I had to go and tell him about the breaking transfer story.

Howard looked at Jim and promptly asked a simple question: "How much have we just saved on Saunders?" Of course, he knew the answer was close to the £2.5m Liverpool had just confirmed, an English record fee.

You couldn't keep Howard down for long. "Nearly £2.5m," he repeated out loud. "We can put that behind the bar for now, Jim," he said, tongue in cheek, adding: "Sit down lads. I've got a treat for you here."

Dean Saunders was now history as far as he was concerned. Howard ordered a bottle of champagne and it appeared to me he was making a bubbly version of an ice cream sundae. He was spooning ice cold lemon sorbet into the bottom of the glass and pouring the champagne on top. Of course, as soon as the 'champers' hit the sorbet it was exploding and flowing over the top. No problem, Howard just topped it up.

"Try one of these, lads," he said, "absolutely beautiful."

Phil and I didn't need much persuading. It reminded me of those sunny days as a kid when the Walls ice cream man would come on his three-wheeler bike to our street in Everton and my mother would concede to pester power, sending me out to buy a large block of vanilla.

This would soon be sliced up in equal portions and out would come the Schofields cream soda. Same logic, when the soda hit the ice cream it would fizz up and I loved it.

Howard's special treat was not dissimilar, except the champagne topping was a little more lethal than Schofields' best.

We had one of these bubbly specials, then another, then another. It was a lovely warm afternoon and everything seemed right with the world as we began to talk about that evening's game against Strasbourg.

Before we knew it a couple of hours had passed and I gave Phil a knowing glance. "I think we had better go and get our gear together," I said, aware that we were travelling with the team by coach straight after the game across the nearby Swiss border where our base was to be the picturesque mountain village of Balsthal.

However, after several of Howard's sparkling lemon sorbet sundaes my words probably came out in 'oddle poddle' – the language of the Flower Pot men from the 1950s BBC puppet series. I therefore probably said something like "Flobadob our gear Phil," but my colleague, speaking the same language, seemed to get my drift and we stood up to walk perilously near to the side of the pool.

I came as close as you can get to falling in fully clothed with a swerve that Trevor Steven would have been proud of, but we made it back to our room where, in our new language of 'oddle poddle', we decided between us that rather than getting packed and ready, we would just get our heads down for five minutes. "Flobadob," said Phil. I assumed that meant: "Great idea, just a quick five-minute snooze."

The team bus was leaving for the stadium at 5pm. It was now 3pm so the time wasn't a problem. One minute later, or so it seemed to us, there was a knock on the door. It was skipper Kevin Ratcliffe. "The coach is about to leave lads," said Kevin. "Are you ready?"

Finally speaking plain English again, I shouted: "Please tell Howard that we'll make our own way to the stadium."

Now this was highly unprofessional. If we had been players, we would have been fined heavily for missing the bus. We launched our gear into our bags, and headed down to the hotel reception to pay for any incidentals.

I immediately handed over my credit card, only for the receptionist to shake her head. "Cash only," she said. "You're joking," I replied. "Isn't this the forward-looking city of the European Parliament? Surely any relevant Visa credit card is acceptable here?"

She just looked at me blankly. "Is there a bank machine nearby?" was my next question. "Only at the airport," she said.

Was I still talking in oddle-poddle? I checked the hotel lobby mirror in case I had a flowerpot on my head. I didn't and so Phil and I grabbed a taxi and raced to the airport for emergency cash funds. We could have simply left the bill unpaid, but being late was one thing, avoiding payment of a hotel bill while travelling with the club was another.

Our round trip to the airport and back took about 30 minutes. Back at the hotel we told a very happy taxi driver to wait, and finally settled up with the receptionist who clearly needed a personality by-pass. Of course, all of this delay left it extremely tight to get to the stadium in time for kick-off and we were lumping two heavy cases that would normally have been safely in the hold of the team coach.

We arrived at the stadium right on kick-off, and I was soon looking down at the pitch from the elevated press box as the game kicked off, still feeling a little woozy from the earlier champagne sundaes.

In sharp contrast, Howard was up on his feet, animated, bright as a button, and issuing instructions from the touch-line as the Blues completed this first tour game with a 1-1 draw and no serious injuries to worry about.

Colin Harvey said: "I remember the night we won at Spurs late in the 1985 title winning season. It set us up for the championship. We stayed over in South Mimms and Howard was elated. I eventually went to bed, but told Jimmy Martin – our coach driver at that time and now Everton's kit manager – to make sure Howard didn't stay up too late because he was due on Breakfast TV the next morning."

Colin added: "I was up early and spoke to Jimmy who said: "I couldn't stop him, he had a very late one celebrating." I immediately switched on the TV in my room and there was Howard in the BBC Breakfast studio, absolutely immaculate in a smart tracksuit and perfectly groomed. He gave the best interview I have ever seen. He had this remarkable ability to bounce back."

There's a school of thought in football that it's crucial to celebrate your victories. Howard had more successes to celebrate than most, a class act who lived life to the full as one of the game's greatest characters.

Conjurer's Cannon and Ball act, and a transfer swoop in Howard's bedroom

WE now left Strasbourg behind to continue Everton's preparations for the 1991-92 campaign, crossing the nearby border for the fairly short hop into Switzerland. Our base would be the small and picturesque mountain town of Balsthal from where the Blues would play four games in a local tournament to celebrate the 25th anniversary of an outfit called – yes, you've guessed it – FC Champagne.

Down the years, players and fans have all amassed personal stories about classic moments during pre-season tours which, by their very nature, have a fairly relaxed atmosphere as the players come back together with the emphasis on preparing for the big kick-off rather than going flat out for results.

I would have to say that Balsthal was arguably the most amazing football trip I have ever been on – and I have been lucky enough to have travelled as far as Khartoum in Africa as well as to almost every capital city in Europe covering football-related assignments.

Of course, few people will recognise the names of the Swiss teams the Blues played and beat that summer: Yverdon Sports (1-0), FC Bulle (1-0), Balsthal (3-0), and SR Delemont (7-1).

The football was a means to an end on the fitness front. It was everything else around the trip that was truly memorable, not least the setting for the games.

We settled quickly at our small Balsthal base and the following morning, after training, I had a coffee with Howard and Jim Greenwood in the small town square outside the hotel front door.

A small but dedicated band of Evertonians were already making themselves at home in the sunshine. It doesn't take long for Scousers to suss out the hot spots, and someone said there was a Chinese restaurant at the end of the street with an unusual little club at the back. With nothing much else to do for the rest of the afternoon, we headed down there.

It was just like any other Chinese restaurant, but we soon plunged into darkness when we went through a connecting door into the adjoining club the fans had described. Clearly, a show of sorts was about to begin and we sat down near the front of the stage and ordered some drinks. In retrospect, we should have grabbed a table at the back.

It was early afternoon, but a manic-looking magician

immediately stepped into the spotlight, his darting eyes carefully scanning his unexpectedly large audience, mostly made up of Evertonians. Struggling to pick up two large cannon balls, he stared down at Howard as if to say: "Give me your undivided attention, or else!"

Howard just giggled and, under his breath, muttered one of his favourite little phrases: "Deary me!" Like all of us, he was wondering what was coming next.

The magician then started to juggle the cannonballs, a little bit too close to our front row table for our liking. Our mad magician paused briefly and flashed another manic stare our way that smacked of: "Who the *!*! are you looking at?"

He then fumbled one of the cannon balls that crashed down on the wooden stage and rolled in Howard's direction. We were all roaring with laughter, but the magician had a face like thunder as he stepped off the stage to retrieve it.

He looked as if he was going to continue with his juggling routine, but instead he shaped up like an international shot-putter and launched a cannonball into the middle of our front row table.

I fell on the floor as we leapt back and the drinks went everywhere with the place in uproar. Of course, the black cannonball he threw was the one made of sponge, but we didn't know that.

We sat back down as a waitress swept in to replace our drinks, and Howard smiled. "I think we're going to like it here," he said.

Back at the hotel, things settled down. Training had gone well earlier and the focus was now on the following day's game against Yverdon Sports, the opener in the FC Champagne anniversary celebrations.

I still have the unusually-designed programme for that game, described as the 'Match De Gala' which translates simply as exhibition match. A banner headline on the cover declares '25th Anniversaire FC Champagne', below which the word JAZZ is overlaid on a drawing of a goal net, accompanied by images of a saxophone and a piano keyboard.

Clearly, the organisers wanted to make music on and off a pitch that had a tiny stand on one side, the other three sides bordered only by a wooden rail. The sight of fans casually walking down the mountainside to reach the pitch and join in the celebrations was a remarkable sight.

Everton won the game 1-0, a stroll in the mountains, and this was immediately followed by a public barbecue by the side of the pitch, attended by home fans and members of that small group of travelling Blues fans. The Everton hierarchy respectfully attended, aware that the hosts had planned a question and answer session in a large marquee. A Swiss official with a microphone, who I assumed was the chairman of FC Champagne, spoke in immaculate English to welcome his guests. He said: "We would like to thank a famous team like Everton for helping us celebrate our 25th anniversary today. Have you any questions for our visitors?"

He was clearly expecting a familiar Swiss voice, but it was a Scouse accent that rang out from the back of the marquee, a travelling fan asking: "Why are we so *!*!*!* crap?"

With the timing of a precise 22 carat gold Swiss watch, the home chairman snapped back with a brilliant retort, saying:

"We are taking questions, not statements," and pressed on to the applause of everyone present. Even the small band of Evertonians present had to laugh.

At the team hotel later that night, I was invited fairly late on to Howard's room where he had clearly been discussing team matters and early season options with Colin Harvey. It was approaching midnight and Howard said: "Have you written anything yet for tomorrow's Echo?"

I said: "We can leave that until tomorrow morning if you want?"

Howard immediately turned to Colin and said: "Have you got a number for Celtic?"

For some time, Everton had been linked with Celtic's prized asset Paul McStay. Clearly, Howard was about to formally swoop for the talented midfielder and he told Colin to put in a call and ask them to name their price. I was more than a little surprised, firstly because it was so late, but mostly because I was suddenly a party to a sensational move for a man who could genuinely help take the Blues to another level. It indicated that Howard could trust me.

I recently spoke to Colin about that night. He said: "McStay was a class midfielder, but he was an out and out Celtic man. We had talked about him and it was a genuine interest because Paul was probably the best footballer around at that time and could have become a big Everton hero if we had managed to sign him."

I went back to my room and penned an exclusive piece that would dominate the headlines back on Merseyside the following day. EVERTON SWOOP FOR McSTAY.

The player would remain at Celtic for another six seasons. The year after Howard's failed bid, Paul was voted a member of Celtic's greatest ever team by the club's fans. He also became member of the Scotland Football Hall of Fame which honours the best players to play in Scotland and is located in the Scottish Football Museum.

There is little doubt that he would have been a class act in the royal blue of Everton and could have been the spark that lifted things during Howard's second spell at the helm, but he was a one-club man who was totally dedicated to the Parkhead cause.

McStay went on to become a successful businessman in Australia. It would have been particularly fitting if he had signed for the Blues because, incredibly, his middle names are Mike Lyons – Paul Michael Lyons McStay!

Everton's pre-season Swiss tour to Balsthal in 1991 was memorable, part of the appropriately-named FC Champagne's 25th anniversary celebrations. In the gala game, Everton beat Yverdon Sports

Great engine:
Classic car for a
classic goalscorer.
He had this work
ethic, on and off
the pitch

Father to son:
My dad Harry
(pictured with
me, left) gave
me my love of
Everton FC

On the ball:
With my Major
Lester school
team (front,
centre)

Big calls:
My break in
journalism
came in 1968

Key moments: These classic typewriters are a world away from the laptops and mobile phones used by journalists today

Pitch invader!: I got the best seat in the house at Wembley for the 1968 FA Cup fina – on the pitch behind the goal with Echo photographer Neville Willasey

Vantage point: In the press box ready to phone the office with my match report

Home run: Posing questions to some baseball players

Prize guy: Former Echo sports chief Vincent Kelly with an award we won, while I hold my son Colin

cross the park: I would clash ith the great Bill Shankly

Legendary duo: Merseyside greats Billy Liddell and Joe Mercer join Ian Hargraves and I at the Echo offices

Title winners: The heroes of 1985 put Everton at the top of English football

The Bernabeu boys:
Everton's friendly in Spain in 1987 gave colleagues Philip McNulty, Charles Lambert and I the chance to tread on Real Madrid's hallowed turf. New Bilbao manager, Howard Kendall, arrived to show his coach the discipline of playing 4-4-2. The bad news was that the Blues crashed 6-1!

A hero in my book:
Howard Kendall helped me launch my 'Goodison Glory' title in 1992

friends and legends: I was grateful when Brian Labone, Colin Harvey and Jimmy Gabriel also turned up to support a promotional date for my book

Big chance:
I got to play alongside Mike Lyons, Terry Darracott and th great Colin Harvey during a charity match at Marine

Chopper Parry:
I evade a scything challenge from former colleague and Sky commentator Alan Parry during a 1987 TV commentators v journalists friendly at Wycombe

Hands on the cup:
Pictured with my hero Dave Hickson. Anfield Iron Tommy Smith put his foot in to join this proud Evertonian momer

Strike partner:
I learned a few tricks of the trade from Dave Hickson while playing for the Over The Hill Mob

smiles:
Echo team
as invited
Colin
arvey to play
ainst some
mous faces
Bellefield

Blue nose:
Duncan
erguson lifts
the FA Cup
wearing an
Echo blue
nose

Cup captains:
We got FA Cup winning captains
Kevin Ratcliffe, Brian Labone
and Dave Watson together for
a feature in 'Everton's FA Cup
100'. Days later we were shocked
to discover the legend that was
Labby had died

eeting of minds: Head down and thinking of Wembley (fourth right) in an Echo
litorial conference before the 1995 FA Cup final. Notice the 'Good luck Blues' bill

Eighties heroes: In the company of Paul Bracewell, Howard Kendall, John Bailey and Derek Mountfield

14th October 1999

Ken Rogers
Sports Editor
Liverpool Echo
Old Hall Street
LIVERPOOL
L69 3EB

Dear Ken

Millennium Giants

With the new Millennium fast approaching our thoughts are now turning to how we will celebrate such a momentous occasion.

As part of those celebrations, Everton Football Club, in conjunction with the Liverpool Echo, is planning to select a group of players and a manager to form our "Millennium Giants".

A player from each of the ten decades of the twentieth century will be chosen, together with a manager of the century.

For this, a panel of judges will, with the help of Everton supporter's votes, ultimately choose which names will form the elite group of legends. I therefore would like to formally invite you to be a member of the adjudicating panel in recognition of your journalistic experience and affinity to Everton Football Club.

The first meeting of the panel will take place at 1.00 PM on Tuesday 26th October 1999 in the Boardroom at Goodison Park.

I hope you will accept what is sure to be a very difficult task, though one, which will form a significant part of our great clubs history.

I look forward to your reply.

Yours sincerely

ALAN MYERS
Communications Manager

Secretary
M.J. DUNFORD
Manager
W. SMITH, O.B.E.

Registered Number
38624, England

Official Club Sponsor
one2one

Official Sportswear Sponsors
UMBRO

Official invitation: I was honoured to accept a chance to help choose Everton's 'Millennium Giants'

True Scousers: I joined John Aldridge and Peter Reid for a superb afternoon as they debat the ultimate Scouse der match

Learning his history: Former Blues boss Roberto Martinez at the famous Everton lock-up

I quiz Seve about Everton before Beagers' motorbike flying circus

PREPARATIONS continued apace during the summer of 1991. After returning from the eventful trip to Switzerland, the team now stepped things up with friendly victories against Glentoran (6-0), Tranmere Rovers (3-1) and Robert Warzycha's old club Gornik Zabrze (3-0).

Next in the friendly timetable was an August 13 trip to Spain for a prestige game against Real Sociedad.

In the San Sebastian press box, I made the acquaintance of a knowledgeable female Spanish journalist who was reporting on the game for the local paper. We exchanged information on our respective clubs and she talked about how impressed she had been with Scouser John Aldridge who had just left Sociedad to begin his spell with Tranmere.

She seemed to know everybody, not just in the press area, but also in the crowd. On the final whistle, I spotted one of my all-time sporting heroes, immortal Spanish golfer Seve Ballesteros, who was sitting about 20 rows further forward. The great man had won two US Masters (1980 and 1983) and the Open three times (1979, 1984 and 1988). So here I was, suddenly shouting out the obvious to my new Spanish reporter friend: "My god! There's Seve Ballesteros."

Yes, even experienced journalists can get star struck at times. She looked at me, smiled and said: "Do you want to speak to him?" She was far too young to be my fairy god-mother, but I jumped at the chance, thinking she was going to walk me to a private lounge somewhere in the main stand to seek permission from a six foot-plus Spanish bouncer.

Instead, she just whistled and incredibly the golfing legend, swamped in this big crowd, looked back. "Seve," she shouted. "Come and talk to my friend Ken from Liverpool."

I couldn't believe my eyes as the Spanish super hero started to climb over row after row of seats to reach the press box.

She hugged him and made the introductions. "Seve, this is my friend Ken Rogers. He would like to interview you, yes?"

My mind was racing. Okay, I've suddenly got an unexpected exclusive interview with one of the greatest names in the world of sport, but what was I going to ask a golf icon in the wake of a goalless Spanish football friendly that had been one step up from a training match?

I asked Seve if he knew anything about Merseyside football, Everton in particular. He said he followed the English league and revealed: "My favourite team is Chelsea!"

I said: "Chelsea. Never heard of them! Are they a small club in London?"

He flashed that famous smile back. Everton (and Liverpool) had won everything in sight in the 1980s. Chelsea had won the second division title in 1983-84 to get back into the top flight before being relegated again in 1988. The club bounced back immediately by winning the second division championship in 1988-89.

I suggested he should adopt Everton as his new English team. He beamed, we shook hands, and suddenly the golf superstar was whisked away.

I filed my report with its unexpected Seve quotes and set off back to the team hotel.

When you are up close and personal with key individuals at major football clubs, as I was for decades, you inevitably witness a lot of personal and private incidents that could have made blockbusting headlines along the way. However, there's an old saying that I very much believe in: "What goes on in Vegas, stays in Vegas." In the tough world of journalism, this was a rule that would be frowned upon by many of the senior editors I had worked for and I had my fallings out over it, but I would never break this unwritten code of trust. Some people might, but I looked on it my own way.

If I picked up a story because of my journalistic expertise and contacts and it was genuinely in the interest of the fans and my paper for me to report it, I would have had no choice but to print and be damned. It was my job.

But if I was invited to travel with a club as part of an intimate group, particularly on the more laid back pre-season tours when I was often on the team coach, staying at the team's hotels, and effectively being treated as part and parcel of this travelling football road show, I would always ask myself one simple question: "Would I have stumbled on this story if I had been operating independently?" If the answer to that was 'no' then I lived by the 'Vegas rule' I alluded to.

Down the years I secured many more exclusives than I ever missed for Liverpool Echo readers. I would like to think this was because I was half decent at my job, good enough to be named Northern Sports Journalist of the Year. But it was also because down the decades I earned the trust and respect of many coaches, managers, chief executives, football club owners, club secretaries and players.

I would have annoyed some individuals at times with certain match reports on difficult days, but that's a completely different kettle of fish. Fans deserve and demand total honesty in match reports, good days and bad, and I always tried to give them that.

I loved the pre-season tours because they provided a rare opportunity to talk to people on a different level in a more relaxed environment. As I've explained, this was often an inner sanctum experience, but here's a question for you. What do you do when a well known player drives a motor cycle through a plate glass window in the front of a big hotel in downtown San Sebastian? Take a bow Peter Beagrie. This escapade unfolded on this Spanish trip and is now so famous that it ranks at number three in a national newspaper's 'all-time top ten list of players behaving badly'.

I can talk about it because it subsequently made all the

major papers, long before the next available edition of the Echo had hit the streets. Peter had been out having a drink (or two) after the goalless draw. A Spanish news agency got wind of his late night shenanigans via the police and it made all the morning news outlets.

Would I have used the story anyway? It was immaterial, taken out of my hands as it happened. He had been out having a post-match drink and flagged down a Spanish motorcyclist to give him a lift back to the hotel where he couldn't raise the night porter.

'Beagers' then commandeered the bemused Spaniard's bike, rode it up the hotel steps and drove straight through the entrance window. It turned out to be the wrong hotel and he required a significant number of stitches. Now you just can't keep stories like that out of the press.

With friendlies behind him, Howard now looked forward to the 1991-92 campaign with a much clearer idea how he wanted to move things forward in this, his first full season back at the helm. Towards the end of the previous campaign he had added Polish international wing star Robert Warzycha to his squad, unexpected in as much as he had always been against bringing in foreign players because he felt they struggled to settle. This view seems outdated now but Howard had been impressed by the Pole's style of play and his attitude to starting a new career in England.

I have already revealed the manager's disappointment in not securing the services of Dean Saunders that summer. The Everton boss had been so keen that he had actually driven down to Derby's Baseball Ground to hand in his sealed envelope bid. But the pull of partnering Ian Rush at Anfield and the fact that Dean's father had once played for Liverpool proved decisive in the end.

But Howard was clearly still thinking big for Everton, highlighted by his unsuccessful offers for Celtic hero McStay and Saunders. He now capitalised on Liverpool's abundance of forward talent by putting £1m on the table for Peter Beardsley who Anfield fans still idolised.

Howard later told me that he had been a Beardsley admirer for years and recognised the player still had a lot to offer.

While we might not look back at Howard's disappointing second and third spells as Everton manager with anything like the excitement we felt during his 1980s glory years, he clearly didn't just come back for the ride.

All Evertonians retain a respect for Beardsley. He was an Anfield hero, but crossed the park without a backwards glance and continued to put his skill, effort and enthusiasm into the Everton cause. The likeable Geordie grabbed 20 goals that season, a superior return to that of his replacement Saunders across the park.

Ultimately, Beardsley would make 95 Everton appearances which produced 32 goals. Along with David Johnson, he became one of only two players to have scored for both sides in Merseyside derbies.

But looking back, fans were not over-enamoured with the wider situation in 1991-92, reflected in some poor attendances. Howard, having settled things and finished ninth in his first part-season back, now dropped back three places to 12th which was clearly below his, and Everton's, standards.

30

Writing a match report? Surely it's a piece of cake – and you get in free!

MANY people think that writing a football report is easy. After all, how difficult can it possibly be to take down a few simple notes, record the build-up to a great goal and get the scorer's name correct, preferably also identifying the individual who made the assist?

How hard is it to track a striker's run into the box, see him crash to the ground under a lunging tackle from a burly defender and decide instantly that it is a stonewall penalty?

And surely the bonus of being a big match reporter is that you get in free!

If you genuinely fancy your chances when it comes to writing 750 colourful, descriptive (and accurate) words on the final whistle of a big match, encapsulating running play, controversies, goal action and analysis of what the result means to both teams then you have my absolute admiration, but beware.

Getting through 90-plus minutes in a press box can be a veritable minefield, even for the best in the business. This is despite the fact that most modern press facilities include the benefit of seeing action replays on a monitor, something that we didn't have in the old days. Having said that, match reports are not just about facts, but writing in an analytical, critical and colourful manner and for those just learning the ropes, pulling all of these things together in the heat of battle can be a nightmare.

Let me paint a scenario that you possibly don't think about as you sing, chant and scream your way through a typical game before going down for your pie and a pint at half-time.

For starters, many press boxes were built for those days when the only thing a reporter needed was a pen and notebook. These days, every journalist arrives at the match with a large bag, a substantial laptop computer, a mobile phone and, yes, the proverbial notebook and biro.

Watching reporters crammed into their seats at many of the big grounds – attempting to command and defend the 18 square inches of bench working space allocated to them – is a sight to behold. Computer cables get yanked out, phone signals drift and tempers flare – and this is before a ball has even been kicked. There is as much elbowing and blocking going on in a typical press box than you will ever see watching a carefully rehearsed corner out on the pitch!

Of course, switching yourself off from everything around you is crucial to ensuring that the contrasting and varied thoughts constantly being expressed by colleagues don't suddenly become YOUR views. Putting this to one side, you must also block out the intensely personal opinions of partisan fans screaming and chanting in all corners of the ground, every one of them determined to highlight who they believe is playing well or, conversely, having a nightmare.

On big European nights, your adjacent reporter might be incessantly shouting in a foreign language as he delivers a radio report and these guys can get as animated as the most passionate fan on the planet.

Multiple mobile ringtones also indicate that newspaper offices locally, and further afield, want urgent updates.

While reporters constantly share information in a press box, it is important you can be your own man. Rudyard Kipling might have had football reporters in mind when – in his famous poem 'If' – he said how crucial it was to "keep your head when all about you are losing theirs."

Deadlines are extremely tight for night matches. Most titles want to go to print within seconds of the final whistle to despatch their early first editions all over the country.

But let's assume that everything is going well. You have been working with a particular mindset for your report and the club you are covering is leading 1-0. You have confidently input your thoughts and comments into your laptop computer, ready to intrigue, inspire and stir the people who will be reading your sports pages the following day.

Suddenly, with the last kick of the 90 minutes, the opposition breaks away to secure a totally unexpected equaliser. Deep into extra time they grab a winner that suddenly renders your initial match report useless.

It's at moments like this that you genuinely respect the ability and focus of the experienced football journalist, as skilful in his own field as any midfield genius on the pitch.

If you write hundreds of thousands of words over the course of a long career you will have at least one personal tale of woe that you might prefer to forget. Let's just call it the football reporter's equivalent of a suicidal back pass.

All football reporters have been there. When my 'own goal' occurred it came in a pre-season friendly against VFB Lubeck, the memory of which will forever make me shiver.

Everton match reports for games against Preussen Hamelin, Haspar Sport and Cloppenburg during their 1992 summer pre-season tour of Germany had gone to plan before the match against Lubeck.

Are you sitting comfortably? Then I will begin . . .

When the 1992-93 summer pre-season fixtures were announced, it was actually the Preussen Hamelin friendly game that fascinated me most, not for the quality of the German opposition, but because of the town's link with one of the most famous fairy tales of all time.

Of course, as a kid I had read about the 'The Pied Piper of Hamelin' who was a rat-catcher, hired by the town to lure away increasing numbers of rodents by playing his magic pipes. When the citizens refused to pay for his services, he retaliated by turning his haunting musical power on local children, leading them away instead, never to return.

I was accompanied on this trip by a colleague from our morning paper the Daily Post, Peter Jardine. It was the first time we had been given the new laptop computers to file our copy from the various match venues, high tech then, but dinosaurs compared with today's modern counterparts.

This new process was initially going to make life a little bit more challenging as we dealt with wires and attached primitive muffs to the phone handset to capture a high-pitched signal from the office. Previously we had just phoned our newspapers and dictated the developing match information to a human being at the other end of the line.

The opening tour fixture was against Haspar Sport where Peter Beagrie scored in a 1-1 draw. Two nights later we were in Hamelin's small but picturesque stadium as they celebrated the installation of a new pitch, track and floodlights. It was a big occasion for them and 3,000 people turned up to see the Blues put on a show.

Beagrie grabbed his second tour goal with Andy Hinch-cliffe, Yugoslavian trialist Preki and Mark Ward also on the scoresheet in a 4-0 win.

We moved on to the next match, a comprehensive 4-1 victory over Cloppenburg, before we faced VFB Lubeck and Mo Johnston's third tour goal gave Everton a flying start. The Germans were fairly non-descript opposition, but I remember a drummer behind one of the goals who hammered away incessantly to create a cup tie atmosphere.

Despite Mo's early opener, a German journalist oozed confidence in the tiny press box, mesmerising everyone around him with encouraging stats about every Lubeck player.

"If you want to know the names of any of our goalscorers in this game, just ask," he said with a beaming smile that suggested a German comeback and victory was all but guaranteed. Cheeky sod!

As it turned out, the game developed into a fairly gruelling encounter for a friendly. Lubeck had a midfielder who was clearly a bit of a character. After 15 minutes he hammered in an angled shot that appeared to beat Neville Southall all ends up. To celebrate, he set off on a long curving run with his arms outstretched, imitating the famous 'aeroplane salute' that was popular at that time.

My German journalist friend wheeled round and, still beaming, declared: 'Peter Harth'.

Along with my Post colleague, I quickly flipped open the lid on my brand new laptop computer and started to key in the goalscorer's name and the goal description. When we looked up, play was in full flow again.

There were no further 'goals' and Peter, because of the Post's overnight deadline, filed his report with the 1-1 scoreline on the final whistle.

The next morning, I met Stuart Barlow on the way to breakfast and we exchanged thoughts on the previous night's action. "Decent game," I said. "Shame they equalised."

He looked bemused, saying: "Oh, you mean the 'goal' that midfielder supposedly scored before he ran back doing that 'aeroplane' celebration? Apparently he always does that as a joke. It looked like he had scored, but it went into the side netting!"

I made a quick retreat to my bedroom and immediately

called my Post colleague. "What score was it last night?" I queried, clearly asking a ridiculous question.

"We drew 1-1," he said, clearly bemused. "Striker Peter Harth equalised and then did that zany celebration. The German journalist confirmed his name."

I had to reveal the shock news that the shot had actually hit the side netting and that the goal was a bigger 'fairy story' than anything written in nearby Hamelin.

By now the Daily Post was out on the streets of Merseyside, reporting: VFB Lubeck 1 Everton 1.

My report was still sitting inside my shiny new computer. I had still not filed because of my later deadline and knew what was coming next from Peter.

"Why don't you report the same scoreline as me?"

Now even though the Evertonians attending the game that night were in quite small numbers at this out-of-the-way German venue, I was being asked the impossible, even though I was as culpable as him for an unforgiveable lapse in concentration.

The Echo ultimately received an amended and correct report, while two journalists both learned a painful lesson about the emerging new computer technology and the definitive rules when it comes to reporting all football matches. Don't believe everything you see. Don't believe everything you hear. Don't take your eyes off the pitch for a second. Check, check and check again.

I love a good goal celebration, but I come out in a cold sweat whenever the old 'aeroplane' salute rears its head.

As that five-game 1992 tour reached its finale, it was good

to finish with a game against one of Germany's elite clubs.

Everton were up against Borussia Moenchengladbach and this game would end up being all about the world class qualities and quirkiness of a goalkeeper. This is how I started my match report that night:

"Evertonians often suggest that Neville Southall is the best goalkeeper in Europe, without having the ammunition to substantiate that claim, but last night the Welshman spoke up himself in a country that is renowned for the quality of its goalkeepers."

I reported that Goodison's undisputed number one had entertained an appreciative German crowd with a string of outstanding saves, including a penalty.

But the most unusual aspect of a fiercely contested match that Everton ultimately lost 2-1 was the remarkable sight of Big Nev handing his goalkeeping jersey to his understudy Jason Kearton five minutes from time and completing the match in an outfield position with Barry Horne feeling a shoulder injury and the Blues fully out of substitutes.

Neville just shrugged when asked about his unusual outfield sortie. It was just another day at the office for him. Absolutely nothing fazed him.

Everton finished 13th at the end of an inconsistent 1992-93 campaign that concluded with a 5-2 win at Peter Reid's Manchester City where Jackson, Beagrie (2), Beardsley, and Preki all found the net.

Beardsley had continued to show his quality during his second season, but returned to Geordieland in July, 1993, to join Kevin Keegan's resurgent Newcastle.

EVERTON FOR SALE!
I stumble on an exclusive that shocks the fans

WHEN Iranian businessman Farhad Moshiri purchased 49.9% of Everton shares in late February 2016 to become the club's single largest shareholder, it took me back 23 years to a day in 1993 when the ownership and future of a club that once basked in the tag 'The Millionaires' dominated the headlines for the very first time following years of stability under the stewardship of the highly influential Sir John Moores.

The Blues were clearly going through a testing transformational spell on and off the pitch in the early 1990s and in May that year I found myself writing an exclusive on the front page of the Echo that would shock all supporters and dominate their thoughts for the next 14 months.

In three simple words, it declared: EVERTON FOR SALE!

It had been unthinkable that Sir John Moores, the club's longstanding majority shareholder and 97-year-old head of the giant Littlewoods organisation had any intention of selling his dominant stake in the club he had guided since the 1960s. But behind the scenes, his age – and the very different priorities of the younger members of the Moores family at that time – was obviously something that was uppermost in the thoughts of the Everton board.

So how did the news come to light? I well recall attending the regular morning news conference in the office of Liverpool Echo editor John Griffith. As we waited for the other heads of department to join us to plan that day's paper, John mentioned that he had been in London that week at Trinity Mirror's Canary Wharf headquarters.

A senior executive on the finance side had mentioned that one of the capital's big merchant banks had been instructed to seek ways of refinancing Everton Football Club. Griffith, an Evertonian himself, asked if I had any way of confirming the story, not least because a spokesman for Sir John Moores had denied that he had any intention of selling his shares.

We were sitting on a potentially explosive item of news that had still to feature in any newspaper. I left the conference and headed back to my desk where I made a quick call to Jim Greenwood, Everton FC's influential chief executive at that time. I had built up a trusting professional relationship with Jim down the years and was able to speak to him on and off the record.

Clearly, this was a day for the latter with Littlewoods playing a straight bat on behalf of Moores. Jim didn't reveal much, but less is more in these situations. He simply responded that it would be in my interest to further investigate the story coming out of the London banking fraternity.

That was good enough for me. It meant that our information had real substance and I immediately set about breaking the bombshell news that a battle would soon be unfolding among as yet unnamed third parties to claim a controlling interest in one of the founder members of the Football League.

In my short conversation with Jim Greenwood, I sensed that it would actually be in the interests of the Everton FC board to get the information into the public domain because they had been working in something of a vacuum.

And so the Echo presses rolled with my front page exclusive very quickly drawing out expressions of interest from two contrasting rivals, existing board member Bill Kenwright, a dyed-in-the-wool Evertonian, and Peter Johnson, head of Merseyside firm Park Foods and the ambitious chairman of Tranmere Rovers.

It was no secret that in terms of Merseyside's Big Two, Johnson had leanings towards the red half of the city, but he declared he had the wealth and the ambition to lead Everton positively towards the 21st Century.

There was little doubt that the club had been stagnating in an investment sense. In the Sixties and Seventies, the Blues had revelled in the tag of the 'Millionaires' with Moores, the man who had inspired a hugely profitable football pools business, able to sanction big money moves for some of the game's finest players.

But he was now in his late nineties and unable to exert the same power and influence that had been his hallmark in the early years. We were now in an era in which football investment went hand in hand with the stock market.

Everton could have muddled on, but within five months of that Echo front page story forcing things into the open, everything suddenly came to a head in the September when the grand old man of Goodison died peacefully at his Formby home. The Everton board now needed to generate significant momentum regarding the club's ownership and it was clearly not going to come from within the Moores family.

Neither John Jnr nor his brother Peter, the men who had inherited their father's controlling interest, appeared ready or willing to pick up the football challenge. Both had other recreational interests. John Jnr was a Freeman of the City of Liverpool, the Chancellor of John Moores University and a successful farmer.

Peter had proved a colourful character in launching the Peter Moores Foundation in 1964 to support the arts and became a trustee of the Tate Gallery. His pastimes were listed as opera, shooting and fishing. Neither of the Moores brothers had football anywhere near the top of their personal agendas.

It had been left to a Littlewoods senior executive Sir Philip Carter to guide Everton FC and he did a magnificent job, helping to inspire the unparalleled successes of the Eighties. But in the Nineties, football inflation was on the up and up and it was increasingly difficult to compete at the top without generating major new funds.

Lifelong Evertonian Kenwright was the first man to show an interest in taking control. Prior to Christmas 1993, he had met Peter Moores and John Moores Jnr along with their sister Lady Grantchester and actually secured a signed document backing his takeover bid. He was convinced that these 'Heads of Agreement' would win him the day.

All of this was unfolding off the pitch while controversy was reigning on it. Howard Kendall was struggling to paper over the cracks of a roller coaster start to the 1993-94 season. The Blues beat Liverpool 2-0 at Goodison in the September, but then lost 5-1 at home to Norwich City whose manager Mike Walker almost certainly struck a chord with the Everton board.

It all came to a head after the Blues beat Southampton 1-0 at Goodison on December 4, Kendall resigning in controversial circumstances following an abortive attempt to sign Manchester United striker Dion Dublin for £1.7m.

It was reported the Blues board had not supported the manager's request. Was this because the club was strapped for cash at that time, did the takeover situation create a sense of inertia, or were they looking ahead and already considering a managerial change? Chairman Dr David Marsh was quick to clarify that there had been no boardroom bust-up and that he had actually tried to persuade the manager to stay on, but Howard clearly felt his position was untenable.

Two former heroes, Peter Reid at Manchester City and Joe Royle at Oldham Athletic, were immediately linked with the vacancy, but Dr Marsh didn't rule out a move for a foreign manager and suggested that there would be no shortage of applications once the job was advertised.

Coach Jimmy Gabriel, a great former player and tremendous character, was placed in temporary charge as the board considered its options. As 1993 drew to a close, a snap phone poll in the Echo, while not scientific, gave an indication of how the fans were thinking with the following poll result:

Jimmy Gabriel 20%; Peter Reid 17%; Mike Walker 16%; Bobby Robson 12%; Joe Royle 12%; Bruce Rioch 6%; Steve Coppell 5%; Ron Atkinson 5%; Graham Taylor 3%; Ray Wilkins 2%; Terry Venables 2%.

It would be January 7, 1994, before a month of deliberation finally delivered the new boss. Everton confirmed that Mike Walker was their preferred candidate to replace Howard Kendall and the man who had been holding the emergency reins, caretaker boss Gabriel. The former Norwich man was immediately handed a pledge from the board that he could spend immediately, certainly unhindered by the takeover situation.

He would inherit a team that had recently claimed an unwanted record, only the second in the club's 115-year history to go six league games without scoring. When it happened previously in 1951, the club went on to be relegated.

Clearly, the Walker appointment was not without risk. He had done well in the less than glamorous surroundings of Carrow Road, but he had no experience of managing or even understanding a giant like Everton and under his short 10-month watch things would get significantly worse.

The manager announcement came as Bill Kenwright displayed supreme confidence in taking personal control of the club. Speaking during an impromptu press conference at Stamford Bridge and aware that Walker was the board's managerial choice, Kenwright declared: "Peter Johnson's bid for the club has as much chance of winning as Graeme Souness has of being Everton's next manager. If I fail I will walk off the end of the Pier Head. Everyone keeps telling me I must be mad to get involved and I'm sending my mum mental, but I'm doing it because I just love Everton."

The ownership issue continued to unravel as Walker settled into the significant challenge of moving Everton forward on the pitch. Norwich had just cause to feel smug two months after their old boss joined the Blues. On his first return to Carrow Road, on March 21, 1994, the Canaries beat Everton 3-0 and the relegation fears of the fans were now rising by the day.

It all reached a tense, even frightening, conclusion on May 7, 1994, the last day of the season, when Blues fans went to hell and back against Wimbledon before we survived by the skin of our teeth.

This was another day when I felt I had to swap my press box seat to think and act like a fan again. Normally the rule is always business before pleasure, but this was never going to be a pleasurable occasion. For every supporter, it was a day when any personal negatives about the manager and the team would be replaced by unadulterated passion and support for 90 crucial minutes with the club's proud top-flight future on the line.

A friend of mine had taken the small sponsorship lounge near Goodison's main entrance with seats in the Main Stand. We even got a pre-match team talk from Mike Walker himself. He never looked anything but laid back and while Everton's chances of avoiding the drop had more permutations than a lottery win, he declared we had nothing to worry about.

Worry? A member of our small group, George Rice, had done so well at the Chester races the previous day that he superstitiously wore exactly the same clothes for the Wimbledon clash, including his undies. Sometimes your mates provide too much information. Walker retreated to the dressing room, presumably to pass on his karma to the players.

In reality, we had to endure 90 nerve-jangling minutes during which we went 2-0 down to Plough Lane's 'Bash Street Kids' before the Goodison gods (and Hans Segers) finally answered our desperate prayers. If someone had started a petition at that moment to erect statues to Barry Horne and two-goal Graham Stuart, I would have been the first to sign.

Instead, as Stuart made it 3-2 with a shot that squirmed under the prostrate Segers, the bloke next to me leapt up and threw his arms in the air, smashing me in the mouth and drawing blood. The fact that I gave him a hug as a deafening roar exploded all round us sums up the sheer relief we all felt, but even then we had to wait for other results before we could truly celebrate survival.

Meanwhile, Kenwright's confidence of taking ownership of the club had been seriously undermined after John

Moores Jnr surprisingly questioned the meaning of his father's will which had stated that any new owner of Everton should be "selflessly devoted to the club and a safe pair of hands." The initial interpretation of this was that only a 'True Blue' should own the club which appeared to undermine Peter Johnson's credentials.

Peter Moores had passed his Everton inheritance to his two sisters, Lady Grantchester (Elizabeth Suenson-Taylor) and Janitha Stubbs. This had the effect of making John Moores Junior the majority shareholder with around 21.2 per cent and he now declared that his father had not been specific about the ownership of the club.

This left Kenwright in some confusion because he thought he had an agreement with the Moores family. It all turned on its head when Everton board member Sir Desmond Pitcher raised a 'point of order' in a board meeting, stating it was not in their remit to favour one candidate over another. With Johnson now offering £4,000 a share, double his original bid, Kenwright was now forced to stand aside.

He declared: "Peter Johnson knows that I love Everton more than anything in the world. I wanted to check out his commitment above and beyond the money side of it. Because of my stand Peter Johnson has vastly improved his original offer and that can only be good for the Blues."

Johnson crossed the River Mersey from Tranmere to become Everton's new owner on July 26, 1994, having paid £10m to secure a controlling interest. A month later the new board posed for a picture in front of the rebuilt Stanley Park Stand. It retained a 'Moores' connection in the shape of the

Honourable John Suenson-Taylor (Lord Grantchester and the son of Lady Grantchester). Bill Kenwright retained his board place and a key member of his consortium, Arthur Abercrombie, joined him.

However, Peter Johnson was now chairman and stood centre stage alongside his key Park Foods executives Clifford Finch and Richard Hughes, who were both lifelong Evertonians. Sir Philip Carter was still in situ from the old board, as was Keith Tamlin, David Newton, Dr David Marsh and Sir Desmond Pitcher.

My 'Everton for Sale' news story had reached its conclusion for now and while the Peter Johnson era would ultimately become a roller coaster ride of emotions for Evertonians, it all started so positively – on and off the pitch.

A Red buys the club and it's all change

IN May 1994 it was always going to be a steep learning curve for new owner/chairman Peter Johnson who was known to have been a Red and whose previous football experience had been confined to Prenton Park, the home of Tranmere Rovers.

Thankfully, the Park End wasn't renamed the Park Foods End in honour of his Wirral company. More importantly, the impressive new £2.3m stand that was now in place, traditionally holding away fans, was now a 6,000-capacity structure that would emit a powerful royal blue roar to back up the traditional passion of the Street End. This move would ensure that Goodison Park now had the ability to intimidate opponents from all sides of the stadium.

It was full credit to the Johnson regime in these early days that the lounges throughout Goodison were now upgraded.

Previously the wall art looked as if it had been sourced from a local department store, perfect for corridors of city centre hotels, but failing completely to reflect the rich history of a club of Everton's standing. Pictures of legends and immortals now covered the walls and I was more than happy to help with key images from the extensive archive of the Liverpool Post & Echo.

Johnson had already shown his hand in this area at Prenton Park where Rovers had stolen a march on Everton by introducing a Dixie Dean Lounge while Goodison had its mundanely-named 300 and 500 clubs. It was now decided that Everton would not only create what would be called the Dixie Dean Platinum Suite, but make it the most exclusive facility in the ground. At the same time, the 300 and 500 Clubs became the Alex Young and Joe Mercer Lounges.

The all-powerful Johnson now had the run of Goodison Park with people like his senior Park Foods executives Finch and Hughes. To mark the opening of the new Dean Suite, Johnson decided they would stage their own football match at Goodison – under the floodlights with the terraces totally deserted.

The teams were made up of a mixed bunch of 22 plus friends, contacts, and business individuals. Even I was invited to play. What an opportunity to run out on the hallowed turf where Dean, Lawton, Hickson, Young, Ball, Harvey, Kendall, Royle, Latchford, Sharp, Gray and the rest had contrived to write Everton history.

In the home dressing room, hanging on one of the first-team pegs, I spotted a blue shirt with my own name on the back, the stuff dreams are made of. I've still got it. Out on the pitch I even scored a penalty at the Gwladys Street end. Later we congregated for a special dinner in the Dean Suite.

I don't know what the groundsman thought about 22 amateurs stamping about and cutting up his pitch on a cold winter's night, but was he going to tell the club's new owner to pick up his ball and go and play elsewhere? I don't think so.

Johnson had paid handsomely for the right to do what he wanted and the impromptu match was a nice gesture at that time.

Many key new initiatives were now implemented with Cliff Finch often at the forefront. He was determined to put his stamp on the club's commercial activities. Towards the end of the Johnson regime, Finch would become a target for much criticism from the fans as he appeared to push the boundaries of his remit to the limit. There was a perception that he was even having an influence on transfer talks. As Johnson began to retreat into his shell, Finch became more of a front line spokesman, too powerful for many supporters.

However, my dealings with him in the early Johnson days were lively and positive. In 1994, as sports editor of the Echo and with a determination to change the focus of our publishing strategy, I recommended to the club that they introduce their own monthly magazine. I saw this as a new way forward to communicate with the supporters in the firm belief that traditional sources of local information, specifically the historic football pinks with their live Saturday reports, had a diminishing shelf life with games now moved all over the place to accommodate the new power in English football – Sky TV.

As it turned out, Merseyside's Football Echo, founded in the late 1800s and always the respected voice of local football, would struggle on until 2004, at which point a sensible decision was taken to insert it free in the Saturday Echo to retain a famous and much-loved brand.

Working with a key member of my staff at that time, sports production editor Richard Williamson, we planned the vision for the first Evertonian magazine in 1994 and I went into negotiations with Cliff Finch to strike a mutually satisfactory deal. The product was to be the same size as a tabloid newspaper, but printed on better quality newsprint. I had tested a few earlier editions in a different format with commercial manager Derek Johnston, a great bloke who was also an excellent photographer and the man behind the early running of the Liverpool Marathon.

I remember meeting Cliff for early discussions at a pub in Walton Road, an unusual place to hold contract talks of any sort. We must have just fancied a pint!

I had a small company Vauxhall Astra at the time and, as I arrived in the car park, he turned up in his large blue Jaguar. I felt it was 1-0 to him before we had even started, but negotiations went well and we settled on an agreeable arrangement.

These deals are always heavily weighted in the club's favour, but because we were the publishers and effectively taking the risk, I registered the 'Evertonian' title copyright in the name of the Liverpool Echo. This would become an important lever years later as contracts came up for renewal with rival publishers from outside Liverpool now competing with us for official club publishing rights. Eventually, we handed over the copyright, but only as part of a broader publishing relationship that would eventually see us also handling the official matchday programme as well as official club books, including well received titles like 'If You Know Your History' and 'Everton's FA Cup 100'.

Having initially nurtured the 'Evertonian' logic with Derek Johnston and then carried the vision through with the support of Cliff Finch, I am delighted that this familiar club product, now entitled Everton magazine, has stood the test of time. It is still going strong as one of the Premier League's oldest and most respected club publications.

In assessing Johnson's early impact, it should also be noted that the club's first ever official shop, with its distinctive tower design, was built on the corner of Walton Lane and Langham Street.

As things moved on apace in 1994, no-one could have predicted that Johnson's brave new world would ultimately come tumbling down with the Park Foods chief transformed from potential visionary into a figure who was mistrusted and disliked by Evertonians.

I ultimately found myself at loggerheads with him, forced to take the unprecedented step of calling for the resignation of an Everton FC owner and chairman in the Echo. But this was for the future.

In August 1994, with the impressive new Park End Stand

now looking down on what we all hoped would be a brave new world, the only priority was to sort things out on the field of play after surviving a desperate relegation fight by the skin of our teeth.

As the new season unfolded, the board and the fans were soon agreeing that Mike Walker was not the man for the present or the future and he would find himself out on November 8, 1994, ironically after another frustrating Everton performance against his old club Norwich.

Like most Evertonians, I can sum up the Goodison career of the so-called 'Silver Fox' in two simple paragraphs.

In a positive sense, he brought Duncan Ferguson to Everton on loan from Glasgow Rangers, a move that would ultimately be made permanent by new manager Joe Royle who helped the big man become a Goodison icon. Walker signed midfielder Joe Parkinson and winger Anders Limpar, and also brought in striker Daniel Amokachi from Bruges for £3m. The latter would eventually write himself into Everton FA Cup history in the most bizarre of circumstances, but with another manager in the dug-out. I'll get back to that later.

For now, no-one was surprised that Walker was sacked after just 10 months in the job. He had managed just six league wins from 31 games, the worst record of any Everton manager. It would fall to Joe Royle to turn around the worst start to a season in Everton's history while bringing fight, pride and direction back into a team that had simply lost its way. Football's most tested fan base would finally get something to shout about.

33

Nev's '10 nuggets and big Dunc' ready to take Wembley by storm

JOE Royle was a battling striker in the great tradition of Everton centre-forwards. He understood the legend of 60 goals and the legacy of Dixie in terms of those subsequent stars that graced Goodison's famous number nine shirt.

Big Joe had played in one of Everton's greatest teams, had an Evertonian's understanding of what made Goodison fans tick, and had proved his managerial potential and his sustainability by spending 12 years developing unfashionable Oldham Athletic into a real force.

He took the Latics to a League Cup final and twice reached the last four of the FA Cup as well as gaining them promotion to English football's top flight. It was always going to be tough for Oldham to compete and survive among the game's elite. They would lose their treasured status after three seasons, but Royle had proved himself as an astute manager who could get the best out of players.

Along the way he had been shortlisted for the England job, highlighting the respect with which he was held in the game. Everton fans knew exactly what they were getting when he returned to Goodison Park on November 10, 1994.

Fittingly, his first test was a home Mersey derby clash with arch-rivals Liverpool. I remember Joe's old playing pal Brian Labone, previewing the game with the words: "You can forget all about the School of Science. This match is all about getting at least one point. We won't be playing any fancy stuff, but you can be sure we will be challenging all the way."

Meanwhile, Anfield Iron, Tommy Smith, predictably previewed the derby and Joe's Goodison Park return with the words: "I can't see anything other than a Liverpool victory. Everton have one mighty weapon . . . the Goodison crowd. I have to admit the supporters have been magnificent, but I can see the final margin being 3-0 to the Reds!"

Bring it on! Royle had urged his players to fight for the right to win by competing in every area. The framework was being laid for the famous 'Dogs of War' tag, but it would be unfair to label Joe's sides as nothing more than scrappers and fighters. He had more about him than that, even though his pal Labby was urging a simple and straightforward: "Get into them!"

I found myself sitting next to Tommy Smith in the Goodison press box. As the derby began to unfold, I glanced at the former Kop hero and he was looking anything but happy as a certain Duncan Ferguson, on loan from Rangers, rose to claim his first goal in a blue shirt. This would, quite literally, be the start of something big. His partner Paul Rideout grabbed the second in a 2-0 victory. I quickly turned to Smithy and gave his 3-0 Liverpool victory prediction my own 'Over the top'.

Tuesday's Echo advised 'BUY FERGUSON QUICKLY JOE', but that was stating the blatantly obvious and Royle would soon be putting his faith in the Scot in every way, signing the striker for a fee upwards of £4m.

Everton would finish 15th at the end of this landmark season and so there was still plenty of work to do on that score, but what had the fans' spirits soaring was instant success in the FA Cup.

The Blues beat Derby on January 7, 1995, to progress beyond the third round for the first time in three seasons, a day when Joe was almost certainly impressed by talented defender Craig Short, who he would sign six months later.

Before the month was out, Royle would face his second league derby of the season. Sometimes, a short phrase spat out in anger by a fierce rival says more than a thousand words about a team's progress.

"Don't talk to me about the School of Science," said Liverpool boss Roy Evans after Everton held their rivals 0-0 in a league clash at Anfield in late January, 1995.

Joe Royle often had exactly the right words to respond in these situations. "Sounds like a few dummies have come out of the pram tonight," he said with a smile, making no apologies for the physical nature of his side's battling performance.

Beyond this, FA Cup dreams were rising following a fourth round away win on a dreadful Bristol City pitch. To be fair, it wasn't an overly impressive performance and one of the home players said: "At least Dick Turpin wore a mask." It was a potential cue for Joe to respond with his "dummies and pram" quote, but he smiled contentedly at progress to the fifth round where his side beat Norwich 5-0.

We didn't know it then, but a late February Goodison win over Manchester United would be an omen of things to come on a famous day later in May. A significant quote from Royle was that matchwinner Duncan Ferguson could "become the biggest thing at Goodison since Dixie Dean. He's that good."

FA Cup dreams were now seriously manifesting themselves following a lone goal quarter-final triumph over Newcastle that set up a semi-final clash with Tottenham at Elland Road.

Sometimes the southern-centric national press clamour for what they see as 'the dream end game' and there is little doubt that they all wanted a Spurs versus Manchester United final. Joe Royle had other ideas.

I opted not to work at Elland Road, sitting among the Evertonians with my fanatical son Peter who was revelling in his first semi-final while David Prentice handled the Football Echo report from the press box. We can all recall Matt Jackson's timely opener and a well deserved Graham Stuart effort that made it 2-0. A Jurgen Klinsmann penalty had the

Spurs fans and the London press buzzing again, but what happened next will stand forever in FA Cup folklore.

Paul Rideout went down injured and physio Les Helm signalled to the bench that the striker would not be continuing, walking him towards the touchline. Big Joe waited for final confirmation as Rideout, like magic, appeared to recover.

Meanwhile, substitute Daniel Amokachi had persuaded a bemused linesman that he was going on and play resumed before the Everton bench could respond. Joe Royle said: "It was the best substitution I never made."

Daniel scored twice in the final eight minutes for a famous victory. I looked at my son Peter, on his feet and surrounded by fanatical Evertonians. He just reminded me of myself as a young fan, so proud to be among supporters of a like mind, thrilled to be part of something special, and earning his royal blue spurs at the expense of Spurs. What a day!

Royle had some tongue-in-cheek words in his press conference. He apologised, saying: "I shouldn't be here, should I? Sorry about the dream final, lads. Having read the previews, we played a lot of good football, which is perhaps surprising to one or two of you. So **!!**** to you, and that's double 'L'. Only joking, lads."

On the eve of the Wembley clash, one man who was still seething about what he viewed as the disrespect shown to Everton was Neville Southall. When asked for a personal view on the final, he said: "Just like our semi-final with Spurs, I suppose we needn't turn up at Wembley tomorrow. Manchester United? They are the biggest name in world football. We are just Duncan and ten nuggets!"

In typically bizarre Nev fashion, he then suggested he would ideally like a draw "so that we can have another day to look forward to at Wembley, a night match when it would be cooler."

Evertonians laughed out loud at his tongue-in-cheek "nuggets" quote, but the big man could forget about a replay.

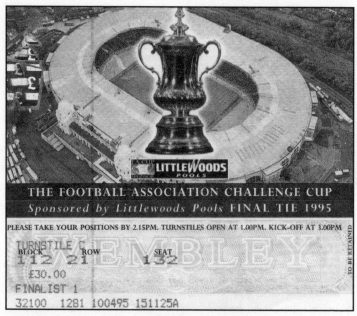

I would shun the Wembley press box to sit among the Blue Nose army in 1995. I retain my ticket: Block 112, Row 21, Seat 132. The £30 price looks a snip now

The drama and elation of what will forever be the Blue Nose Cup Final

HAVING beaten Ipswich in mid-May, Everton could prepare for the FA Cup final against Manchester United without the burden of a last-gasp relegation fight.

I had reported on Howard Kendall's moment of managerial glory against Watford in 1984. At that time, the press box was high in the roof above the royal box which meant that when the players climbed up the steps to pick up the cup and their medals, they disappeared below us. I therefore never witnessed the magical moment Kevin Ratcliffe hoisted the famous trophy above his head following the victory over Watford. Instead I had to focus on the touchline to watch the faces of Howard and Colin Harvey.

First they displayed pride and relief as Kevin began the

long climb up the steps. Then smiles of sheer delight told me that the trophy was in a pair of Everton hands for the first time since 1966, a year Labby was the most elated man on the planet.

The mood before the cup final against United was upbeat and aspirational. If John Bailey's famous top hat was the humorous sideshow in the Eighties, the fun in 1995 was all about thousands of plastic blue noses that the Echo's marketing team had purchased and shipped in ahead of the May 20 showdown. These were given away free on a first come, first served basis at our office in Old Hall Street and Everton's official club shop.

They were snapped up overnight and so, in tandem with the club, we ordered several thousand more, taking the total to 30,000. Everybody was wearing them. You would see taxi drivers sporting their blue noses as they picked up bemused visitors at Lime Street station. The mid-Nineties equivalent of 'selfies' – snapped on old fashioned instant cameras – were up on walls in offices and factories across Merseyside. Pet pooches would be pictured with their own blue noses – genuine 'Dogs of War'.

This might have started out as a marketing gimmick, but the fans picked up on it in every way, determined to show their allegiance on the trains and buses heading for London. When the second batch of several thousand blue noses arrived at the Echo office, queues began to build around the block and into the middle distance, just like the famous snaking lines you used to see at Goodison in the Fifties and Sixties for derby match tickets.

As sports editor of the Echo, I naturally qualified for an automatic place in the press box, unlike in 1968 when the FA had deemed that the Liverpool Weekly News was not important enough, resulting in me using a messenger's pass to sit just behind the goal-line with the massed bank of photographers.

However, as I'd done at Elland Road in the semi, I opted for a Wembley seat among the blue and white hordes, once again sitting alongside my proud and excited son Peter, then aged 15. Of course, he was wearing his blue nose and wouldn't take it off.

The game was a delightful blur, but in my mind I still see the winning goal in pin sharp slow motion. Dave Watson made a solid interception just outside the area. He moved the ball on to Anders Limpar as Everton broke on United down the right, four-on-two. Graham Stuart was screaming for the ball wide left, but Limpar opted to move it right to Matt Jackson who showed fantastic composure and skill to play in a cross in front of the desperate Peter Schmeichel. Stuart, still alert, came in and smacked a shot against the crossbar, the ball looping in the air.

The action now appeared to switch into a frame-by-frame scenario with the ball hanging up there for what seemed like an age. It was a real live case of football suspended animation. Every Evertonian took a deep breath as Paul Rideout's header finally evaded Steve Bruce on the line and hit the back of the net. At that moment slow motion switched into utter pandemonium as the royal blue army officially became the Royle Blue Nose Army.

I was up on my seat, screaming like one of those manic South American football commentators . . . GOAAAAAAAAAL! And as if to confirm in my mind that it had gone in, a second GOAAAAAAAAAL! My son's Blue Nose fell off, soon recovered as we hugged everyone around us and took in the enormity of the moment.

Immediately 40,000 Evertonians had to remind themselves there were still 60 minutes to go. It's amazing how an hour can seem like a lifetime. Fortunately we were in the safe hands of people like Neville Southall and man-of-the-match Dave Watson, senior players who had seen it all before and who were immensely influential.

And as I watched Nev come out at the death to barge past team-mates and opponents to calmly claim a United centre with one massive hand, I smiled inside and remembered his 'Big Dunc and ten nuggets' gem.

One final image lives with me. As the players circled the pitch with the FA Cup, I caught sight of Duncan Ferguson who had come on for the last 30 minutes along with semi-final hero Daniel Amokachi. Dunc was proudly wearing his Blue Nose and it became one of the classic images of a fabulous day. The big man has always demonstrated that he understands the club. These days he is proving that he understands the game as well, as an ever-improving coach.

As for Joe Royle, his beaming smile and bubbling sense of satisfaction mirrored that of Howard Kendall 11 years earlier and, like his great friend, Joe glowed inside in the knowledge that here was an Everton managerial success story that no-one could ever take away from him.

35

Banned by Everton, banned by Liverpool – at least that's consistency!

PETER Johnson now reflected on the way things had turned around. He had taken decisive action in sacking Mike Walker and the appointment of Joe Royle had brought a major piece of silverware back to Goodison for the first time since 1987.

In confirming that he would now spend big to build on a wonderful FA Cup win, Johnson declared: "I'd like to think this could be the start of another Everton dynasty. There's no reason why the FA Cup should not be the first of many more trophies for the club."

For his part, Royle followed up his FA Cup success with a winning return to Wembley in the Charity Shield on August

13, 1995. However, the attendance against Kenny Dalglish's resurgent Blackburn Rovers was a disappointing 40,149, suggesting that Rovers were still not the draw their owner Jack Walker wanted them to be, while the Blue Nose revolution at Goodison still had some way to go before supporters bought into Peter Johnson's brave new world.

Nevertheless, it was uplifting to see another trophy secured thanks to a lone Vinny Samways goal after 57 minutes against the new champions.

Everton began the new season with a goalless draw at Chelsea before losing 2-0 at home to Arsenal. The fans immediately received a boost when Joe captured flying winger Andrei Kanchelskis from Manchester United. No hard feelings about Wembley then? United had unloaded their top scorer to Everton and the fans now applauded a 2-0 home win over Southampton.

Having survived the first hurdle of the European Cup Winners Cup against KR Reykjavik, the Blues now crashed out against Dutch side Feyenoord. But while that was disappointing, Royle once again proved that he had the measure of arch-rivals Liverpool with a 2-1 victory at Anfield, always something to celebrate.

Indeed, the Everton manager would build on his FA Cup success by finishing sixth at the end of 1995-96, an improvement of nine places on the previous campaign that had begun so disastrously under the 'Silver Fox'.

For Joe Royle to have transcended the panic of the short Walker regime and turned Everton from a side going nowhere into a club full of renewed determination and hope was an achievement in itself. Sixth place promised to be a solid springboard, but I recall that Joe gained an insight into a potential area for improvement as he prepared for his third campaign at the helm with a friendly at Wrexham. Andrei Kanchelskis now bagged all four for Everton at the Racecourse, but the manager was not happy to have conceded three at the other end.

However, it was all smiles when the league campaign kicked off with a 2-0 win over Newcastle United at Goodison Park. Duncan Ferguson, a towering figure on the day, overshadowed Kevin Keegan's record signing Alan Shearer. This was also a game in which the remarkable Neville Southall made his 700th appearance.

The Blues moved on to Old Trafford where they held Manchester United 2-2, big Dunc grabbing a double in an all-round battling performance.

This inspired United boss Alex Ferguson to actually tip Everton as genuine title contenders. But roll on to September and that particular prediction was under serious debate when Everton lost 4-0 at Wimbledon where murmurings of discontent began to surface on the terraces about the side's style of play.

Towards the end of September, the Blues lost a Coca Cola Cup tie 3-2 at second division York where a famous cobbled city street in the city centre is quaintly called The Shambles. Echo reporter David Prentice linked the name of the street with the performance itself, recording how frustrated fans chanted: "What the hell is going on?"

His match report described the performance as "the most

appalling capitulation in living memory." For some, this might have been over the top, but not for the fans that had travelled across to Yorkshire. I can't say the report brought big Joe and the Echo sports desk closer together. When hopes are raised, disappointments magnify themselves in the minds of supporters, particularly a group that had been spoiled during four remarkable years in the mid-Eighties and had, more recently, seen the FA Cup back at Goodison.

In particular, the Echo's senior football columnist Philip McNulty was cutting and hyper-critical at times about results and performances.

In his 2005 book 'Joe Royle – The Autobiography', the Everton manager highlighted his increasingly difficult relationship with the local and national press towards the end of 1996 and moving into 1997. The chapter was entitled 'Poisoned Pens'.

He wrote: "People may think I was becoming paranoid by the time I told the local reporters working for the nationals as well as the local Merseyside newspapers that they no longer had the freedom to walk into our training ground and chat to the players. In my view McNulty and his newspaper (the Echo) were nothing but destructive in a series of carping, critical articles that did not take into account the mitigating circumstances of our situation, namely a cruelly long injury list that seriously weakened my squad. I could not ignore the nagging suspicion that the press was conducting a vendetta against me."

Joe's reaction to media criticism was not confined to the Echo. He took issue with the nationals, annoyed that the Daily Mail's Colin Wood had described him as being "prickly." He was unhappy with the Daily Star's Matt D'Arcy for continually linking Everton with Wimbledon's Dean Holdsworth, despite this being regularly denied by the manager.

In a later book chapter, Joe would pick up on the media theme again. He reflected on my Echo sports editor's role in overseeing what he viewed as incessant negative coverage after a series of results that many fans found very hard to swallow.

"I like Ken Rogers as a bloke," he wrote, "but I do believe the way the paper treated me should be on his conscience."

Joe was fully entitled to use his book to target those who he deemed had targeted him in those difficult months towards the end of the 96-97 season. He's a big character with big opinions – and he's an Everton legend.

Of course, football is a game of wildly different views. At one extreme reporters and fans revel in moments that can be hugely uplifting, inspirational and awe inspiring. At the other end of the spectrum, when things are not going well, emotions and frustrations inevitably spill over in a tribal sport that dominates the lives of everyone involved.

Newspapers seek to reflect the mood of their readers. The views of fans tend to dictate editorial policy, not controlling sports editors.

Rightly or wrongly, it's always the managers who find themselves at the sharp end rather than their massively rewarded players who tend to keep a very low profile when the going gets really tough. And clearly, sports editors are also at the sharp end when a manager chooses to vent his frustration against a specific newspaper.

Before he was sacked, the vastly experienced Steve McClaren clashed dramatically in the St James' Park press room with a national newspaper reporter towards the end of the 2015-16 season with the relegation-threatened Geordies at the height of yet another survival dog fight. Louis van Gaal's constant war with the media was also never far from the headlines at Old Trafford. Things get personal and it's understandable.

But often it's not just what's happening on the pitch that can lead to an explosive outcome. News and sport departments have always been like oil and water, each with their own specific writing teams and different agendas that often bring them into conflict. It could be over something petty, like the news team breaking an exclusive about the club's new kit ahead of the official launch. The sports desk would always feel the backlash when this happened.

Back in the mid-1990s I can remember the Echo news team reporting a prominent story on the front page about the official Liverpool FC players Christmas party. It was held at a city centre hotel where there was fighting in the street in the early hours.

For absolute clarity, team members were not involved in the outside mayhem, but John Barnes was photographed leaving the hotel early the following morning and the image was used on that day's Echo front page.

Even though this was completely out of my area of responsibility, I found myself called up to Melwood by Liverpool manager Roy Evans. Barnes was a powerful and influential figure at the training ground at that time and the Echo sports desk was banned for weeks from speaking to the manager or the players, even though we had absolutely nothing to do with the story.

I always found in these situations that our football coverage was at least as good, if not better, because we had to work much harder on lateral features to generate relevant content, using former players and other key figures to analyse the ongoing football scene.

I clearly wasn't happy that Joe Royle banned us for a spell from Bellefield, but he had the right, he felt the need, and he exercised it. As an Evertonian – and as a sports editor – my duty during that spell was to ensure that the level of Blues coverage in the Echo was never overshadowed by the column inches afforded to the team on the other side of the park.

This has always been a contentious area. Evertonians would claim we were biased towards the Red half. Liverpudlians would complain we were biased towards the Blues. At one stage I took to measuring the column inches every night to ensure we were being scrupulously fair so that I would have the definitive answer whenever the phone rang, which it often did, but then I realised I was getting paranoid and this was no way to run a sports department.

The one thing that did upset me was that Joe felt our reporting was having an effect on his elderly father, Joe Royle Senior, who had been an Echo reader all his life. Mr Royle Senior was a lovely man who I had come across on numerous occasions. He was a well known local musician in an excellent band called The Saturation Seven.

In my younger days I was actually lead singer in various Liverpool pop groups you will never have heard of, including The Circulation, Action Line, and Hurles Jinx.

We'd appeared with recording artistes like Eddy Grant and the Equals, and Manfred Mann and played at all the leading Liverpool venues like the Cavern, the Mardi Gras, the Blue Angel, the Peppermint Lounge, the Beachcomber and so on.

Towards the end of this little phase I was in a trio called The Kenny Simon Set and we did a gig in Norris Green at the Broadway Club where The Saturation Seven performed in their own right as well as backing the solo acts that needed their support. They had a drummer, saxophonists and Joe's dad, a truly excellent musician, on the piano.

We didn't need any backing, but halfway through our first song, these guys unexpectedly joined in. Suddenly, our little threesome was blasting out the classic 'In The Midnight Hour' like a fully fledged Atlantic Records soul band and while it failed to make my voice imitate my hero Wilson Pickett, I turned round and smiled knowingly at Joe's dad. Keep playing Mr Royle! You're making us sound as if we actually know what we're doing!

36

Lies, damned lies and statistics – but sometimes they make sense

MY previous relationship with Joe Royle had been extremely positive. Even during his time at Norwich and Oldham, I had travelled to Carrow Road and Boundary Park to interview him for the Echo to revel in his wonderful Goodison Park playing memories, but now things had become difficult.

After the significant improvement in league position in 95-96, Everton had struggled to find the kind of traction and momentum that would satisfy the fans as the 1996-97 season headed for a tense conclusion with the team – severely affected by injuries – up one minute, down the next.

As a sports editor in a football-mad city, and regardless of my own thoughts, it's wrong to over-control reporters and columnists when they start to write critical reports during times of stress. It didn't help Joe that the fans were increasingly losing faith in the club's owner.

The Echo wasn't and isn't Pravda, the famous Russian paper that always reflects the government line. It's when it gets personal that you finally have to rein things back and it was certainly moving that way as Joe clashed with some of our football columnists.

Of course, football can be a tantalising roller coaster existence. In November, 1996, Andrei Kanchelskis was looking unstoppable and with Gary Speed showing the class every fan recognised, Everton slaughtered Southampton 7-1 at Goodison, even with Duncan Ferguson on the sidelines.

A week later, a solid away win at Leicester suggested the season might be taking a positive turn, but fast forward another week and Evertonians found themselves reflecting on a frustrating 3-1 home defeat against Sunderland.

Seeking to find the missing link that might provide the consistency he needed to regain the momentum of his first two seasons, Royle captured Nick Barmby from Middlesbrough for a club record £5.7m and when the skilful midfielder scored a lone goal winner at Derby County on December 16, 1996, Everton shared seventh place in the league table with Manchester United with a string of home matches to come.

Injuries never come at a timely moment and such a crisis rarely comforts impatient fans. Everton would now lose three successive games, culminating with a 2-0 home defeat to Blackburn Rovers on January 2, 1997.

Could the FA Cup offer some respite as it had done in

1995? This competition can always lift supporters at the start of a new year and in his first season it had been the catalyst for Joe to inspire that winning run to Wembley glory.

But giant-killers always have the potential to stalk and undermine the high and mighty, as had happened 12 months earlier when Everton succumbed in a fourth round replay at Port Vale. Now the Blues were losing again at the same stage to less than glamorous opposition.

In a season in which Bradford City would be fighting desperately to avoid relegation to the third tier, they pulled the rug from under Everton with a 3-2 win at Goodison.

I can remember the mixed emotions in the Echo's match report, written by David Prentice.

It was penned amid a growing clamour for the head of the manager. David, who had retained a decent relationship with the Goodison boss, began with a question:

'What do you do once you've sacked the man who has presided over two years of topsy-turvy Evertonia? Give a Goodison wannabe – Peter Reid say – two years in charge? And if he only wins one FA Cup before hitting a turbulent patch, boot him out as well? That kind of stability worked well for Manchester United, didn't it?'

Clearly David was urging caution, laced with reality, his report adding:

'There were screams of anguish at another cup embarrassment and screams of anger at manager Joe Royle. Everton are a club in crisis, no-one can deny that now.

'But adopting a knee-jerk reaction of axing a manager would not improve matters. Not yet anyway. Patience, however, is the rarest commodity in modern football. Martin Edwards showed it, giving Alex Ferguson seven years to restore Manchester United to their current position.'

Dave continued: 'Football pressures have increased, even in that short time. Royle is likely to receive only 15 matches, from now until the end of the season, to prove his value.'

The Echo laid out the statistics that suggested Joe had earned the right to fight on.

Prentice pointed out that the manager inherited the worst team in the Premiership, saved them from relegation, consolidated, and even won the FA Cup.

He then highlighted the stats from the two years before Royle arrived: Won 27, drawn 22, lost 47. He compared them to Royle's two-year reign: Won 42, drawn 32, lost 24.

'Tangible progress,' said Dave. 'But that was up to December 16, 1996. Since then the wheels have fallen off!'

Joe was to get little respite from the mounting pressure when Everton travelled to Newcastle and lost 4-1. Even though one Everton banner at St James' Park declared 'True Blue Joe Royle must stay', the situation now had the potential to be the start of a perfect storm.

Clearly, the inspiration for that banner stemmed from the fact that here was a man battling in the hot seat who was a former playing hero, a trophy-winning manager and an acknowledged Evertonian.

Having tasted success with him at Wembley, many fans so desperately wanted Joe to succeed, but we all know that when the going gets tough, emotion and sentiment can evaporate as quickly as an Andrei Kanchelskis dash down the wing. Indeed, as if to make the point, the next throw of the dice actually saw Everton selling the Ukrainian to Fiorentina for £8m. An Everton career that had started so positively had lost its way.

In the Echo's Bradford match report, David Prentice had declared: 'Kanchelskis is world-class at his best, but a lazy liability when he isn't. He has wandered through the season showing less commitment to the cause than Liz Taylor to one of her marriages.'

The fans wanted to see new faces and Joe Royle was determined to acquire them to solve his side's inconsistency. At the end of March he moved to bring in Brann Bergen centre-half Claus Eftevaag and striker Tore Andre Flo. Sources in Norway revealed that £2.5m had been offered against the £4m Brann Bergen wanted.

When chairman Peter Johnson refused to support the manager's transfer judgment, Royle lost patience and finally resigned with the traditional club statement suggesting 'mutual consent'.

This was an uncomfortable case of déjà vu in that Howard Kendall's second spell at the helm had ended with his failure to gain backing for a big centre-forward deal.

There is no doubt that near the end Joe Royle felt he was the victim of a negative, hostile and unsupportive local and national press campaign.

I accept this was a very uncomfortable period and understand his pain and anger, but I also recognise the frustration of fans whose hopes in the glorious Eighties had reached an all-time high, inspiring expectation levels that always had the potential to strangle the managers that followed. Joe himself had raised those expectations with that sensational early FA Cup win.

The Echo stats I highlighted earlier prove how he significantly turned things around in his first two years, but football is about narrow margins and managers live and die by them.

Modern sports scientists can now pinpoint how many miles a player might have run in a game; chart and highlight positional play across the 90 minutes; provide analysis of successful and unsuccessful passes – and so it goes on in ever-increasing detail.

Managers once operated on pure football instinct, knowledge and experience, but now they find themselves walking a very different path, often clutching an iPad under their arm.

I'm prepared to acknowledge the famous saying that there are lies, damned lies and then there are statistics.

Nevertheless, I will use stats to finish this chapter, reflecting on those fine lines between success and failure with tables that relate to Everton bosses since the appointment of the club's first acknowledged 'proper' manager Theo Kelly (hot seat years 1946-1948, not counting the regional football of his war years).

These statistics don't reflect the situation a boss might have inherited, whether or not he was supported by his board at important moments, or what expectation levels he might have had to live with, but they are nevertheless quite illuminating.

Everton Managers Chart (league games only)

Manager	Era	P	W	D	L	Pts	Pts ave
Kendall (1)	1981-1987	252	131	59	62	452	1.79
Catterick	1961-1973	500	225	137	138	812	1.62
Harvey	1987-1990	126	51	37	38	190	1.51
Moyes	2002-2013	427	173	123	131	642	1.50
Martinez	2013-2016	113	43	34	36	163	1.46
Lee	1977-1981	188	69	63	56	270	1.44
Royle	1994-1997	97	36	31	30	139	1.43
Bingham	1973-1977	146	53	48	45	207	1.42
Carey	1958-1961	111	45	21	45	156	1.41
Britton	1948-1956	313	109	90	114	417	1.33
Kendall (2)	1990-1993	129	46	33	50	171	1.33
Kelly	1946-1948	96	36	17	43	125	1.30
Buchan	1956-1958	93	29	21	43	108	1.16
Smith	1998-2002	143	41	42	60	165	1.15
Kendall (3)	1997-1998	38	9	13	16	40	1.05
Walker	1994-1994	31	6	9	16	27	0.87

* Assuming 3pts for a win, 1 for a draw, 0 for a defeat. Up to end of 2015-16 season

The first table reflects league games only with the rankings based on points average per game.

The second table looks at all games – league, domestic cups and Europe.

For ease of comparison, all games assume three points for a win and one for a draw, regardless of whether it is league or cup action.

In each table, Howard Kendall is given three separate

lines to highlight his three periods as Everton management – 1981-87, 1990-93, and 1997-98.

You won't be surprised to learn that these stats, taking first his supremely successful 1980s figures, demonstrate beyond doubt that he stands alone as the most successful Everton manager of all time.

His league games points average (1981-87) sits at 1.79 with his great mentor Harry Catterick on 1.62 points per game. It is interesting and encouraging to see one of the club's greatest servants, Colin Harvey, in third place in this statistical area. He averaged 1.51 points a game in the hot seat between 1987 and 1990, with David Moyes fourth on 1.50 points per game.

Intriguingly, despite being sacked with one game remaining of the 2015-16 season, Roberto Martinez is in fifth place ahead of Gordon Lee, with Joe Royle completing the top seven of 16 post war managers.

Things play out slightly differently looking at the points average based on all matches.

There is no change in the top three positions with an order of Kendall, Catterick and Harvey, but surprisingly, Martinez moves up to fourth ahead of Moyes, while Royle moves up to sixth ahead of Lee. However, Moyes was in charge of significantly more games than Martinez (518 v 143).

Fans trying to get their heads around the Martinez scenario will find themselves focused totally on his final season when he reigned over the worst home league record in any season in the club's history, 23 points (using three points for a win), three of those points coming after he was sacked.

LIES, DAMNED LIES AND STATISTICS

Everton Managers Chart (all games)

Manager	Era	P	W	D	L	Pts	Pts ave
Kendall (1)	1981-1987	338	183	78	77	627	1.86
Catterick	1961-1973	594	276	157	161	985	1.66
Harvey	1987-1990	176	75	52	49	277	1.57
Martinez	2013-2016	143	61	39	43	222	1.55
Moyes	2002-2013	518	218	139	161	793	1.53
Royle	1994-1997	118	47	36	35	177	1.50
Lee	1977-1981	234	92	72	70	348	1.49
Bingham	1973-1977	172	64	55	53	247	1.44
Carey	1958-1961	122	51	22	49	175	1.43
Kendall (2)	1990-1993	162	63	40	59	229	1.41
Britton	1948-1956	336	124	91	121	463	1.38
Kelly	1946-1948	103	39	19	45	136	1.32
Smith	1998-2002	168	53	50	65	209	1.24
Buchan	1956-1958	99	32	22	45	118	1.19
Kendall (3)	1997-1998	42	11	13	18	46	1.10
Walker	1994-1994	35	6	11	18	29	0.83
Kendall spells combined		542	257	131	154	902	1.66

* Assuming 3pts for a win, 1 for a draw, 0 for a defeat. Up to end of 2015-16 season

Roberto's Everton career started much better for him. He had 21 league wins in his first season, but that was followed by just 23 in the next two campaigns combined.

He is the definitive example of the phrase 'there are lies, damned lies, and statistics.' He went from averaging 1.9 points per game in 2013-14 to just 1.2 over the next two seasons. On a downwards stats curve, this highlights why he had to go.

The fans began to pull out their hair in Roberto's last season with his reluctance to change his philosophy which makes it strange to see him higher in a table like this than certain other bosses, for instance, 1995 FA Cup winner Royle.

Clearly, statistics can be made to mean anything you want them to mean, although one stat is undeniable.

Howard Kendall is, without doubt, the most successful Everton manager of all time, even when you combine the stats from his three periods in charge. The 'all games' table, incorporating his three managerial stints, drops his points' average to 1.66 per game, exactly the same as Catterick, but their comparable win percentage across all games sees Howard return a 47.42% score with Harry on 46.46%.

While both managers won the same number of domestic honours, Kendall secured that famous European Cup Winners Cup success in 1985 which leaves him unassailable.

37

It's your move, says Johnson, but fans group has grounds for concern

ALL a manager can do when he inherits a very difficult situation – and they don't come any more difficult than a potential relegation nightmare – is to review, consolidate and gradually make the necessary improvements to move things forward. Even then, there are never any guarantees.

Joe Royle had quickly put the lid on Mike Walker's can of worms and, almost in the same breath, put some jam on the table in a silver bowl. He had so desperately wanted to build on that FA Cup success, but it wasn't to be.

I remember his thoughts on the day he resigned as manager. He said: "I've always been an Evertonian and I'll remain an Evertonian. If I ever had to write a CV for another manager's job, right at the top would be my achievement in keeping Everton in the Premiership after taking over a side with just eight points from 14 matches."

It's interesting that Joe put the safety of the Blues' top-flight status at number one on his CV ahead of his 1995 FA Cup triumph – and he's probably right.

I would add something else about Joe Royle. Like Peter Reid, Bill Kenwright, Graham Stuart and Duncan Ferguson, he spoke magnificently at Howard Kendall's funeral, a powerful Evertonian tribute to a friend and former playing colleague that came from the heart. Up until his shock death, Brian Labone, for me, was undoubtedly Everton's proud godfather, a local lad who achieved greatness as a player and later became the respected voice of Evertonians.

I watched Joe sum up Howard perfectly at that cathedral service, and I have witnessed him first hand at various Everton fan dinners of late, talking with a dignity, modesty and understanding of the club that his old skipper Labby would immediately recognise.

With Dave Watson in temporary charge at Goodison, a significant story broke on May 6, 1997, when the Liverpool Echo confirmed that Peter Johnson was considering a revolutionary plan to build a new home for Everton, 105 years after the opening of historic Goodison Park.

In producing a glossy brochure entitled 'It's Your Move' the chairman declared that any final decision would be taken in consultation with the fans. A lively and constructive 'Goodison For Everton' group had emerged to argue the case to stay, producing a rival 'Grounds for Concern' document.

I remember writing that the vocal GFE faction did not want civil war, but rather an open debate, not least on the potential to redevelop Goodison itself. The passion of the stay campaigners was compelling from a history and heritage standpoint and I fully understood it.

The Echo had taken a stance to support the new stadium plans, simply because it seemed to me that the Blues were getting left behind in the new world that was the business-dominated Premier League. Just 10 years earlier, in 1987, Everton had been the undisputed Kings of England on the pitch. Thirty-one years earlier Goodison Park was one of the country's most admired venues, good enough to stage key World Cup games in 1966. One hundred and five years earlier the brand new Goodison was deemed "the finest and most complete ground in the whole kingdom."

Now others were driving ahead of us. Our famous stadium, with its commercial and attendance limitations, plus its obstructed views, was beginning to look and feel its age.

It remains tortuous to consider a move away from the pitch where Dixie grabbed his 60 goals and where the 'Holy Trinity' of Ball, Harvey and Kendall had inspired us along with Labby and the rest. This was not to mention Howard's magnificent Eighties boys.

Fans will always have personal reasons about not wanting to leave a treasured spiritual home. Whenever I go to Goodison, I always think of my late father Harry who gave me my lifetime passion for all things royal blue. And so I recognised the emotion behind the stay campaign as it gathered pace. A large group of fans protested outside the Echo office in Old

Hall Street. They wanted to know why we were supporting the potential move away. I went outside to speak to them.

As it turned out, 84% of fans who voted in the club's independently-audited official poll appeared to support Johnson's ambitious plans, but the big question was: "Where to?"

It was generally assumed that the site of Kirkby Golf Course near the M57 was favoured, but club members and some local residents were seriously opposed. Protestors even blocked the entrance and a planned Everton inspection of the site was aborted. The South Docks were mentioned which, in the future, would become a massive thrust for the Bill Kenwright consortium. I shuddered when the former Cronton Colliery site near Widnes got a mention.

The 'Goodison for Everton' campaign wanted the club to review every option possible for redeveloping the existing stadium site. As it turned out, Peter Johnson would soon have more important issues to deal with, like keeping his Park Foods dynasty in power at Goodison.

Johnson had been convinced that Andy Gray was about to return to Goodison to take on his first managerial role. When Gray shocked the club with his late decision to continue with his Sky TV career, Everton had to go back to Howard Kendall and ask if he might still be interested. He was never going to turn them down. Kendall's passion for all things Everton immediately brought him back from a hastily taken holiday, but he should have steered well clear of a Johnson regime that was under increasing pressure.

Howard had already failed to turn back the clock in his second spell. His third tenure would last just 42 games.

Do you want a shave, a close shave or an Everton? It really was that close!

HOWARD'S third spell at the helm would last just 261 days, a lifetime compared with Brian Clough's 44 at Leeds United in 1974, but not what Everton's greatest ever manager would have put in the script 12 months earlier when he took over from his great pal and former team-mate Joe Royle.

Having survived a panic-stricken relegation fight under Mike Walker four years earlier, the fans would now find themselves staring down the barrel of a relegation shotgun for a second time at the end of the 1997-98 season.

This was not how Howard had envisaged it. A season of increasing frustration ended with an all or nothing final day home clash against Coventry City on May 10, 1998.

Survival was reliant on Chelsea doing the business at home

to Bolton, but the Stamford Bridge side were just days away from a crucial European Cup Winners Cup final against Stuttgart and predictably reported a long list of pre-match injuries, highlighting that they had their own agenda.

It started well enough at Goodison when Gareth Farrelly sent a rocket of a shot into the net after just six minutes to secure the lead. Fans, who had provided remarkable support, raised the roof, and when they suddenly began to chant "Vialli, Vialli, Vialli" in the 73rd minute, it told the players that Chelsea had rocked Bolton at the Bridge.

And as the Blues retreated deep into their own half to try and run down the clock, Dion Dublin rose to equalise with a firm header past Thomas Myhre.

One more goal from Coventry or one from Bolton at Chelsea now had the potential to send Everton down, but when Jody Morris grabbed a second at Chelsea the final whistle confirmed it was Bolton who would suffer. Scenes of unbridled joy swamped Goodison Park. This soon turned to anger, however, with supporters chanting: "We want Johnson out."

Within 24 hours, Howard Kendall's contract was terminated. It was a sad way for an Everton legend to sign off his Goodison career.

A national newspaper now featured a cartoon showing a shocked fan sitting in a barber's chair with his hairdresser posing the question: "Do you want your shave close, very close or Everton?"

It was clever, but what the fans had just been through was no laughing matter. The Echo, in a page one lead, asked the chairman a question on behalf of the club's beleaguered supporters: "Can you hear us Mr Johnson?"

It related to the demands of the minority shareholders, Johnson remaining untouchable based on his significant majority holding. In a nutshell, those shareholders were demanding change and it was revealed that the board would meet at 10am on the Monday to discuss Peter Johnson's long-term commitment to the future of the club, and his ability to conduct club affairs from a tax haven in Jersey.

Glasgow Rangers manager Walter Smith was the man handed the task of picking Everton up off the floor. Walter was a great football man who had experienced success north of the border, but this was a very different challenge.

It would not take long, indeed less than five months, for him to get caught up in a controversy that was not of his own making and which appeared to make his chairman's position at Goodison completely untenable.

I will never forget November 23, 1998, because it was the day before my 50th birthday. The Blues were entertaining Newcastle at Goodison that night and won 1-0, but events off the field dominated the next day's headlines.

While the action had been unfolding on the pitch, Johnson was settling the shock £7m transfer of fans' hero Duncan Ferguson to Newcastle. The Geordies got their man without the final sign-off of manager Smith who was surprised, rather than shocked, to hear the news after the final whistle.

That summer Johnson had encouraged Smith to lavishly spend £19m, a spree that, realistically, the club could not afford. It was therefore no surprise when Walter was told that he would not receive a penny of the Ferguson cash for further rebuilding.

Evertonians felt betrayed by Peter Johnson. The Echo, the fans, and respected bodies like the Shareholders Association were all vocal in their criticism of the owner. As far as the Echo is concerned, the relationship became virtually non-existent and I recall my former colleague David Prentice writing – in his book 'Ten Year Blues' – how Johnson introduced him to someone at an awards dinner with the words: "I was just explaining that you're that sh** from the Echo!"

Johnson's mounting disdain of the fans had surfaced the previous December when he arrived at an Annual General Meeting that had been described by the Shareholders Association as the most important in Everton history.

Johnson, with his 68 per cent majority shareholding, could do what he pleased and his long-awaited address began with the words: "This meeting will be over at 8.30pm."

Johnson used the short time he had to talk about "hurtful" articles written about him in the press. He handed out a pre-prepared document entitled: 'The Real Facts About Everton' in which he addressed spending, the potential move from Goodison Park and his commitment to the club.

He indicated that Everton had spent more money than any other Premiership club since he became chairman, a total of £43.1m against a return of £16.4m. What he didn't say was that this deficit had the potential to put Everton in serious trouble. Fast forward 11 months and the Duncan Ferguson controversy was now on the lips of every supporter.

The Shareholders Association always invited me to its

annual dinner at Goodison. I recall sitting on the top table next to Johnson. Lord Grantchester, the grandson of John Moores, was another guest. Johnson stood up to speak and absolutely slaughtered the Echo, blaming us for all the problems and issues he was encountering. Yes, newspapers can be influential, but we don't sign players, snub shareholders and fans, pick teams, or organise league tables.

When Johnson had finished his tirade, the response was muted, to say the least. I leaned across and indicated to the chairman of the Shareholders Association, in Johnson's hearing, that I needed to respond. He said he would speak to the owner and asked me to wait until after the break which was now swiftly taken. I remember Lord Grantchester coming to me and quietly apologising on behalf of the shareholders about what had been said.

Of course, Johnson had every right to speak his mind. Criticism has to be a two-way street, but I felt I had to respond.

When people gathered again for the second part of the evening, it was clear that Peter Johnson had already left the building. When I spoke, I was on the same page as the majority in the room who, for some time, had been highlighting their frustration with the Johnson regime.

There were now moves behind the scenes to finally relieve the owner of his majority shareholding. On November 30, 1998, Johnson announced his intention to resign as chairman, but it would take over a year, until December 26, 1999, before the ownership issue was finally resolved. Bill Kenwright, after losing out all those years earlier, now secured the majority shareholding on a day when Walter

Smith's side beat Sunderland 5-0 at Goodison. Bill immediately extended Smith's contract and explained his delight at taking control by saying: "My dream used to be to afford to be able to go somewhere better in the ground than the Boys' Pen. Then it was to get a season ticket, so assuming control is much more than a dream. It's extraordinarily important to me, particularly with the situation the club is in."

As for Johnson, he picked up his previous love affair with Tranmere Rovers, a club where his influence and money did a huge amount of good. He remains the last Everton chairman and owner to bring a major trophy to Goodison Park. That it all went so dreadfully wrong for Johnson; well, I'd like to be able to say that it was all the fault of the Echo. I'll leave it to Evertonians to make up their own minds.

A national newspaper cartoon tried to put humour into the precarious position Everton found themselves in

Bill Kenwright's ambitious Kings Dock dream rolls in and rolls out

BEHIND the scenes and in terms of getting exactly the right message across, I had worked extremely closely with Bill Kenwright on his takeover bid, as I had done during his first attempt to secure the club before Johnson grabbed centre stage. Newspapers don't normally give any individual sight of the material they are going to use ahead of publication, but Bill had lost out once and desperately wanted every word he uttered and every quote he gave to come across with the meaning he intended.

From where I was sitting, as sports editor of the Echo, I wanted to ensure that each story we carried was totally accurate as far as it could be, aware that the ownership issue had the potential to change by the hour, let alone the day.

I would therefore find myself speaking to Bill in the middle of the night if necessary and I was delighted when the club was finally in the hands of a dedicated and loyal Evertonian.

Perhaps the most ironic fact about Everton FC is that the club has never played in Everton, although that could have changed as we moved into a new millennium following the collapse of the club's ambitious Kings Dock stadium project. Kenwright had formed the ambitious 'Kings Dock Consortium Limited' on October 9, 2000, with the project sufficiently well advanced to merit consideration.

A plan by previous chairman Johnson to relocate the club had gained fan support, only to fail three years earlier.

This new vision for the future, on a spectacular riverside site, was aimed at creating a world-class leisure and family entertainment facility. At its heart would be a 55,000 capacity international stadium/arena. In typical fashion, Kenwright wanted to carry the supporters with him on this ambitious quest for a new ground and produced a smart brochure entitled "Moving to a vision in blue."

The front cover declared: "Supporters are requested to state their declared option as we approach the final phase of the decision making process."

Everton's interest in the Kings Docks had emerged eight months earlier when the options were clearly laid out. Option one was to remain at Goodison, necessitating an extension of the existing footprint from 8 to 15 acres.

This would have allowed the club to build a mixed commercial and retail development which, in theory, would have supported the project financially. It would have entailed the closure of Bullens Road, the purchase of 91 residential properties and the relocation of the Gwladys Street School.

There was an offer to re-house the school and half of the residential properties on the nearby Eileen Craven School site on Walton Lane. However, the club was informed by financial advisers Deloitte and Touche that revenue created by any ancillary development was unlikely to be substantial, putting the net cost of the new stadium directly on the club at £50m. This was the first indication that this was going to be anything but straightforward for the Everton board.

This was not helped by the view of Liverpool City Council at the time. They had indicated that there would be enormous problems with the Bullens Road plans and that substantial opposition would come, not only from local residents, but also from the city planners. The suggestion was that any application might take years before an eventual outcome became known.

Looking back, this is infuriating, not least because of the support Liverpool Football Club were ultimately given for the development of their giant Main Stand at Anfield, an exercise that has seen several streets demolished with residents caught up in frustration and inertia for years.

Further options for Goodison would have involved a phased redevelopment over three to four years, and so the board felt they had to investigate alternative sites within the city boundaries. The Kings Dock, owned by The English Partnership, very quickly moved to the top of the list.

In August 2000 I was given a unique opportunity to fully understand the vision Everton were applying to their Kings

Dock dream. I was invited by Bill Kenwright to fly to Holland and Germany in a private jet to view two world-class venues that offered all of the pluses Everton were considering for their proposed new arena.

First stop was Amsterdam where we were quickly transferred to the 53,000 capacity Arena, built between 1993 and 1996 at a cost of 140m euros. This multi-purpose venue is the home of the famous Ajax. It was hugely impressive.

We then jetted to Germany to view an amazing club facility at Schalke. Known as the Veltins Arena, it not only featured a fully retractable roof, but also a roll-in, roll-out pitch. The pitch itself could not be damaged during indoor events such as concerts. The stadium's external area, when not accommodating the pitch, could be used as a major parking facility for buses during football matches. It was a remarkable experience to stand on the Schalke pitch and actually sense the movement as the roll-out motion was activated.

We flew home with Kenwright further motivated and excited by the opportunity for the Kings Dock. Here was a key development opportunity, not just for the club but for the city as a whole, a destination of international significance.

The stadium itself would have had a capacity of 55,000. It was highlighted that the retractable roof and roll-in, roll-out pitch, mirroring the Schalke example, would enable the Arena to be transformed into a multi-function facility capable of staging other international sporting events, concerts, conferences and exhibitions. The site would include a 20 screen cinema, a family entertainment centre, a health club, a nightclub, bars and restaurants, specialist retail facilities, a high quality hotel and 200 waterfront apartments.

The Waterfront Development Brief declared: "The Kings Dock is a dramatic site, demanding a dramatic and dynamic architectural statement. A stadium/arena lends itself to this approach. The consortium will aim to achieve the highest standards of design and establish a character and style which are both unique to the site and yet complement the cityscape and reflect the highest quality established elsewhere on Liverpool's waterfront."

If Everton could have pushed this dream to a successful conclusion, the club would have been transformed in every way, the arena reinforcing our standing in the game.

Immediately, the club's architects produced a fantastic DVD that provided a fly through and flyover vision of the new stadium that filled us all with excitement at the time.

It certainly knocked previous possible sites like Kirkby, Gilmoss and Cronton Colliery into a cocked hat.

In every club's existence, opportunities like this are few and far between. West Ham United's opportunity to move from their historic yet old and restricted Upton Park stadium in east London to the magnificent Olympic Stadium in London will completely transform them. Likewise, Manchester City's fortune in being able to claim the Commonwealth Games stadium has gone hand in hand with their dreams to step out of the shadow of Manchester United.

Everton's ultimate failure to secure the stadium support funding required at that time is understandable. It was always going to be a mammoth challenge. I will forever applaud Bill Kenwright's vision and the stage he reached, but I believe we will rue the chance we had to put Liverpool FC's Anfield, even with its latest facelift, in the shade.

By 2003 the Kings Dock dream was finally over. Ironically, an impressive indoor arena would later be built on the Kings Dock and after a mutually beneficial sponsorship deal, it became the Echo Arena.

As the debate continued about a potential site for a new Everton ground, I found myself thinking about the fact that Everton FC had never actually played in Everton. I recall that the substantial Everton Park site, with Heyworth Street on its upper boundary and Great Homer Street at its lower extent, was very much in my thoughts at that time, being close to where I once lived. A major part of the site had replaced 110 former inner city streets that had been demolished as part of the controversial 1960s slum clearances.

The park that took its place felt disjointed at that stage, unloved and even dangerous at times, and I found myself walking its upper area, close to Everton Village where, in 1879 at the Queen's Head Hotel, St Domingo's FC took the historic decision to become Everton FC. The rest, as they say, is history. Nearby, stands the famous 1787 Lock-Up Tower, an iconic feature on EFC's famous crest.

The North Liverpool Academy on the opposite side of Heyworth Street had still not been built at this time. I paced the park itself and it seemed to offer a genuine opportunity for the club to build a spectacular stadium on the hill, bringing to the Everton district jobs and regeneration. I went back to the office and penned a column on the potential for

Everton to 'go home' and solve their long-standing issues.

Many years on, and I find myself an active and enthusiastic supporter of the Friends of Everton Park whose remit is to use the space for the benefit of the local community and the many visitors who come to take in the greatest elevated view in Liverpool. I have helped organise events there, contributed to a heritage trail, and devised street reunions and even archaeological digs, one at the site of the Queen's Head in Village Street that I have already alluded to as the birthplace of big time football in Liverpool.

I have no doubt that, in its old form, Everton Park could have provided the perfect new home for EFC. But in 2016 the community use of the park has advanced dramatically. It is seen as a key local facility, and its glorious summit view remains one of the unheralded jewels of the city. There is a time and place for every opportunity and the opportunity for Everton Football Club to return 'home' has gone.

The ground issue trundles on, another proposed venue – Walton Hall Park – being deemed unsuitable in May, 2016.

Having leapt forward on the stadium story, I need to track back and reflect on the football action as the year 2000 drew to a close. The club encountered an old friend on a visit to Manchester City where their manager Joe Royle masterminded a 5-0 annihilation of his former club. It was the signal for Walter Smith to cancel the annual players' Christmas party, never a sign that all is well.

By the end of January 2001, a second symbolic defeat – 3-0 in the FA Cup at Goodison to Peter Johnson's Tranmere Rovers – inspired the first calls for the head of Smith.

Seasons flash by when things are not going well and as 2002 dawned, we had the unprecedented scenario of senior Everton players, led by Paul Gascoigne, contacting the Echo to publicly back a manager they clearly didn't want to lose.

But on March 10, 2002, after a 3-0 FA Cup exit at Middlesbrough the die was cast for Walter and four days later David Moyes, the emerging young Preston boss, arrived at what he described as the People's Club.

Without the resources of his big Premier League rivals, the gritty Scot would create decent teams, gain Everton long overdue entry into the Champions League in 2005, and take the Blues to the 2009 FA Cup final. He would secure three Manager of the Year awards but his 11-year reign failed to produce the silverware the fans craved.

I was able to see Moyes close up, ghost writing many Evertonian magazine columns for him. I saw a man who cared deeply about his job and who was always keen to learn. I knew he was fascinated by American sports, and in one column he revealed how he had studied Stateside training regimes in sports such as baseball and American football, correctly believing that there were many overlaps in terms of good practice that he could use in football.

But Moyes is well aware that there is nowhere to hide when things go wrong. Managers carry the weight of the world on their shoulders and if that is at a club that has always been their life – as it was for Howard, Colin and Joe – everything is magnified a hundred fold. Of course, this means that the great times are also a hundred times better.

Outed as a Blue at the official Liverpool Supporters Club AGM

IN the opening chapter of this book I highlighted how a 1969 headline in my first newspaper, the Liverpool Weekly News, led to me being thrown out of Anfield as a 20-year-old journalist by a furious Bill Shankly.

He had seen red after my paper had suggested in a fairly impacting sports page headline that Liverpool fans might boycott Anfield in the aftermath of legendary striker Roger Hunt being substituted for the first time in his career during an FA Cup clash with Leicester. Hunt, known as 'Sir Roger' by his adoring Kop fans, had uncharacteristically thrown down his red shirt in front of Shankly who sat fuming in the Main Stand dug-out.

Roger Hunt would inadvertently cause me another problem at Anfield, although by now 25 years had passed and I was sports editor of the Liverpool Echo.

I was often asked to speak at events, but one invite came right out of the blue, or should I say out of the red!

The phone rang on my office desk one midweek afternoon and the voice on the other end identified himself as a committee member of the Liverpool International Supporters Club. He revealed that their Annual General Meeting was taking place the following night in Anfield's impressive Main Stand trophy room and asked if I might be available to act as the main guest speaker.

I knew instantly that someone had dropped out at the last minute and they were in need of a substitute at very short notice. However, it was important for the Echo to be supportive of events like this involving fans and readers of our newspaper. I agreed to the request and was asked to turn up around 7.15pm.

When I got there I realised it was going to be a big evening for the Supporters Club with the trophy room packed to the rafters. I was asked to wait in a side room while they completed the AGM formalities – and while sitting in that tiny room I suddenly realised who I was replacing.

The Supporters Club chairman wasted no time in apologising to all and sundry in the room. He said: "Ladies and gentleman. As you are well aware, we were due to have that Liverpool and England legend 'Sir' Roger Hunt as our main guest tonight. I'm very sorry, but Roger cannot make it."

There was a collective and clearly disappointed 'Ahhhh'

from members throughout the room. The chairman quickly added: "However, I am delighted that we have a late substitute for Roger and I would like to introduce him now. The mood brightened up immediately. There was clearly a belief that they would be introducing an Ian St John or a Tommy Smith. The supporters' chairman said: "So please welcome Ken Rogers, the sports editor of the Liverpool Echo."

Once again there was a collective 'Ahhhh' from inside the room. Still sitting in the small side room, I felt like a pub singer who had been called in to replace Frank Sinatra at the Royal Albert Hall. Once again, a substitution involving Hunt was about to give me a testing moment.

I stepped out to a muted welcome from the gathered Reds. Of course, I had plenty of stories to reveal to them, having been the Echo's Liverpool correspondent in my time as well as following Everton. I had clearly had my moments with the likes of Shankly, Paisley and Fagan. I had travelled as far as Khartoum in Africa to cover a Liverpool match and had broken many of the big club exclusives down the years on the back pages of the Echo. The room fell silent as I introduced myself, ready to give the supporters the benefit of my tales of a career following their beloved Reds, a period in which I had been a ghost writer for Shankly's colossus Ron Yeats and the Anfield Iron, Tommy Smith.

I was just about to start when a gentleman on the front row put his hand up. I said: "If you don't mind, I'll take questions at the end."

He said: "This will only take a moment. Can you confirm that you have been a lifelong Blue?" He had the kind of self-satisfied smile on his face that suggested he wanted to shout out: "Gotcha!"

I said: "You are absolutely right. Brought up in Everton, lifetime Evertonian, but I'm not here to talk about that. Among other things, I wanted to give you an insight tonight into my experiences after the Hillsborough Disaster."

The self-satisfied smile of the questioner disappeared and I immediately had the full and undivided attention of the entire room.

As explained in my earlier Colin Harvey chapter, I was not at the April 1989 Liverpool FA Cup semi-final at Sheffield Wednesday. My colleague Ian Hargraves covered that tie while I reported on the Everton v Norwich City semi-final at Villa Park. That is where I started my talk.

I looked out into the Anfield AGM audience and said that I was fiercely proud of the response of Evertonians in those days after Hillsborough. There was an instinctive round of applause supporting this sentiment. Roger Hunt was now the last person on anyone's mind.

In the days that followed the Sheffield disaster, I would walk the Kop many times to write articles for the Echo as that sea of flowers built up on the pitch below. The terrace itself had scarves tied to the crash barriers from all manner of rival fans. Whenever I saw an Everton scarf – and there were hundreds of them – it filled me with pride and I would get quite emotional.

I had been to derby games in Glasgow between Celtic and Rangers and witnessed the kind of bigotry that makes your heart sink. It was the same in many other big football cities, but Merseyside had managed to rise above this which made us fairly unique as a soccer stronghold.

I turned the Echo sports desk after Hillsborough into a 'media embassy' for journalists who started arriving from all over the world. A German reporter walked in one day and said: "Take me to where the hooligans live!" I shrugged and indicated that there was no such thing as a hooligan ghetto in Liverpool. He then said: "Well take me to Toxteth," clearly aware of the riots that had once unfolded there and oblivious to the fact that it had absolutely nothing to do with football.

I was asked by a French TV station to attend the so-called 'Chain of Hope' in Stanley Park with red and blue scarves intertwined from Goodison to Anfield. It was a truly remarkable sight. As I started to speak in the middle of the park, holding up the chain, a huge crowd gathered. I spoke out powerfully for the people of Merseyside. Such was the weight of frustration and high emotion with outrageous accusations already flying around, inspired by the South Yorkshire Police and people who should have known better, like Nottingham Forest boss Brian Clough, that the crowd clapped their support. They were desperate to hear a positive voice.

I was happy that there was now attentive silence in that Anfield trophy room as the Liverpool Supporters Club AGM continued. I explained that there had been a time when I felt a certain amount of cynicism for the so-called 'Gulf War Syndrome' identified by many soldiers returning from the battlefields. I had now firmly changed my opinion on that score. The reality was that whenever I was asked to publicly comment about Hillsborough, the football equivalent of a war zone with those heart rending and shocking images locked in my mind, I would find myself almost unable to speak.

I couldn't begin to think how it affected the families of the Hillsborough 96.

I now felt ready to move on in the meeting to some less traumatic football stories and was happy at the end that the 'Ahhhs' that had greeted my name being announced at the start were now replaced by some applause, although I'm certain Roger Hunt would have raised the roof. This Blue Nose substitute had hopefully demonstrated that Evertonians might continue to be the enemy on derby days, but that when push comes to shove at times of pain and stress, Merseysiders always stand together.

This, of course, was demonstrated perfectly towards the end of the 2015-16 season when the inquest jury finally ruled that the Hillsborough victims had been unlawfully killed. Before Everton's home match against Bournemouth, family members of the 96 walked out onto the Goodison pitch, including Hillsborough Family Support Group chairperson Margaret Aspinall, Jenni Hicks, Sue Roberts, John Traynor and Jim Wafer. All the players wore '96' shirts bearing the words "Truth & Justice" and a large banner was unfurled at the Gwladys Street end declaring "Justice at Last, 96 Brothers in Arms."

From the 'Chain of Hope' to the very end there had been total solidarity and this should never be forgotten.

In your dreams!
Reidy and Aldo play
the ultimate
Scouse derby match

I'VE had some hilarious and inspiring moments in my time as a writer and sports editor, but very few matched an amazing afternoon I once spent with two of Merseyside's greatest football characters – Peter Reid and John Aldridge.

The appropriate subject matter I placed on the table for Reidy and Aldo to discuss was 'Scousers' and my challenge, on paper, was a simple one.

I named each of them as manager or player-manager of their very own fantasy football team in an imaginary Everton v Liverpool derby clash in which they could select stars and immortals from any generation with the proviso that they had to be from Merseyside.

Of course, even before a ball was kicked in earnest we

had a heated debate. For the purposes of the exercise, what was the definition of a Scouser? If you live in London, a Cockney is someone traditionally born within the sound of Bow Bells. In reality, this does not define someone from London, but rather someone from an area of London . . . the East End.

There are several variations that can identify the exact borders of Scouseland and it is not necessarily the boundaries of Liverpool, although clearly some people would think that it is.

The Collins English Dictionary confirms Scouse as a British informal noun.

No help so far, but it goes on to say:

1. Also called Scouser – a person from Liverpool.

2. The Liverpool dialect (adjective).

3. Of Liverpool, its people, or their dialect (from lobscouse, a sailor's stew).

There are some key words there: The Liverpool dialect; of Liverpool; its people.

The Scouse dialect doesn't end at Kirkby or Bootle's boundary with Waterloo/Crosby. Likewise, the width of the Mersey doesn't stop people in downtown Birkenhead from speaking with an accent that is at least as strong as anything you will hear in Walton or Kirkdale. Dixie Dean would have confirmed the latter.

The only exception to the rule is probably St Helens, although there are actually lots of people there with Scouse genes through parents and grandparents. This all suggests that there are varying levels of Scouseness across Merseyside and with both Reidy and Aldo benefiting from this widening of the boundaries we agreed that they could select any player born within the five Merseyside metropolitan districts of Liverpool, Sefton, Knowsley, Wirral, and St Helens.

This opened up the opportunity for Peter to potentially name the legendary Dean in his side (from north Birkenhead) as well as Paul Bracewell (from Heswall, Wirral). The balance was that Aldo could consider European Cup winning captain Phil Thompson, whose family are from Liverpool, but who has always looked on himself as a Kirkby lad (Knowsley), as well as helping to deal with a potentially tricky goalkeeping dilemma which forced him to call up a Wallasey custodian.

With both managers happy, we settled down in the lounge of the Crowne Plaza hotel, fittingly towered over by two legendary Pier Head Liver Birds. For balance, we deemed that one bird would be a Blue and the other a Red!

I ordered a limitless supply of wine or beer on the basis that it was going to be a long – and enjoyable – afternoon.

I handed out the squad lists which indicated that Reidy had 170 player options while Aldo had 120 which immediately proved to Peter that Everton FC are more 'Scouse' than Liverpool FC! John countered with the fact that the Blues had been in existence for 14 more years (1878-1892). It was going to be one of those days.

This exercise was to have an intriguing end product. It was my plan to produce two separate magazines, one on 'Everton Football Club's Scousers' and the other a Liverpool Football Club version, and it wasn't just about naming two teams with substitutes. I wanted Reidy and Aldo to consider every aspect of a typical derby match: tactics; pre-match team talk; what might happen in the tunnel before the kick-off; first half outcomes; half-time team talk; second half outcomes; post-match celebrations.

My only stipulation was that the score heading towards the 90th minute mark would be 4-4, thus replicating the now famous FA Cup fifth round replay at Goodison Park on February 20, 1991. The twist was that both managers would now determine who would score their injury time winning goal in a 5-4 victory for their respective blue and red magazines. We clearly had a lot of fantasy football ahead of us and settled down into the big armchairs in the Crowne Plaza lobby. I had brought along my Trinity Mirror Sport Media colleague Simon Hughes to tape the proceedings and ultimately write up the outcomes.

My god, I should probably have arranged for a professional boxing referee to preside over this gathering.

Even before we reviewed both squads, questions were zipping over my head, like: What happens if a player has turned out for both clubs, like Steve McMahon, David Johnson, Dave Hickson or Johnny Morrissey? Who would have first grabs on these players? Which team would have the benefit of home advantage? Who would be the ref? The latter was a hot debate because both teams have traditional hate figures when it comes to the man in the middle.

I settled on the venue query straight away. It had to be Wembley Stadium for a good Scouse day out, but obviously with a sensible 3pm kick-off time. I wasn't having any of this

5pm or evening kick-off nonsense to satisfy TV schedules.

Venue and kick-off time sorted, everything else was for the lads to battle and fight over and they were both up for it. The gloves were off and battle was about to commence in the ultimate Mersey derby, but not before we opened another bottle of wine!

FANTASY DERBY PHASE 1:

Challenge number one in our Mersey derby fantasy football clash was to study the squad lists and name the teams.

Funnily, both Reidy and Aldo spotted an immediate flaw in their selection plans when I handed out the squad lists. Neither boss had a Scouse goalkeeper of real international quality. They had decent goalkeeping options, but not a Neville Southall or a Ray Clemence.

Peter observed: "I'm struggling for a Scouse keeper. I'm only selecting players with at least 100 appearances, so that narrows it down. Andy Rankin from the Sixties was one of few local goalkeepers who made it into the big time (107 Everton games). Old 'Sheepdog' used to have a great haircut and he once helped us knock Borussia Moenchengladbach out of the second round of the European Cup. So he gets to wear his old green goalkeeper's jersey one more time."

Aldo said: "Initially I was going to pick Tony Warner, but then I realised he never actually made a first-team appearance. He was on the bench for about 200 consecutive games which is crazy, so I had to choose Frankie Lane, even though he only played twice. Unfortunately, Frankie stands out in my mind because I still remember his debut mistake against

Derby when he caught a cross and then stepped back over the line!"

Both managers were shaking their heads, although Reidy was definitely the happier of the two at this stage.

Peter's back four was a bit more straightforward with Brian Labone and Dave Watson immediately named as his giant centre-backs, with Tommy Wright at right-back and John Bailey on the other flank. "Labby was a great player and a true Blue," said Reidy, "everything you could want in a centre-half. I would trust him with my life. Waggy is a cracking lad and would complement Labby very well. He would also be a threat from set-pieces.

"Tommy Wright was a magnificent full-back, very underrated. He got into England's 1970 World Cup team in Mexico, a side many said was better than the 1966 team.

"John Bailey was brilliant, one of the best chest-to-feet men ever to have played for the club. Front men would love him because he always hit the spot. He was a real character and great for team spirit. And I don't mean drink. In the 1984 cup final he was excellent. Fit as f*** too!"

Leighton Baines had still to make his international impact when we conducted this exercise in the 2007-08 season, having made just 17 appearances at the time. He would certainly be in contention for any revised Reidy line-up.

Aldo smiled as he named Phil Thompson and Tommy Smith as his centre-backs with Chris Lawler and Gerry Byrne as his full-backs.

He said: "No player has ever given as much to Liverpool FC as Tommy. He cared so much and wouldn't accept second best. Tommo's also a proper Scouser, a Red through and through, and a good talker. He'd get the lads going in the tunnel.

"Chris Lawler's goals-per-game ratio was phenomenal for a full-back. There was no-one better ghosting in at the far post. Bobby Collins hit Gerry Byrne with one of the worst challenges I have ever seen in football in the 1965 FA Cup final, studs first into the left-back's shoulder. It dislocated his collar bone, but he played on, even through extra time, to help us lift the trophy. What courage!"

With midfield a crucial area, both 'managers' were more than happy with their selections, Reidy in particular because he had the opportunity to name himself in a 4-3-3 formation, partnering his old mate Paul Bracewell, and also naming his ex-coach and manager Colin Harvey.

Leon Osman didn't make his Everton breakthrough until 2004-05. Whether Ossie would get in now, despite his fantastic Everton career, is debateable, the same for Ross Barkley. Would Reidy leave himself out (no!); his championship winning mate Brace (no!); or Colin Harvey, one of the Holy Trinity (no!). Sorry Leon and Ross, but you would give Peter a fantastic option on the bench.

Peter said: "I know there would be a lot of pressure on me because I'm the boss as well, so I would lead by example. I would try and sit in front of the back line and break things up to allow the other lads in midfield to play a bit.

"I had to name Brace because he'd have a f****** go at me if I didn't. To be fair, we made a good partnership. He's a top lad. He's still a miserable b****** though!

"What an honour and pleasure it would be to name Colin Harvey on the left, a brilliant and intelligent player. To make your debut in Europe against Inter Milan as a young lad, you knew he was destined to become a giant in the game."

Aldo's 4-4-2 formation would now accommodate a midfield of Ian Callaghan, Steven Gerrard, Terry McDermott and Jimmy Case. "I couldn't pick an all-time XI without Cally, let alone a Liverpool Scouse team," said John. "There probably hasn't been a better crosser of the ball in history over an astonishing 857 games.

"Steven Gerrard? What a player! I have never known anyone like him. He could be my captain, but I'm going to let him get on with his own game. He's had more than enough time dragging other players out of the s***.

"Terry Mac? What a legend. If he played today, everyone would be talking about him. All the players loved him too because he was such a funny fella.

"Jimmy Case was a hard b******. He'd get stuck in and had a fearsome shot, but it was the way he allowed players like Dalglish to play that made him special."

I'll let Aldo finish his selection with his attackers. He said: "Like Reidy, I'm naming myself as a player-manager. I'd be looking to work down the right and make sure Chris Lawler was also getting down there to exploit John Bailey's ability to have eight pints before the game. Only joking Bails!

"Robbie Fowler would be my attacking partner. His record at Liverpool (and in derbies) was phenomenal. We tend to overlook his heading ability so I would be asking the wingers to get the ball into the box."

This left Reidy to name his three strikers and he was rubbing his hands as he opted for Wayne Rooney, Joe Royle . . . and Dixie!

He said: "People have a go at Wayne because he left, but I think he was the saving of Everton because that £27million allowed us to rebuild the side bit by bit. We're all professionals and would love to stay at one club for our whole career, but it never works that way. If he had stayed he would have become the symbol of the club.

"Big Joe was a great player and just as good as a manager. I don't know a person who would say a bad thing about him. He won us the FA Cup, showing strong leadership and organisational skills, something he always showed when he was on the pitch in a blue shirt.

"Finally, how magnificent would it be to be able to pair him with Dixie whose goalscoring record was amazing? Just look at the great Dean. He was awesome and if I was a defender, I wouldn't fancy playing against someone like him. I could have picked Labby as captain, a great player and a true Blue, but I couldn't ignore Dixie's credentials and his 60-goal legend."

So there we had it, two fascinating Scouse teams, just leaving the lads to name two very strong-looking substitutes benches with no limit on numbers. Everton: Johnny Morrissey, Alan Harper, Derek Temple, Terry Darracott, Mike Lyons, Leon Osman, Ross Barkley and Dave Hickson. Liverpool: Sammy Lee, David Fairclough, Steve McManaman, Steve McMahon, David Johnson, and Jamie Carragher.

Let battle commence . . .

FANTASY DERBY PHASE 2:

One of the great disappointments of my journalistic career was that I did not film that afternoon when Reidy and Aldo went head to head for their fantasy Scouse derby match. Both lads were different class, but then I always knew they would be.

They picked up on the challenge, they bounced off each other, they got right into the mood – and the Scouse humour that flew from one side of the table to the other symbolised everything that is good about Merseyside derbies and how important it is to have local lads at the heart of these epic battles with a complete understanding of what it means to the fans.

It's almost impossible to translate the mood, the rivalry, the camaraderie and the sheer fun of that session into a match report for a book, let alone a magazine, but here goes.

On the basis that you always get the first blow in, mentally and physically, Peter spotted what he believed was a flaw in John's attacking 4-4-2 shape. He said: "He's made a massive mistake. I'm playing Rooney in the hole behind Dixie and Big Joe. I'm not sure who's going to pick him up. Mind you, I've just seen Jimmy Case so I take that back!"

Aldo reminds us that he's also got Tommy Smith in there. "Bloody hell," mused Peter. "There could be no-one left on the pitch because everyone would be getting fouled or injured by Smithy, or getting sent off for fighting with him."

Aldo quickly made the point that Smithy could play as well as intimidate. He must have been meeting the Anfield Iron that night. John was confident that his attacking line-up would stretch the Everton defence, but Reidy was having none of it.

"We'll defend narrow and not let them play through us," he said. "That Aldridge and Fowler would never win anything in the air against Waggy and Labby. I rest my case. In fact, we'd just boot everything out for throw-ins and corners, then we'd boot it long, get it up the pitch into the box, then Dixie would be on the end of it . . . bang, 1-0."

Aldo said: "It really is intriguing when you look at it, with Reidy going with three up front and me with two."

Peter was clearly having other thoughts above and beyond his initial route one plan to capitalise on Dixie and Joe's aerial power. Laughing, he said: "I know Aldo probably thinks we would knock it long, but we have class and other options. None of us here will have seen Dixie, but we can't ignore his goalscoring record."

Aldo suggested an Everton weakness up front would be pace, but he was immediately shot down by Reidy. "You're wrong, Aldo," he said. "I've been led to believe that Dean was electric. He had pace and lots of it, brilliant in the air too. It's interesting because I'm usually a 4-4-2 man myself, but having looked at my squad and the quality I've got, I'm confident in our tactics.

"There's also a month's curfew before the game by the way. No drinking for four weeks. That goes on record (laughter). That's to nobody specific. I just want us to be fit."

I assume you've gathered by now that our two Scouse managers were turning this fantasy clash into something that was a lot more real in their minds. Reidy insisted that the referee would be instructed to play the old fashioned way, with proper tackling and with red cards only issued for second degree murder. Aldo signed up to this.

While he was on the question of discipline, Peter made it clear that he was not having Clive Thomas as the referee, the man who disallowed Bryan Hamilton's 'perfect' goal against Liverpool in the 1977 FA Cup semi-final that would have taken the Blues through 3-2.

Both lads opted for Neil Midgley, a Manc but one who understood players and gave as good as he got.

Both 'managers' accepted that a Scouse derby would be tough and would need common sense officials. They were also asked why Scousers were so tough. Aldo said: "It's the way we've been brought up. There's no silver spoon in our mouths."

Reidy said: "It comes back to that story when they were building Knowsley Safari Park. A lady stood up at a local council meeting and said 'What happens if a lion escapes?' A councillor responded: 'It's gonna have to take its chances!'"

With laughter ringing around the room, we agreed to move on to the team talks. Peter's eyes lit up. He said: "I'd just say: 'Listen Dixie, Smithy never stops talking as you know, and he says you're not going to have a kick'. I rest my case! Seriously though, they're a quality side and it's important to stop the likes of Gerrard and McDermott shooting and making runs. Aldo and Fowler are two of the best when it comes to finishing so I'd get Labby to make sure the defence stays narrow.

"Let's use what I think is our strength by getting wide and

getting loads of crosses in, and wait for Rooney to do it in the hole. That would be my team talk."

Aldo said: "I'd just tell my lads to get in their faces. It would be the same from both sides, but f****** hell, who's going to win that battle?"

Reidy's final response brought more laughter. "If it becomes a kicking game, I'm calling for Johnny Morrissey from the bench."

Enough said! The lads were asked about mind games in the Wembley tunnel. Peter said: "All that stuff that went on in the tunnel. F****** hell, that was part and parcel of it. Let's forget about political correctness. We'd get into each other. There would be plenty at it in this game. I'd pick on Terry Mac cos he's my mate and I'd leave Brace to have a go at Smithy (laughs). Dixie and Smithy would be left to get on with it. Tommo would probably talk Joe Royle to boredom!"

Aldo said: "We're talking about Scousers here. We've got too much mental strength on both sides. It would be water off a duck's back. A lot of the lads who would be playing against each other were brought up in the same districts and have played against each other all their lives. The respect would be immense. Game on."

FANTASY DERBY PHASE 3:

I know I was once the supposed unbiased sports editor of the Liverpool Echo, covering Everton and Liverpool home and away on a month about basis, but I've given up my Wembley press box seat for this all-Scouse derby. I'm in the middle of a sea of blue and white at the Everton end.

I might be in the middle of the travelling Goodison hordes, but I'm still taking notes because I've got to file my Football Echo runner on my mobile phone as the action unfolds. So here we go.

Reidy, never slow in coming forward, is straight in with fantasy move number one. He pictures Bails getting up the field with Liverpool trying to shut him down. Bails knocks in a raking cross towards the edge of the box. The Reds fail to spot Dixie running in with his raw 13 stone. Bang, top corner. And Frankie Lane's still singing!

Everton 1 Liverpool 0.

Aldo says: "Yeah, you may have scored one right at the start, but we are the ones playing real f****** football. Lots of our players link in midfield. The ball goes out to Cally who plays in a right-foot cross to where I've pulled away from Watson and Labone. I lay it off for Robbie who has run in and scored with a side-foot volley from six yards. Goal! We're Scousers and we don't celebrate. At least, none of that running over and punching the corner flag sh**."

Hang on Aldo, who are you talking about there?

Everton 1 Liverpool 1.

Reidy is unmoved. He says: "Aldo was worried about his team's ability to defend set-plays and he was right because we've just scored again, this time from a corner. We've all piled in and I know John is keen on zonal marking, so we've exploited the space and the corner's gone short to Rooney on the edge of the box, played perfectly by Colin Harvey.

Rooney's volleyed it right into the top corner and Frankie Lane's still singing while rooted to the spot."
Everton 2 Liverpool 1.

The interval is approaching and Liverpool desperately want to level before the break. Aldo tells Lawler and Case to double up on Bails. 'Silent Knight' goes on the overlap and pings a ball to the far post. Aldo says: "Again, I've peeled off Watto, nodded it back to the edge of the box where Stevie G's come in like a train and smacked one in the bottom corner. It's right on the interval and a sickener for Everton."
Half-time: Everton 2 Liverpool 2.

Reidy declares: "Waggy and Labby are going to get some stick. Aldo's pulled away from them twice. 'What have I told you before, Waggy and Labby?' Liverpool have got quality movement and you can't let Aldo on your shoulder'."

Aldo counters with his team talk: "We can't give too many corners away. Get your leg round it and put it up the pitch."

Just like the first half, Reidy immediately chirps in with another bit of vision. He says: "We finally get some joy in the middle of the park and Rooney breaks free. Tommo has to come out to stop him, but Wayne plays a one-two with Dixie and puts him in. Then Tommy Smith comes in with a great flying challenge. Luckily for me, I have got up with play for once and the ball rebounds into my face, looping over Frankie Lane's head and into the open net (and he's still singing!). I'm absolutely delighted because it's a fluke."
Everton 3 Liverpool 2.

Aldo's fuming, but he won't lie down in this derby of derbies. He says: "My choice of Chris Lawler is vindicated because there's a great six-man move with Cally, Gerry Byrne, Robbie, Steve Gerrard and myself all involved.

"I have made a near post run. This has taken the two centre-backs away from the back post – they didn't listen to Reidy at half-time. They also didn't expect 'Silent Knight' to get forward, but there was Chris Lawler, volleying through the f***** goalkeeper's legs. Poor old Rankin."

Everton 3 Liverpool 3.

Reidy starts to lose it. "I'm not having this, Aldo. You've been involved in all the goals and Waggy and Labby are having a nightmare. The goalie's also had a mare (more laughter).

"And you've led every time," responds Aldo. "Now it's our turn. Robbie gets involved in midfield. Six or seven passes and Jimmy Case blasts it from 30 yards. For once, Andy Rankin pulls off a worldie, but there I am all on my own at the far post – just pulled off Watto (laughs) – I tap it in."

Everton 3 Liverpool 4.

Reidy grimaced, but a half-smile became a beam when he said: "I would usually like to keep my back four in shape, but Bails is off and Morrissey is on because we need a physical presence. I say 'Come on Bails, you've had a great game, but come off son, the centre-halves let you down badly'.

"It immediately pays dividends because Johnny, or Mugsy as he was called (that's not my nickname for him, by the way), hoists a ball into the box with the clock ticking down. Dixie goes elbows and beats Tommy Smith to the ball. It whistles past Frankie and he's still singing!"

Everton 4 Liverpool 4.

At this point, any LFC readers might want to turn to the next chapter. While there were two endings when we first played out the Scouse fantasy derby match project, this book only has one. You'll have to check your fantasy result with Aldo so over to you, Reidy.

Peter points out that, for once, it's not the fluky Kopites grabbing a decisive late goal. He sits back in his chair, thinks for about two seconds and then paints a brilliant verbal picture of the final explosive minute.

He says: "Gerrard's racing through the centre and I get a great tackle on him, studs showing. Ref, Neil Midgley, says 'play on' and I turn to knock it to Rooney who's on the half-turn. He fires it in to Joe and Dixie comes in again.

"Tommo's hanging on to his shirt, but he brushes him aside and rushes past Smithy who's gasping for air. Dixie just blasts it from 12 yards out into the top corner of the net. Hat-trick Dixie Dean. Get in! (laughter)."

"Even I enjoyed that goal," admits Aldo. "It sounded great!"

This was Peter's cue for the final word: "It was the best ever goal in English football! Dixie does it again. It's his 61st goal of the season and he sets a new league scoring record that will never be beaten."

Everton 5 Liverpool 4.

A CELEBRATION TO END ALL CELEBRATIONS:
Reidy decides it's only fair that Wayne, on mega millions, finances the joint post-match piss-up.

The lads agree that the teams will travel home separately, but meet up in a Liverpool city centre bar later on. Peter says: "I met Dixie a couple of times and he seemed to enjoy a drink. If only I could sit with him again and discuss his fantasy Scouse derby hat-trick. I'd get Brace to organise the 'do' because he's a miserable so and so and we'd just ignore him and get on with it. Of course, I'd get Wayne to finance it all based on his mega millions contract, so it would be a great occasion. Dixie earned 15 quid a week so he could keep his hand in his pocket!"

I know the fantasy action was all in the minds of two remarkable Merseyside football characters, but Reidy and Aldo genuinely inspired an afternoon of predictions, laughter and out and out Mersey passion that I will never forget. I swear that, at that moment, Peter was up for an open-top bus tour of the city – and a few drinks, of course.

On behalf of myself and my colleague Simon Hughes, I couldn't thank the lads enough for their company, vision, and Scouse humour.

It was an afternoon I will personally never forget, not least because I picked up the wine and beer bill on the way out. Where's Wayne when you need him?

The Last of the Great Corinthians – Labby's amazing final interview

I ONLY need to type the words 'Brian Labone' and I get incredibly emotional. I was lucky enough, not only to watch him play in the heart of one of Everton's greatest ever teams, but also get to know him as a personal friend.

Labby actually helped to guide my career in those early years in the late Sixties when I was a teenage journalist trying to find my way at the imposing Bellefield training ground in West Derby. My school mentor Ken Webster, an outstanding sports master and former school friend of Brian's at the Liverpool Collegiate, had asked him to help me get through those difficult early days.

It was the start of a long and happy relationship with the giant Blues centre-half who I will always acknowledge as being the greatest Evertonian of all time. His love of the club he served so magnificently knew no bounds.

Ironically, I'm not going to start at the beginning with my personal story of Labby. I'm going to start at the end because, by some remarkable quirk of fate, I conducted his final full length media interview, just three days before he tragically died on Monday, April 24, 2006.

Fittingly, his last night on this earth was spent in the shadow of Goodison Park, handing out trophies at the Everton Supporters Player of the Year celebrations.

I couldn't believe it. On the previous Friday I had entertained him for lunch in a small Italian restaurant near the Liverpool Echo building in Old Hall Street along with my Sport Media colleagues Will Hughes and James Cleary. We were completing the words for a brand new book entitled 'Everton's FA Cup 100' as we began to celebrate the centenary of the Blues' first FA Cup success in 1906.

It was a special gathering because we were joined by two other Everton FA Cup-winning captains, Kevin Ratcliffe (1984) and Dave Watson (1995). Brian, of course, had held the trophy above his head on a famous day in 1966. It was one of the most enjoyable couple of hours I have ever had, sitting back and listening to the memories of three men who, between them, had made more than 1,500 appearances for Everton.

Labby was in great spirits, but then he was what I would call a 'man's man'. By that I mean he liked to be in good social company while having a beer or a glass of wine. He was different in that he also liked to be in the company of fans and he was always at ease in these situations. Most current players steer clear of supporters in a social sense, but Brian was the opposite.

After his football career was long over, Brian would sell insurance and I would often see him at lunchtime in pubs near the Echo building like the Exchange in Old Hall Street and the Pig & Whistle in Chapel Street. He had a million stories and confidently held court during these 'working lunches' as he happily mixed business with pleasure.

One of his final roles for Everton was to act as the main 'meeter and greeter' at Goodison Park on match days. I used to marvel at his ability to retain the names of thousands of Evertonians, greeting each of them as if they were friends and making them feel very special in the process. It was a gift and Labby revelled in his role, also making sure that any former players who turned up were also looked after. Another who enjoyed socialising with supporters on match days was Dave Hickson and he and Labby were among the best ambassadors any football club could wish for.

When I launched the Echo's Dixie Dean Memorial Award in the early 1990s to counter balance the company's long-standing Bill Shankly Memorial Award, Brian instantly agreed to join the panel. Again, happy working lunches ensued at which we discussed the merits of some of the club's greatest servants.

I have always been fascinated by our club's rich history and once identified the Everton Football Heritage Trail which is now on the forward agenda of the Friends of Everton Park. Starting point for my trail was the lock-up tower that stands above Netherfield Road South, at the foot of old Everton Village. The tower, of course, features on Everton FC's famous crest.

I asked Brian if he would join me to test the trail and he instantly agreed. The first thing I did was ensure a photograph was taken in front of the tower. I had never seen an Everton captain on such an image, and would later repeat the process with Dave Watson.

Having looked at the tower and the adjacent site of Molly Bushell's legendary Everton Toffee Shop, we set off up Village Street to view the site of the Queen's Head Hotel where in 1879 St Domingo's FC changed its name to Everton FC. Unfortunately, we couldn't have a beer there because the old pub was demolished in the Sixties, by which time it was the Everton Labour Club, but we would soon put that right for the second phase of our trail tour.

We stopped at the site of the former St Domingo's Church on the corner of Breckfield Road North and St Domingo Grove that is occupied these days by a block of flats. Inside the hallway is a plaque on the wall highlighting the Everton FC link and also Dixie Dean's record-breaking 60-goal Football League record.

It was now approaching lunchtime and fittingly the next stop for Labby and I was the Sandon Hotel in Oakfield Road, Everton FC's headquarters when the club played at Anfield in the 1880s. We had a pint and Labby wondered what it must have been like for those early Everton stars to change at the pub and actually walk through the streets to the Anfield ground, having to make the return journey in uncomfortable circumstances after a defeat. We had a good laugh, imagining Brian's team changing on matchdays in the Winslow pub opposite Goodison Park before battling through the crowd to reach the players' entrance.

Brian was looking forward to seeing the site of Everton's original pitch in Stanley Park, our next stop. Many years before, I had met Dr John Rowlands, a collector of Everton memorabilia, who had conducted some excellent research to pinpoint the pitch on what would become the corporation's football car park, effectively opposite the Sandon Hotel in Arkles Lane. It stood close to the back of Stanley House, the former mansion on Anfield Road of John Houlding, the former Everton club president and owner of the Sandon Hotel who, as the club's effective landlord at Anfield, tried to escalate the rent, leading to the migration across the park to Goodison. Houlding, of course, would then form the new Liverpool FC.

We drove past the Anfield Kop and I reminded Labby of his famous quote: "One Evertonian is worth 20 Liverpudlians." He smiled and said: "I actually meant 100." This was the signal for me to put my foot down and head towards Goodison Park where we sat together in an empty Stanley Park Stand, looking out across that famous pitch as Brian regaled me with some of his favourite stories.

What a treasure of a day and what an honour to have taken the heritage tour with such an Everton legend. This flashed back into my mind as I tried to take in the news that Labby had died. However, uppermost in my thoughts was that last big interview.

Dave Watson and Kevin Ratcliffe will recall that we never stopped laughing from start to finish. It began with Brian's first observation after we asked about the differences between their three FA Cup finals. "Well, ours was in black and white," was Labby's first comment.

We spoke about Dave's 1995 final against Manchester United and the thousands of blue noses the Echo had produced which became one of the memories of a remarkable day with Duncan Ferguson wearing one after the game.

Brian said: "I was working for Littlewoods at the time and was involved in a former players' match before the game. We beat them 1-0, which was a good omen. I was manager of the Everton old boys and after the game we were getting changed when Andy King, in his distinct Cockney accent, said: 'Flipping 'eck. Here I am, I've ran my ******** off, I've scored the winning goal and all I can see when I come off are fans holding up a dirty sheet with 'Bob Latchford Walks On ******* Water' on it!' Bob was also playing and he came off looking like a tailor's dummy with not a hair out of place!"

Brian's best mate, of course, was the great Gordon West – the first Everton player I ever interviewed. Labby recalled how he and Westy continued to play tricks on each other, as if they were still in a 1960s Everton dressing room. He recalled doing an after-dinner talk at Goodison on a day when Neville Southall was also present.

Brian said: "One of the questions was: 'Who was the best goalkeeper between you?' West said that Nev was a bit prickly on occasions and in the end they decided that

Gordon was the best in black and white and Neville was the best in colour!"

This was the lunch I did not want to end as we ordered one bottle of wine after another with Brian, Dave and Kevin clearly revelling in each other's company. We then stepped out into the Old Hall Street sunshine and took several pictures of the three captains, which I treasure.

Brian looked in great shape, full of beans as we hugged each other and said our goodbyes. I didn't think for one second that it would be the last time I would see him.

Our priority was to get back to the office and write up the taped interviews which would form the opening chapter of 'FA Cup 100'.

On the Tuesday, as news broke of Brian's shock death outside Goodison, I rushed across to Will Hughes' desk and said: "We have something very special on tape, a piece of real Everton history."

He looked white. "Sorry," he said. "I wrote up the interview but because we recorded much of it in a restaurant with lots of background noise the sound quality isn't great."

It was a disappointment, but at least we had the words and the pictures.

I immediately checked with Brian's family if we could have permission to go ahead and publish and they were very keen for this to happen.

Everton was the only club Brian Labone ever played for. He made 534 Everton appearances – only Neville Southall made more. Brian won two league titles and an FA Cup, but more importantly never lost his love for the club.

Unassuming and modest, when youngsters asked him who he was, he would reply: "I used to be Brian Labone."

He should have said: "I used to be the one and only Brian Labone," because they broke the mould when we lost Labby.

In late 2014, I attended one of the fantastic dinners organised by former Everton winger Ronny Goodlass, shortly after I had retired from my role as managing director of Trinity Mirror Sport Media, the Echo's nationwide football publishing unit.

I was sitting on the top table with Howard Kendall, Joe Royle, Derek Temple, and Tony Kay. I knew that Ronny had instigated a 'Brian Labone Memorial Award' the year before and when we reached that part of the evening I sat up in my chair to take it all in. I was looking down at Pat Labone and her family and wondering how they had coped with the loss of such a giant.

Suddenly I heard my name being mentioned and didn't quite grasp it for a moment. I then realised that I was being presented with a trophy in Brian's name for my lifetime's work in local sports journalism, but notably for my years chronicling the achievements of Everton FC. I gratefully stepped up and received it from Pat who said that Brian would have been delighted.

I tried to respond, but I would have needed a week to compose something that did real justice to my admiration and respect for Brian, the footballer and the man.

As I walked out of the door at the end of the evening, clutching the trophy, I took heart from the fact that I could also call Labby my friend.

43

Living by the maxim 'Evertonians are born, not manufactured'

THERE is a famous Everton FC maxim that states: "Evertonians are born, not manufactured!"

I have already explained how my father ensured that I became steeped in all things royal blue at the start of the 1950s.

At the end of the 2014-15 season I had the opportunity to pass the baton on to two of my young grandsons – Harry and George. I wanted the experience to be about much more than the game itself, which was just as well. We lost to Sunderland!

I had arranged to meet my son Peter and his lads at St Luke's Church, adjacent to Gwladys Street, where we went upstairs to enjoy the informative displays provided by the

EFC Heritage Society. This hard working group fully lives up to our famous 'If You Know Your History' battle hymn.

We then walked down Goodison Road past the main entrance, pointing up at the stars in the 'Walk of Fame' montage that runs the full length of the Main Stand and right around the stadium. This, of course, reminds us of some of our greatest characters – a wonderful touch inspired by Bill Kenwright.

Taking both lads by the hand, we stood in front of Dixie's statue. It seemed right and proper on their Goodison debut and I reminded them that Dean was the legend of 60 goals and the hero of my father and their great grandfather Harry Rogers. For different reasons, it was the chance to remember two great men as far as we were concerned.

We moved through the crowd to the Bullens Road stand where, in the summer of 1950, I was formally 'baptised' as a Blue. It seemed right that young Harry and George should experience their special memory in exactly the same place.

The point I'm making is that football symbolism is important. Yes, first and foremost we should look forward, but we should also revel in our history and should pay due respect to those who have gone above and beyond for our clubs.

In a previous chapter I mentioned statues and stands being named after immortals.

In Everton's case, I also believe there should be a plaque with a 'Scroll of Honour' – symbolically placed in the area of St Luke's Church on the corner of Gwladys Street and Goodison Road – to highlight Everton FC's unbreakable links with St Domingo's Methodist Chapel. This should name and acknowledge those early pioneers like Rev Ben Swift Chambers. He had the vision to launch the St Domingo's football team to further his support for the 'Muscular Christian Movement' that believed a healthy body inspired a healthy mind. Of course, St Domingo's organist George Mahon had the vision to take us from Anfield to Goodison Park in 1892 after the historic falling out with club president John Houlding who would later form the new Liverpool FC.

In leading the 'Kicking of King John' – to recall a contemporary cartoon of the day – Mahon was a true Everton giant whose name deserves a much bigger profile. Another of those St Domingo's stalwarts was Will Cuff, who served our club for 40 years, a wonderful chairman and later a respected president of the Football League.

The EFC Heritage Society, with the help of statistician Billy Smith, continue to research Everton's early history and have seen a newspaper article in which Cuff states that he was also a member of the St Domingo's team, although he didn't play for the new Everton.

This particular 'Scroll of Honour' should also include the names of the seven St Domingo's players we have been able to identify who went on to play for Everton. These include the likes of Alfred Riley Wade, a St Domingo's man who would become an influential forward for the new Everton FC and later an influential director. It was Alfred's father, Joseph Wade, a trustee at St Domingo's, who in 1870 laid the foundation stone at St Domingo's Church at the junction of Breckfield Road North and St Domingo Vale.

The magnificent seven who definitely played for the original church team and continued to play for the new Everton are: John Asbury, George Bargery, Edwin Berry, John Josiah Thomas, Alfred Riley Wade, Edward Williams, and Harry Williams. The research continues.

At present there is no reference at our stadium to the great St Domingians who were the pioneers of everything we hold dear today, except within the Heritage Society's informative presentation in St Luke's Church. This should be rectified with a formal plaque somewhere on the stadium walls as soon as is feasibly possible.

A club slogan that sums up how we feel about following the Blues

How good was the Golden Vision? An interesting question from Sharpy

IN September, 2014, I prepared to bring down the curtain on 47 inspiring and eventful years as a local journalist with Swale Press, the Liverpool Echo and its parent company Trinity Mirror.

During this time, I had the great fortune to report on some of Merseyside's greatest ever games while meeting and interviewing stars who had been my personal heroes and others who I had watched develop into giants and legends.

I had begun with the Liverpool Weekly News as an apprentice journalist, becoming a sports editor at 18, progress that gave me inspiring access to both the Bellefield and Melwood training grounds in the late 1960s.

I joined the Liverpool Echo in 1974 as a sub-editor/writer,

and quickly progressed to become sports production editor on a newspaper I had once delivered as a young paper boy with the steepest round in the city in my home district of Everton.

My dream was to become sports editor of Merseyside's leading title, but I had to undergo a steep learning curve that would see me leaving the sports desk in the late 1970s to help run the Echo features department.

When an opportunity arose to claim one of the most prestigious football writing roles in the business at the start of the 1981-82 campaign, the season Howard Kendall returned to Goodison Park as the club's new player-manager, I was about to embark on arguably the most enjoyable period of my entire career, covering both Everton and Liverpool throughout this remarkably successful era.

In this role, I would travel all over Europe, cover eight championship seasons on both sides of Stanley Park, record four FA Cup triumphs and three League Cup successes, and report on Everton and Liverpool as they claimed the European Cup Winners Cup and European Cup respectively.

Of course, as an Evertonian it was those amazing Kendall/ Harvey years that filled me with joy. I was there the day the Blues beat Watford to win the 1984 FA Cup, I was at Goodison in May 1985 when a 2-0 win over Queens Park Rangers brought the title back home for the first time in 15 years.

I saw the pride of Germany, Bayern Munch, blitzed in April, 1985, in a clash that will go down as arguably the greatest Goodison Park match of all time and was in Rotterdam when we completed the job against Rapid Vienna.

HOW GOOD WAS THE GOLDEN VISION?

I was reporting from our famous stadium in May, 1987, when a 3-1 win over Luton Town actually won the Blues two title trophies on the same day, the newly sponsored Today league trophy and the more historic league championship trophy.

I covered the so-called 'Match of a Lifetime' in February 1991 when the Blues refused to lie down against arch-rivals Liverpool in the fifth round of the FA Cup, resulting in a 4-4 draw that would lead to Kenny Dalglish's shock decision to quit as Liverpool boss.

In February 1993 I would achieve a major career aim and become Echo sports editor. I had been able to live out every boy's football dream and while I never achieved my ultimate ambition of playing for Everton, I still had a hugely fulfilling role, working on the inside with people who would go down in club history; travelling and living with the team during famous pre-season get-togethers; and capturing all of the golden personal memories that I have been seeking to reveal in this book.

I was delighted that on my retirement in late 2014, two of Everton's media team, Mark Rowan and Darren Griffiths, organised a leaving lunch for me to mark my 47-year relationship with the club as a journalist. Graeme Sharp, a key figure in that great Eighties revival and a man who continues to play a key role for the club on the community and communications side, joined us at the San Carlo restaurant in Castle Street. Graeme arrived early and we were able to catch up on some great memories as well as discussing Everton legends past and present.

He asked me an intriguing question about another illustrious Everton centre-forward: "Just how good was the Golden Vision, Alex Young?"

I sensed it was a conversation Graeme had had before with other Everton watchers, not least those on the inside who knew and worked with Alex. While clearly recognising the skills of his fellow Scot, I got the impression that Graeme was seeking an understanding about Alex's work rate and his ability to turn it on away from home as well as in front of the fans that idolised him at Goodison.

Graeme was right in repeating a view that suggested Young could disappear for lengthy periods when the going got tough. He was slight for a striker and not built for the fight, but that's not what made Alex so special.

He had a grace about him, a perfect balance and he could turn a game with one classical flick and accurate finish. For a small forward, he also had a remarkable leap that allowed him to rise above bigger defenders, and he could direct the ball with real accuracy.

It was Tottenham Hotspur's famed double-winning captain, Danny Blanchflower who first coined the Golden Vision phrase in tribute to Young, later used in a BBC play based around football passion. This highlighted the manner in which Evertonians idolised their skilful blond forward. Ironically, it was Young's Everton team that took over from the fabled Spurs side in 1963 as the best in the land.

I therefore tried to answer Graeme's question this way: "I can remember days at Goodison when a boring, fairly uneventful game would suddenly be transformed by one moment of sheer Young genius, the kind of skill that Evertonians treasured and revered and which conformed to the club's proud reputation as the 'School of Soccer Science'.

"And when Alex produced one of these magical moments that transcended normal centre-forward play, I would see grown men get almost tearful, proud of the fact that Everton FC, at their best in the early Sixties, were on a different planet to their rivals."

I didn't need to see Young running a marathon or knocking opponents over with a physicality that reflected the power and the brawn of other strikers. It was precisely because he was so different that he was the subject of unashamed hero worship among fans who had been starved of success for far too long and who suddenly had a focal point for their joy and affection.

As was often the case, the Liverpool Echo's correspondent of the day summed up his talents perfectly after he had made his debut against Spurs on December 17, 1960. He reported: 'Young is a thoroughbred, a great mover with the ball; fast, active and razor sharp in his reactions. For his size, he is a good header of the ball. He is clever, artistic and can score goals.'

Ironically, the one key person who was never an Alex Young fan was manager Harry Catterick who inherited a newly-signed Alex from Johnny Carey, famously sacked in a London taxi by chairman John Moores. Alex said simply: "Harry just wasn't my type of boss."

By the time I interviewed him for the first time in August, 1968, his Goodison career was on the wane after 275 games and 89 goals. I was so proud just to sit with him at Belle-field that day and talk about his Everton career and his dreams for the future. Reflecting on his own style of play for Everton, he said: "I could afford to concentrate on my skills. Tony Kay had arrived on the scene and he was some player, a real powerhouse with ability to match. He could sit on the ball and play and also bully opponents off the ball with his aggression. We had two outstanding ball winners in Kay and Jimmy Gabriel.

"I grew to love Goodison due to the atmosphere generated by our fans which made rival players freeze against us. A lot of cities leave you feeling cold, but I felt a special affinity with Liverpool and a real love for Merseyside. I was proud to play with so many terrific players in front of those terrific Everton supporters."

What impressed me most was Young's honesty about his own play. He said: "There were times when I had out-of-this-world games, matches in which everything I attempted turned to gold, duels in which, with a minimum of effort, I've run rings round floundering defenders and laid on goals for my colleagues in the Everton attack.

"Yet there have been times when I've exasperated myself and must have stretched the patience of manager Harry Catterick."

That frustration reached its peak in 1966 when Catterick dropped Young for a game at Blackpool during the cup final season, replacing him with a budding 16-year-old star by the name of Joe Royle. The manager was allegedly confronted by an angry mob in the Bloomfield Road car park although it was overplayed by the media. Nevertheless, it was an unhappy episode.

What infuriated Alex was Catterick's reaction the following week. The manager recalled the fans' Golden Vision and also included Jimmy Gabriel in the side, saying he was "Picking the hooligans team."

Alex revealed: "For several games after that, Catterick never came into the dressing room before matches. He took the reins again when it looked as if his 'hooligans team' might win the FA Cup, which they duly did."

Clearly no love lost between manager and player.

As I completed my first and only interview with Alex at Bellefield that August day in 1968, I asked him one final question: "What are your plans for the future?"

He looked at me knowingly, started to say something and then changed his mind. What he did say was that it was in his mind to move into management. I went back to the office and introduced my article with the news for Evertonians that the great Alex Young was beginning to think about the future by planning a new career for himself as a football boss.

The Liverpool Weekly News used to publish on a Thursday with the press day on a Wednesday. On the Tuesday evening, I was heading home and sitting on a 17C bus alongside Central Station when I suddenly noticed an Echo newspaper bill.

In very large letters it declared: 'ALEX YOUNG IN TRANSFER SENSATION.'

I immediately jumped off the bus and bought an Echo

which revealed that Alex had agreed to become player-manager of Glentoran across the Irish Sea. I raced back to the Weekly News office in Bold Street and just about had time to update my own 'Young wants to become a football manager' interview.

He later apologised to me, saying the deal had still not been confirmed when he spoke to me. The fact that the Golden Vision was worried about upsetting a young journalist says everything about his character.

If you've ever met him you would realise that he is quietly spoken and extremely modest, despite the adulation that was heaped on him. As it turned out, he spent just two months in Northern Ireland before returning to join Stockport County where he retired with a knee injury in August, 1969.

With all respect to those two clubs, it was not the manner in which the Golden Vision should have finished his career.

The Echo found the words to sum him up perfectly on the day he retired . . .

'Young was one of the classiest players in post-war football. Not for him the storm-tossed battles of brawn and ill-will. He brought a fluency, grace and charm to football, but for all that he possessed a vicious shot and a heading ability way above the average.

'His fans idolised him and his name appeared on gable ends throughout Merseyside – always followed by the words . . . THE GREATEST!'

In answering Graeme Sharp's earlier question, yes, the Golden Vision – from a fans' perspective – was very special and someone we will never forget.

Digging for our spiritual roots and finding the pub where it all began

HAVING highlighted in an earlier chapter the debt we owe to those St Domingo pioneers, it's even more important to fully understand how we progressed from a park team to first become kings of the district, then city – and ultimately one of the genuine power brokers of the English game.

You will be aware that at the foot of Everton Village stands the 1787 lock-up tower, erroneously known in modern times as Prince Rupert's Castle. The incorrect nickname relates to the royalist prince who encamped on Everton's imposing ridge with his 10,000-strong Civil War army in 1644 before capturing the town of Liverpool below.

These days, every Evertonian recognises the tower as the

central image on one of football's most famous crests, but Rupert's Civil War 'derby game' had unfolded more than a century before the 'Stone Jug' was built.

Across the path from the lock-up would ultimately be built Molly Bushell's nationally famous Toffee Shop. The tasty sweets she made, to a recipe given to her by a local doctor as a cure-all for children's coughs, would become a favourite of world famous author Charles Dickens. Even Queen Victoria was a patron. It is no surprise, therefore, that Everton FC became known nationwide as 'The Toffees'.

Add to all of this the Queen's Head Hotel link, the former pub in Everton Village where the pioneering players of St Domingo's Methodist Chapel took the momentous decision to become Everton FC, and you can begin to understand why club and district will forever be inextricably linked.

In the winter of 2013, in almost complete darkness and on a bitterly cold and wet evening, Roberto Martinez led a parade of local schoolchildren down Village Street like a modern-day football pied piper as the 'Friends of Everton Park' fulfilled a pledge to bathe the Everton lock-up in a mesmerising blue light that remains illuminated every winter.

All of this unfolded in front of a packed local gathering, an occasion that confirmed to the fairly new manager at that time that he had not just joined a great football organisation, but a true 'People's Club'.

My two times great grandfather Peter Rogers had arrived in Liverpool from Northwich, Cheshire, in 1853 from a family of blacksmiths, men of iron for whom a hard day's work was about blood, sweat and tears.

Peter took up residence with new wife Maria in Tatlock Street between Vauxhall Road and Scotland Road. This was where my great grandfather Thomas McLaughlin Rogers was born.

The Rogers family, revelling in their tough, uncompromising, but community-driven surroundings, settled quickly and subsequently rented houses in nearby Kirkdale before returning to 'Scottie' and the well known Hopwood Street. The family's next stop was to move up the hill into heartland Everton, occupying a tiny terraced house just a few hundred yards from ancient Village Street.

This coincided in 1879 with that landmark meeting at the Queen's Head Hotel that transformed St Domingo's FC into the ambitious new club that was Everton.

This was the birth of big time football in our city and the importance of this date should not be underestimated.

Within 12 years Everton would be elected to the new Football League (1888) and claim a first league title (1890-91). A year later they would cross Stanley Park from their former Anfield ground with its basic facilities and develop what, by comparison, was then a world-class stadium at the new Goodison Park (1892). As the new century began to unfold the club would claim its first FA Cup (1906).

My fascination with the fact that St Domingo's chose to become Everton FC rather than Anfield FC, Walton FC or even Liverpool FC in 1879 has intrigued me all my life, while filling me with pride as an Everton boy.

Oh to have been a fly on the wall at that landmark Queen's Head meeting when the only thing on the St Domingo committee's agenda was the potential name change. What if 'Everton' had not received any support? Who organised the gathering and how long did it take to reach a consensus? Clearly, no longer than it took to down a couple of pints!

Early in 2015 I decided to stop thinking about it and undertake some serious research on the birth of Everton Football Club. Back in 1992 I'd already written the official centenary history of our famous ground – '100 Years of Goodison Glory' – and on my bookshelf at home I have about 60 other Everton books penned down the years by respected authors and football historians. But in terms of where it all began, I was beginning to wonder if we had all missed something in relation to that momentous Queen's Head Hotel meeting of 1879.

As a journalist and author, I'm well aware that once an incorrect fact gets into a publication it can easily be repeated down the years in subsequent titles. Things that were not quite right can subsequently become irrefutable facts.

To go back to the very beginning and to focus the hearts and minds of some key people who I knew could help me, I decided that we needed to do more than just dig for new information. We needed to dig for history and this entailed persuading the archaeological team at the Museum of Liverpool to consider a full scale excavation of the Queen's Head Hotel site where the Everton FC story began.

To ensure I would get a positive response to my unusual request, I began to investigate the building's relevance, not just through previous football books, but by studying Victorian maps, images and plans and, more importantly, the official census records closest to 1879 that would not only reveal who lived at the Queen's Head Hotel at that time, but also information about its neighbours, the other businesses in the village, and the characters who would have been patrons of this heartland Everton pub.

Sadly, there is not a single property still standing on Village Street following the 1960s slum clearances, but intriguingly the road itself is still in situ, effectively the southern boundary of the modern Everton Park.

I made an appointment with Dr Mark Adams, lead archaeologist at the Museum of Liverpool, to enthuse him about the site and its place in local football history. It took just a couple of minutes for him to grasp its importance and within a matter of weeks we had agreed a date for a full scale excavation of the Queen's Head site . . . Saturday, July 18, 2015. Dr Adams immediately visited Village Street to understand the lie of the land.

The shape of the street has remained unchanged for over 200 years, wider at the top than the bottom to accommodate the former Village Cross that stood in a central position at this point, adjacent to the large terraced property on the south side that would become the Queen's Head Hotel.

Having returned to his museum base, he was able to overlay old maps onto modern aerial photographs to accurately pinpoint the pub site.

Mark has worked on over 100 different excavations since the 1980s, ranging in date from 5000 BC to the late 1800s. This makes the Queen's Head one of the youngest sites he has dug. Both Mark and his Museum of Liverpool colleague

Liz Stewart were confident they would unearth the birth-place of big time football on Merseyside, but at the same time they were aware that it's not unusual to draw a blank.

Mark said: "Even with map evidence as good as we had for the Queen's Head there are never any guarantees that anything will be found and there was always a possibility that everything, including the pub's foundations, had been removed when the site was finally demolished in the 1960s.

"Normally this is just part of the excitement of archaeology, but in this case there was also the risk of disappointing the hundreds of Evertonians who we knew would turn up on the day to watch the dig. Luckily no-one was to go away feeling let down."

The property that ultimately became the Queen's Head was constructed around 1830, originally as a domestic house, probably one of the many 'beer houses' opened that year after the 1830 Beer Act allowed any ratepayer to sell beer after paying two guineas for a licence.

Over 24,000 opened nationally in the year after the Act was passed. Most of these were in domestic terraces and often consisted of a single room. A lot of similar pubs were rebuilt in the later 19th century as a result of changing legislation and most of the remaining ones closed down between 1904 and 1920s as regulation tightened. It's therefore remarkable that the Queen's Head building survived into the late 1960s.

Mark's experience indicated that if any remains of the pub had survived, they would be deeply buried. He said: "We were going to need something big to get to the remains in one day and to get the hole filled in again at close of play for safety reasons and to protect the site. Most people believe archaeology is all about painstaking work and patience, but sometimes you need the heavy brigade to help sort things out and we called in a 20-ton tracked excavator."

As it turned out the use of such a large machine wasn't overkill. The remains of the Queen's Head were covered by three separate layers nearly two metres deep in total. The upper metre was a layer of top soil, modern bricks and concrete laid down when Everton Park was landscaped in the early 1980s. Below that was another layer, about 0.75m thick and mainly made up of handmade bricks, containing the walls of the pub. This layer also had a few timbers, plus fragments of Welsh slate from the Queen's Head roof and this was the first sign that we were close to touching Everton football history.

Beneath this was a black layer, about 15cm thick, mainly made up of coal dust and soot. Mark explained this came from the walls, floors and ceilings of the pub and represents the accumulated debris from about 130 years of coal fires.

At the bottom of the trench were the intact foundations of the building where a royal blue football dynasty had begun to take shape.

Mark said: "Without excavating a much larger area it's impossible to be 100 per cent sure, but we believe we found the front parlour of the Queen's Head and therefore the most likely location for the bar area where that landmark name-change meeting would have been held."

A small quantity of finds were recovered from the dig's lower layers, mostly late 19th and early 20th century pottery, exactly the sort of material you would expect to find on the site of any Victorian house in central Liverpool. We know the Queen's Head was later used as a cow keeper's house to supply locals with fresh milk, later becoming a traditional dairy. It also housed the Everton Labour Club in the 1960s.

Despite the pub's later use, Mark said: "We unearthed a few items that are likely to be from the Queen's Head. One of these is a fragment of decorative tile, possibly part of a small arch. Surviving photographs of the pub show a plain brick façade so it's most likely to be from the inside of the building. Other items likely to relate to the building's days as the Queen's Head are oyster shells found in the rubble."

Today oysters are thought of as a food of the rich, but things were quite different in the 1800s when they would have been a common pub delicacy.

Some of the other finds from the site are of the right date, but are harder to link directly to the pub.

A stoneware inkwell is of a type which is very difficult to accurately date. It is probably 19th century, but could be as late the 1940s. Mark said: "Of course, it would be great to think that we found the container for the ink used to write the minutes of that first Everton FC meeting."

We can never prove it, but it's nice to dream and it shows that even archaeologists, who deal only in facts, can share a romantic vision!

Extra time winner on the research front as we revise club history

WHILE preparing for the archaeological dig at the Queen's Head Hotel, I continued with my own research and gained permission to study the files and records held at the respected city centre Athenaeum Club. This enabled me to review contemporary Victorian Street directories.

These would not only tell me who was living at the Queen's Head in 1879, but would also pinpoint the year it stopped functioning as a local pub.

Back home, I found myself reading a Sixties book on Merseyside football by Dr Percy Young who named Everton FC's first secretary as John W Clarke, describing him in time honoured fashion as the landlord of the Queen's Head. As it turns out, Dr Young had got it half right.

The middle initial – W – jumped out at me. I was now able to review official census files for the period, cross checking with the information I had secured via the street directories. This revealed that the Queen's Head pub landlord was actually John Clarke and that it was his 26-year-old son, John William Clarke, living with his father at the Village Street licensed premises, who was Everton's first secretary and who arranged that historic name change meeting.

This suddenly made absolute sense. Clarke the younger was well educated – initially a schoolmaster and then an engineer – well capable of handling meeting notes and organising games with increasingly bigger opposition.

His father John would have been hectic in his pub on Saturday afternoons when the new Everton FC played in Stanley Park.

So not only did the archaeological dig help re-discover the birthplace of big time football on Merseyside, it also helped to correct a crucial chapter in our history in terms of the identity of Everton's FC's first influential club secretary.

Peter Lupson, author of the excellent book 'Across the Park' which, in its own right, unearthed some previously unknown links between Everton and St Domingo's, attended the dig with members of the EFC Heritage Society whose headquarters are in the upstairs room of St Luke's Church on the corner of Gwladys Street.

Lupson said: "I thought the dig was an outstanding and historic day. The locals who attended told me how proud they were to come from the community where the club was born.

"One lady said that she had lived just a stone's throw away from the site for years and didn't know the history of it."

Peter described as "breathtaking" the moment the foundations of the Queen's Head emerged from Dr Adams' deep trench. He said: "Suddenly we were looking into the parlour where, in 1879, the St Domingo's football committee held that momentous 'name change' meeting. Some of the first players to turn out for the new Everton FC would have been in the room that night."

Peter added: "For anyone with a pride in the history of the club, the excavation in Village Street was a truly emotional moment. I even took away a couple of bricks from the walls of the Queen's Head, one for my son who is a big fan, and another for the Everton FC Heritage Society. When I got home I scrubbed them clean and they are now valued treasures of a defining moment in the club's history."

For me, a huge box had been ticked in terms of bringing club and district even closer together. I don't know where the future might geographically take our club, but whether we stay at historic Goodison Park or move to a new home, the importance of remembering our roots has never been so important.

We were the first senior club in this city. We were pioneering founder members of the Football League. We have enjoyed more seasons in English football's top flight than any other club and as far as I am concerned that makes us unique and very special indeed.

We were – and will always be – our city's first football giant . . . genuinely the People's Club and always respectful of those important people who have been a massive part of our story.

This is the history and tradition that new manager Ronald Koeman will very quickly have to learn and understand, not least because of all the nonsense written in some quarters prior to his arrival about Everton no longer being a big club. Koeman is experienced and astute enough to understand what nine league championships, five FA Cups and one European Cup Winners Cup add up to, despite the barren years that he must now end. What a wonderful opportunity he now has to earn his own place in Goodison folklore as he starts his new challenge on the banks of the royal blue Mersey.

These two road signs may not look spectacular but they have real significance in the history of our great club

47

We idolise our stars and legends, but how do we remember our immortals?

DURING the writing of this book, on October 17, 2015, we lost Everton's greatest ever manager. Like all Evertonians, I was devastated.

As a fan, I was fortunate enough to have been able to salute Howard Kendall from the Gwladys Street terraces. As a young journalist, I had the honour of interviewing him as he stormed through games alongside Alan Ball and Colin Harvey to help inspire the legend of Goodison Park's 'Holy Trinity'.

Later, as the Liverpool Echo's chief football correspondent, I communicated almost on a daily basis with Howard during his glorious 1980s managerial reign and we became great friends.

Here was a man steeped in all things Everton. He wore the royal blue jersey with pride and quality between 1967 and 1974 before returning in 1981-82 to become Everton's first player-manager. Howard figured in four league games and two cup games during that first season of change and challenge.

However, he quickly realised that while pulling on his famous boots again might take his influence to the very heart of the matter, it was a romantic gesture compared to the total focus required in one of the hottest managerial seats in football.

Supported admirably by Colin Harvey, Howard would ultimately build the most successful team in Everton history. He would eventually manage us three times, but it would be those four seasons from 1983-84 to 1986-87 that would transform him from a Goodison great into an Everton immortal.

As soon as I heard he had died, at the age of 69, I was thinking about how the club might remember him.

I love going to football grounds that have a real sense of history, stadiums with statues and stands that remind us of giants from the greatest game in the world.

Anfield has its Bill Shankly statue, and the Shankly and Bob Paisley Gates. Deepdale, Preston, has its classic Tom Finney statue and Shankly Stand. Old Trafford has its imposing stand and statue tribute to Sir Alex Ferguson, also commemorating the legend of three European Cup giants, Messrs Charlton, Law and Best. At Stamford Bridge, Chelsea's Sixties striker Peter Osgood is cast for perpetuity in bronze while Pride Park, Derby, salutes both Brian Clough and Peter Taylor. And so it goes on.

Now let's be absolutely clear. Every one of these individuals fully deserves to have their memories enshrined forever at the stadiums where they achieved so much.

But my focus is on Goodison Park. For years we have been able to admire that imposing statue to William Ralph 'Dixie' Dean. It always fills me with pride whenever I walk past this monument to the greatest centre forward the world has ever seen.

At the time of writing, discussions continue as to how Everton might not only salute Howard, but also Colin Harvey and Alan Ball via a composite 'Holy Trinity' statue – a fantastic salute to three remarkable former team-mates.

All fans would support this project in every way, but because Howard achieved so much as a player, manager and club servant, I always hoped and prayed that the Blues might name a stand after him.

In 2013, I was at Goodison for the launch of Kevin Sheedy's new book, an occasion that was jointly organised by the EFC Heritage Group and book publishers Trinity Mirror Sport Media. Journalist and author John Keith, who had worked with Sheeds on the book, was compere for the evening and the audience was delighted when Duncan Ferguson turned up to offer his support.

I was grateful for the opportunity to be able to get to my feet and add some personal thoughts about Kevin whose sweet left foot and quality midfield play was one of the key building blocks of Everton's unmatchable 1980s side.

I also took the opportunity to make a personal point about Howard Kendall while standing within the great man's stadium of royal blue dreams. I mentioned all of those giants at other clubs who had been granted immortality with statues and stands named after them, and said that the club I had supported and worked with all my life needed to follow suit – and quickly – in Howard's case.

The word 'quickly' had nothing to do with any inside knowledge I might have had about his health. I just knew how thrilled Howard would have been to have had such an honour bestowed on him during his lifetime.

On the basis that we already had Dixie's statue, I said that it would be a wonderful thing for Evertonians to be able to sit in and admire a newly named 'Howard Kendall Stand'.

In November, 2014, I found myself at another big Everton event, the annual Ronny Goodlass charity fundraiser at Devonshire House in Edge Hill. These are brilliant affairs, always superbly supported by a mainly Everton audience in the presence of many former Goodison greats. This particular occasion had extra resonance because it was a tribute night to Howard. Joe Royle was among the principal guests and as the evening wore on, compere for the night Darren Griffiths, from Everton FC's media team, began to interview the top table guests.

With a twinkle in his eye, Darren put me on the spot with a fairly blunt question. "Ken, you worked with Howard, Joe and Harry Catterick, so who was the greatest Everton manager of all time?"

I answered it this way:

"All three achieved so much for the Blues throughout their careers. Catterick won two league championships and the FA Cup. As manager, Joe inspired that memorable 1995 FA Cup final success over Manchester United, and so I have to thank him on behalf of us all for the part he played that day in providing us with such a wonderful moment, the last Blues boss to achieve a major trophy success.

"In the first of three managerial stints, Howard guided us to two championships, one FA Cup, plus the European Cup Winners Cup. Those combined achievements confirm his standing as the greatest Everton boss of all time."

Howard was not on the top table, choosing to sit with some friends and guests in the main body of the room. I looked towards him and added this rider, repeating the statement I had made at the launch of Kevin Sheedy's book: "In my mind Everton FC should act now and name a stand after Howard Kendall to salute everything he achieved."

The response from the packed crowd at the Devonshire spoke for itself. I sat down and moments later I caught Howard's gaze. He smiled and nodded at me in typically modest fashion. It was something he would never have said himself, but I knew just how much such an accolade would have meant to him.

In a room full of Evertonians, I was pleased to have been able to make the point for him. Later, as we said goodnight, he quietly said: "Thanks lad, I appreciated your words."

Fast forward another 12 months to November, 2015, and I was back in that Devonshire House venue, jam packed with many of those same vociferous and passionate supporters as

Ronny organised the latest gathering of the royal blue clans, this time a special salute to big Joe.

On this occasion, it was Ronny who repeated the HK stand logic himself in the presence of former stars like Derek Temple, John Hurst, John Bailey, and Tony Kay.

The one giant character missing was the man himself. We had lost Howard suddenly just weeks earlier and Joe, in the presence of Howard's wife Lil, managed to find the right words to pay a moving tribute to his great pal and former team-mate, showing all the respect and admiration he had displayed during a moving cathedral remembrance service.

I looked down into the Devonshire audience and focused on the table where, exactly a year earlier, Howard had flashed back his knowing glance.

This time, that great Evertonian and 1984 FA Cup final hero John Bailey was in my direct line of sight. Down the years, we had been in each other's company with Howard on countless happy occasions.

Bails idolised Howard, always respectfully calling him Gaffer, like all the lads did. Whenever they were together, laughter was never far away, supported by a genuine mutual respect between men who loved life and lived it to the full.

Tears were flowing down John's face. Alan Jackson, formerly of Radio Merseyside, held a microphone towards Bails, hoping he might offer a thought or a funny story about Howard, but our normally bouncy and ebullient former left-back was unable to move, let alone speak. He managed to get the word "Gaffer" out – then choked.

However, his reaction said more than a thousand words.

HOW DO WE REMEMBER OUR LEGENDS?

You think your heroes will live forever, from the parents and grandparents who guide you early in life to the sporting heroes who later inspire you.

Before it's too late, it's always important to tell the people you love and admire how special they are and how much they mean to you. Howard knew how much Evertonians admired him for filling us with such pride and giving us so many wonderful moments.

I went across to say goodnight to Bails and thanked him for being such a great friend to Howard. John still couldn't speak, and we settled for a hug and a thumbs-up which was all that was needed.

Immediately after Howard died, I knew the subsequent gathering of the royal blue family at Goodison Park would be hugely emotional, but one image will live with me forever. Watching later on our TV screens, a camera picked up Howard's brother in arms, Colin Harvey, in the Main Stand and his devastation at losing a man he had been through so much with was etched across his face.

Colin later told me: "I had been to watch my grandson play in the morning. He is into his football. Then we got a phone call and it was Jimmy Martin, the club's kit man. He told me about Howard.

"Joe Royle rang and said he had spoken to him the previous day. Howard was worrying about a speaking engagement he had in his diary, and asked Joe to do it for him. Joe also had a commitment and couldn't, but Ian Snodin stepped in. Howard would have been happy with the thought that he was not letting anyone down.

"Then he deteriorated quickly and was taken to hospital. I couldn't believe the news that he had died. I had been with him just a couple of weeks earlier at the derby game and he was his usual boisterous self. I said I would see him again shortly. The last thing I expected was that call from Jimmy.

"My wife Maureen asked me if I was still going to Goodison. I said I had arranged to take my grandson, but it was a difficult day. It was the shock more than anything."

Colin's desolation summed up how every Evertonian was feeling at that moment. But when we all think about Howard, we smile and remember his passion for football and his love for Everton. He was astute, he was such fun to be with, and he was a remarkable player and football manager.

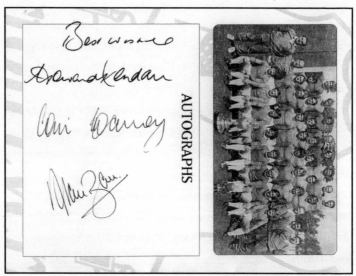

A menu card from a 'Three Legends' dinner signed by Howard Kendall, Colin Harvey and Alan Ball in 2000

'Once Everton has touched you, nothing will ever be the same again'

AS a journalist, I have a passion for great quotes and special facts. As I complete this book, I offer you some of my favourites when it comes to Everton Football Club.

You will be aware by now that I am first and foremost a dyed-in-the-wool Evertonian and Blue Nose which goes hand in hand with my pride in having been brought up in the historic district of Everton.

I was lucky enough to have followed and chronicled the achievements of Everton Football Club through some of its greatest seasons, indeed its most successful era in the glorious 1980s.

During that time I have researched AND written my own books on the club and admired and read the publications of many other 'Everton watchers'. I have also been fortunate enough to meet and interview Goodison legends, some of them immortals, and this only served to increase my pride and passion for our great club.

So here are some famous quotes and observations made by various notable people down the decades, not in any particular order, which sum up just what it means to be an Evertonian . . .

"Dave Hickson belonged to an earlier mould. Unpretentious, courageous, born with a will to demolish the opposition, he thundered across the scene like some hero of Scandinavian mythology. He was not built for finesse, nor particularly did he try to cultivate it. He had fire in his nostrils."

– Dr. Percy M. Young, author of the book Football On Merseyside, published 1963

"Once Everton has touched you nothing will be the same."

– Alan Ball

"One Evertonian is worth 20 Liverpudlians."

– Brian Labone in typically tongue-in-cheek mode, but really meaning it

"Visiting teams to Goodison Park must survive matches at this ground in the certain knowledge that if Everton don't get them, the crowd will. This stadium has become an inferno – frightening, ferocious, and often with some of the malevolence of the latter-day Rome in it. No footballer in the world could face up to this easily. Even Alfredo Di Stefano of Real Madrid would be hard pressed to earn applause on this pitch. This crowd is interested only in Everton and victory in the same breath."

– Bob Ferrier of the Observer, previewing an Everton game in 1963 as the Blues continued their march towards Harry Catterick's first championship success

"We owe a great deal to Everton. No matter where they play, and no matter whether they are well or badly placed in the league table, they always manage to serve up football of the highest scientific order. Everton always worship at the shrine of craft and science and never do they forget the standard of play they set out to achieve."

– Steve Bloomer of Derby County, Middlesbrough and England fame, writing on the subject of Everton in 1928 when Goodison Park was first touted as 'The School of Soccer Science'

"I was running back to the centre circle after I scored the second goal against Liverpool and pure elation welled up inside me. I remember thinking, 'I just love this place – I want this place forever.'"

– Alan Ball

"Everton have always been noted for going out on the pitch to play football. We got called the 'School of Science' quite rightly. The other lot, the Reds, well they were a gang of butchers. They should have been working in an abattoir. McNab, McKinlay and the Wadsworths. God bless my soul, they'd kick an old woman."

– Dixie Dean

"Alan Ball would sit in the dressing room before a game and say: 'If they want to run us, we will out-run them; if they want to fight us we will out-fight them; and if they want to play we will sweep them off the park."

– Joe Royle, recalling the supreme confidence of the 1969-70 championship winners

"Throughout its history, Everton had been noted for the high quality of its football. It had always been the unwritten but rigid policy of the board, handed down from one generation of directors to another, that only the classical and stylish type of player should be signed. The kick-and-rush type had never appealed to them."

– Will Cuff, Everton's famous chairman throughout the Dean era, 1921-1938, speaking to the Liverpool Daily Post in 1946

"I'd break every bone in my body for any club I played for, but I'd die for Everton."

– Dave Hickson

"When you come from a city like Liverpool, you are always going to suffer knocks, and I mean that in a nice way. So there was a lot of dark humour around the dressing room. Nothing was sacred among the players and everyone made a fool of themselves at times. We all knew that at some point on a Saturday afternoon, we would at least do the same once."

– Neville Southall in typical self deprecating mood, reflecting on his view of Scousers

"Brian Labone . . . the Last of the Great Corinthians."
– Harry Catterick

"Labby was a great player and a true Blue; everything you could possibly want in a centre-half. I would trust him with my life."
– Peter Reid

"I always had an ambition to play for Everton as a boy. When I was at Laird Street School in Birkenhead, we wore blue jerseys and so on the night before a match, I would sleep with mine because it meant so much and I'd dream of playing in Everton blue. It was a dream that came true and I loved every minute."

– Dixie Dean, on his lifetime's passion for all things blue

"Throughout the bad times, as well as the good, Evertonians have demonstrated an unbridled devotion and loyalty towards all men in blue and white. They routinely convert Goodison Park into a cauldron of emotions. On some occasions the atmosphere is blood-curdling. On others it's simply spine chilling. During my days as a player, the Goodison roar from the massive crowds of 70,000-plus enthused us and intimidated our foes. In fact, Merseyside folklore says that Gwladys Street has been responsible for more goals than any one player, including Dixie Dean."

– Alex Young, the Golden Vision, on playing at Goodison Park

"I am joining the people's football club. The majority of people you meet on the street are Everton fans."

– David Moyes

"When you talk about a love affair with Manchester City, you are talking about a marriage with Everton."

– Howard Kendall, reflecting on what Everton meant to him when he quit Manchester City to return to his beloved Goodison Park on November 6, 1990. The bonus was to see Colin Harvey once again by his side after it had seemed as if his Everton career was over a few days earlier

"The glories of the past are gone. No-one can live on memories. The future is important, and the future starts today. So for God's sake let's get off our backsides and do something about it."

– Wise words from the one and only Alan Ball that should be permanently displayed in a sign on Goodison's home dressing room wall

"It was the best 10 years of my career, in fact they are the only team I ever actually played for. That's what happens

when you play for Everton, you forget the rest, the rest mean nothing."
  – Duncan Ferguson

"I'm a Scot by birth and an Evertonian by choice."
  – Alex Young

"Evertonians are born, not manufactured."
  – A contemporary sign at Goodison Park

Evertonians are a special group of supporters I have been so proud to be a part of throughout my life.

In one of the early chapters I reflected on how my father Harry Rogers claimed me for Everton Football Club from the moment he brought me home from the Walton Hospital maternity ward on November 27, 1948.

Like every proud royal blue father, he couldn't wait to formally steep me in the Evertonian creed and I have already highlighted how he plotted and planned my first game at Goodison Park, a home clash with Manchester City on May 6, 1950, when I was just 18 months old.

I was in the lounge at the Park End when Howard Kendall beautifully described his relationship with Everton Football Club as a marriage. The twinkle in his eye summed up his own personal joy at being a long adopted and now fully fledged Blue Nose.

If his famous quote made the hairs on the back of your

neck stand up, then by birthright you are also part of that special football family.

And while we might not sing as often as we once did a famous battle hymn that echoed around Goodison Park for decades, the words will always sum up perfectly our defiance as proud Evertonians . . .

WE'LL FIGHT, FIGHT, FIGHT WITH ALL OUR MIGHT FOR THE LADS IN THE ROYAL BLUE JERSEY.

Bibliography

Football on Merseyside (1963) by Percy M Young (Stanley Paul)

Everton – The Official Centenary History (1978) by John Roberts (Mayflower Granada)

It's All About A Ball (1978) by Alan Ball (WH Allen)

Everton Greats (1989) by Ken Rogers (Breedon Books)

Only The Best Is Good Enough (1991) by Howard Kendall with Ian Ross (Mainstream)

100 Years of Goodison Glory (1992) by Ken Rogers (Breedon Books)

Everton – A Complete Record (1993) by Ian Ross and Gordon Smailes (Breedon Books)

Ten Year Blues (2003) by David Prentice (Bluecoat Press)

Everton's Z-Stars (2004) by Ken Rogers, with Howard Kendall's exclusive dressing room secrets (Sport Media)

Dixie Dean Uncut (2005) by Michael Charters (Sport Media)

Joe Royle: The Autobiography (2005) (BBC Books)

Everton's FA Cup 100 (2006) by James Cleary and William Hughes (Sport Media)

Dr Everton's Magnificent Obsession (2008) by David France and David Prentice (Sport Media)

Alex Young, The Golden Vision (2008) by David France (Script Publishing)

Snod This For A Laugh (2011) by Ian Snodin, with Alan Jewell (Sport Media)

Colin Harvey's Everton Secrets (2015) by Colin Harvey with John Keith (Sport Media)

Everton – the official autobiography (2012) compiled by James Cleary (Sport Media)

Special thanks to:

THOSE WE HAVE LOST:

Howard Kendall – for not only being Everton's greatest ever manager and a superb player, but also for being the game's finest communicator in the 1980s, something that helped to make my daily journalistic life so easy and enjoyable. My treasured memories of life working with the incomparable Howard are captured throughout this book.

Brian Labone – for supporting me as a young reporter and becoming a man I admired, first as a great Everton captain and then a wonderful club ambassador – Everton's godfather.

Sir Philip Carter – for showing statesmanship and leadership in the 1980s, thus helping to inspire Everton's greatest era.

TROPHY WINNERS WHO MADE US SO PROUD:

Harry Catterick and the men who contributed to his championship seasons (63 & 70) and FA Cup triumph (66) – Gordon

West, Alex Parker, Mick Meagan, Jimmy Gabriel, Brian Harris, Brian Labone, Johnny Morrissey, Dennis Stevens, Alex Parker, Alex Scott, Roy Vernon, Alex Young, Fred Pickering, Billy Bingham, Tony Kay, Derek Temple, Alan Ball, Sandy Brown, Colin Harvey, John Hurst, Jimmy Husband, Howard Kendall, Mike Trebilcock, Ray Wilson, Tommy Wright, Joe Royle, Roger Kenyon, Alan Whittle, Andy Rankin, Keith Newton, Gerry Humphreys, Tommy Jackson, Frank Wignall, George Heslop, Ray Veall, George Thompson, Albert Dunlop.

Howard's men who helped change history, 1984-1987 – John Bailey, Paul Bracewell, Wayne Clarke, Andy Gray, Pat Van Den Hauwe, Alan Harper, Adrian Heath, Mark Higgins, Alan Irvine, Gary Lineker, Bobby Mimms, Derek Mountfield, Paul Power, Peter Reid, Kevin Ratcliffe, Kevin Richardson, Graeme Sharp, Kevin Sheedy, Ian Snodin, Neville Southall, Trevor Steven, Gary Stevens, Dave Watson, Paul Wilkinson, Andy King, Jim Arnold, Neil Adams, Terry Curran, Kevin Langley, Neil Pointon, Warren Aspinall, Ian Marshall.

Joe Royle and his 1995 Blue Nose Wembley heroes – Neville Southall, Matt Jackson, Dave Watson, David Unsworth, Gary Ablett, Anders Limpar, Joe Parkinson, Barry Horne, Andy Hinchcliffe, Graham Stuart, Paul Rideout, Duncan Ferguson, Daniel Amokachi, Jason Kearton.

THANKS ALSO GO TO:

Colin Harvey – for being such a great Evertonian, as a player, coach and manager, and for the time he so patiently gave me to share and exchange memories in the writing of this book.

Bill Kenwright – for being a proud Evertonian in the boardroom in an era in which the men in football's corridors of power are often anything but loyal supporters.

Gavin Buckland – Everton FC's official statistician for helping me to check a lifetime of facts and figures.

David Prentice – for his EFC knowledge.

Ronny Goodlass – for our many enjoyable chats putting the world to rights on EFC matters. Ronny not only cleaned Alan Ball's famous white boots with such pride as a young Bellefield apprentice, but achieved the dream of every local boy with an Everton heart by going on to play for our club. His Everton FC tribute dinners continue to remind us that we are definitely 'Born, Not Manufactured'.

Dr Mark Adams and Dr Liz Stewart from the Museum of Liverpool archaeological team – for expertly leading the dig in Village Street, Everton, to help me find the club's first headquarters, the Queen's Head Hotel, the birthplace of big time football on Merseyside.

EFC Heritage Society – for their support at the Queen's Head dig, and for their ongoing work to record the remarkable history of our club.

Index

FOLLOW
EVERTON
HOME AND AWAY

WITH
KEN ROGERS

ECHO